American Prince

AMERICAN PRINCE

A MEMOIR

TONY CURTIS
WITH PETER GOLENBOCK

LARGE PRINT PRESS
A part of Gale, Cengage Learning

Detroit • New York • San Francisco • New Haven, Conn • Waterville, Maine • London

Large Print Press, a part of Gale, Cengage Learning.

The text of this Large Print edition is unabridged.
Other aspects of the book may vary from the original edition.
Set in 16 pt. Plantin.
Printed on permanent paper.

LIBRARY OF CONGRESS CATALOGING-IN-PUBLICATION DATA

Curtis, Tony, 1925–
American prince : a memoir / by Tony Curtis with Peter Golenbock.
p. cm.
ISBN-13: 978-1-4104-0930-0 (hardcover : alk. paper)
ISBN-10: 1-4104-0930-9 (hardcover : alk. paper)
1. Curtis, Tony, 1925– 2. Motion picture actors and actresses—United States—Biography. 3. Large type books.
I. Title.
PN2287.C698A3 2008b
791.4302'8092—dc22
[B] 2008039882

ISBN 13: 978-1-59413-362-6 (pbk. : alk. paper)
ISNB 10: 1-59413-362-X (pbk. : alk. paper)

Published in 2009 by arrangement with Harmony Books, a division of Crown Publishers, Inc.

Printed in the United States of America
1 2 3 4 5 6 7 13 12 11 10 09

To my wife, Jill Ann VandenBerg Curtis

Bring your visions to me clearly
Let me hear the sight of you
Reach out and know the wind is trembling,
Sighing silently your shade of blue.

CONTENTS

PREFACE

Truly, Tony Curtis has led an extraordinary life. He and I have been together for almost fifteen years now, and even for me it has been an amazing experience to read these pages. Of course we've always shared the most intimate stories of our lives, and yet Tony never talked much about the tragic deaths of his siblings, or what it truly was like to grow up in poverty, or in fear of being beaten up for being Jewish. I see more clearly now how Tony became such a fighter — there was no other way to survive, much less to make his amazing journey from living in an abandoned tenement building to becoming one of Hollywood's biggest stars, a member of America's royalty. And now I know that so much of what is special about Tony — his generosity, his grace, his charm, his kindness, his enthusiasm for life, and his instinct for making every moment somehow grand — he taught himself by going to the movies and immersing himself in the cinematic lives of actors like Gene Kelly and Cary Grant, whom he so admired. I have never known anyone more romantic, more poetic, or more *alive* than Tony.

Tony may not have dwelled on the hardships he faced growing up, but he certainly never lost sight of what it's like to have to work hard just to get by. From time to time we travel to New York City, where we sometimes stay at the St. Regis Hotel. When Tony was a boy, he shined shoes outside this very hotel, wistfully watching all the rich and famous people coming and going. Nowadays, when Tony pulls up in a chauffeured sedan and is warmly greeted by the doorman, he greets him graciously in return before pausing and looking at the spot near the sidewalk grate where he stood as a little boy, shoeshine box in hand. I have always loved that about Tony, his appreciation for just how far he has come.

Tony Curtis loves people, whether they are doormen or billionaires, and he is supremely comfortable in his own skin, which inspires me to live the same way. Shortly after he and I started dating, he said, "Come on, we are going to my friend Frank's house for dinner." Starting to learn that I always needed to be on my toes with Tony, I asked him the usual barrage of questions, so at least I would have some sense of what to wear. Tony's response was simple, "It's just my friend, Frank Sinatra." Just like that. For Tony, the most important word in that sentence was "friend." Not long after that dinner, Frank's health declined, and Tony and I would go over to visit and play poker so that Frank could have a little company and remember the good times. At some point in the evening Tony would always sneak off to Frank's bedroom, just to sit and be with his friend. From the living room Barbara and I could hear laughing, and sometimes a few tears. Tony and Frank were like brothers, and I think a little piece of Tony died the day Frank passed away.

After Tony and I were married in 1998, we moved to Las Vegas, where we live now. Vegas is a wonderful town. We have some great friends here and Tony really enjoys his life. People who live here somehow seem less judgmental than anywhere else I've ever lived. I guess you have to have a sense of humor to live in a city with an Egyptian pyramid that shoots the most powerful light in the world out its top.

One day after we moved to Vegas the telephone rang, and Tony was offered a job performing in the stage musical of *Some Like It*

Hot. He had not done theater work since he was very young, and he thought it would be an interesting challenge. Little did he know! For months, he trained, practiced lines, and rehearsed; there was Tony, seventy-seven years old, tap dancing and singing with his coach out in his art studio overlooking the Vegas strip. I was amazed at how hard Tony worked. After months of lessons at home, it was off to New York for rehearsals, and then to a year of touring and living out of suit-cases. At age seventy-eight, Tony performed in all 237 shows in thirty-seven cities across the United States. People loved the show, and he was hilarious in it. What an experi-ence!

The worst day of my life came in Decem-ber 2006. That morning started much like any other. I woke early, spent some time with Tony, and left the house to tend to the horses at our ranch. A few hours later, I re-ceived a call that Tony had been taken by ambulance to the emergency room at St. Rose Hospital in Henderson, Nevada. Our housekeeper, Luz, had been at the grocery store, and Tony's assistant had not yet ar-rived at work, so to this day none of us knows exactly what happened. We do know that Tony called 911 and told the dispatcher he was having difficulty breathing. Paramedics arrived within minutes, and placed a breathing tube down his throat, which is standard procedure. It was all downhill from there.

By the time I arrived at the E.R., Tony was already on a ventilator. The situation got worse when fluid began to accumulate in his lungs and he developed pneumonia. It was truly a horrific cycle: as Tony's lungs filled with fluid they grew weaker, so the doctors couldn't take out the breathing tube that was causing the fluid buildup. Worst of all, Tony was so confused that he fought the tube down his throat, forcing the doctors to keep him heavily sedated, and then to put him into a drug-induced coma. He stayed that way in the intensive care unit for thirty days.

It was the longest month of my life. Family and close friends came to town to help me with my bedside vigil, but all of us felt terribly helpless. Finally, the doctors came to me and said, "We've done everything we can. He's either going to turn the corner or he's not. Now it's up to Tony."

Christmas and the New Year came and went, and still Tony showed no signs of coming out of his coma. Finally, two weeks later, the clouds parted: he regained consciousness and came off the ventilator. But our happiness was short-lived. Now that Tony was conscious, we discovered that he was almost completely unable to move. All he could do was blink. It took everything I had not to break down completely when the doctors told me they didn't know if his condition would ever improve.

But in a manner nothing short of miraculous, Tony slowly began to grow stronger. There have been poems written about the beauty of a nightingale's song, or the joy in a baby's laugh. I will tell you, though, that the sweetest sound I have ever heard was in a Nevada hospital room. I was sitting by Tony's bed, passing the time watching a movie on my DVD player, when all of a sudden I heard that unmistakable gravelly voice: "What movie are you watching?" I turned to Tony, hugged him, and wept for joy.

After that, Tony underwent months of intensive rehabilitative therapy, learning to walk and talk again — all the things we take for granted. The amazing staff at HealthSouth in Henderson, Nevada, even taught him how to write his name, which may give you some sense of how far he had to come back. This was a man who had signed millions of autographs all around the world!

It has been a long and difficult fight for Tony, but the man is nothing if not a fighter, and he is doing wonderfully now. He is still in a wheelchair sometimes, but only when he gets tired. Not long after Tony finished his last rehab session, he was offered a role in the movie *David & Fatima,* and off we went to L.A. At one point between takes, he wheeled past me and my mom at high speed, shouting, "I am having the time of my life, girls!" Tony Curtis was back.

These days Tony is dedicating himself to painting, something he has enjoyed doing all his life. In April 2008, he had a sold-out art show in London, and another very successful art show in Paris. He also takes great pleasure in meeting people who have followed his movie career. There is nothing in the world like his laughter when he's chatting with a fan that has waited a lifetime to meet Tony Curtis.

When Tony is not busy in the art studio, writing his poetry, or traveling the world, he's actively involved in our ranch, a nonprofit foundation that he and I set up in 2003 called Shiloh Horse Rescue (www.shilohhorserescue.com). *Shiloh* is a Hebrew word meaning "a place of peace," and on our forty-acre ranch in Sandy Valley, thirty miles outside Las Vegas, we take care of horses rescued from slaughter or from abuse or neglect. Tony and I have been very active in our support of the American Horse Slaughter Prevention Act and we have traveled to Washington, D.C., many times to walk the halls of Congress and the Senate trying to gain support for this worthy cause. Tony, my mom Sally, and I work hard to make Shiloh a place of peace for horses and other animals in need. Little did Tony know when he married me that one day he would have so many animals in his life; in addition to our many dogs and cats we usually have nearly two hundred horses at Shiloh at any given time. Our life is fulfilling and very busy.

One of Tony's favorite poems is "Richard Cory" by Edwin Robinson, and there's a stanza in the poem that always makes me think of Tony:

And he was always quietly arrayed,
And he was always human when he talked;
But still he fluttered pulses when he said,
"Good-morning," and he glittered when he walked.

Tony truly does glitter among us. And it's not just for the 122 movies he's made, or for the hundreds of amazing stories you're about to read. He also has been knighted by the Hungarian Government and has received the Chevalier de l'Ordre des Arts et des Lettres from the French Government;

among his countless awards is an honorary doctorate from the University of Nevada at Las Vegas; his art is in the permanent collection of New York's Museum of Modern Art and in the homes of some of the world's most influential people. Tony is a generous sponsor of the U.S. Navy Memorial in Washington, D.C. (he always refers to the Navy as his "other mother"), and he feels very strongly about supporting the men and women in our armed services. He also helped restore the Dohány Synagogue in Budapest, in honor of his family.

As you will see in the pages ahead, Tony Curtis may be a film icon, but he's no saint. He's very much flesh and blood, a human being with his share of faults and weaknesses. Yet there really is something about him that is larger than life. You can't help but smile when you hear his loud burst of laughter, see his mischievous grin, or hear that mellow, baritone voice. A bit of Tony's glitter rubs off on everyone he meets, and all our lives are richer for it.

Jill Ann Curtis

July 2008
Las Vegas, Nevada

Working with the Stanley Wolf Players in the Catskills, 1946.

1
New Kid in Town

All my life I had one dream, and that was to be in the movies. Maybe it was because I had a pretty rough childhood, or perhaps it was because I was always more than a little insecure, but as a kid I longed to see myself ten feet tall on the big screen. Through no fault of my teachers, I received almost no formal education, but after I spent three years in the Navy during World War II, the GI Bill allowed me to go to acting school on the government's nickel. I may not have had much schooling, but it turned out I had a gift for acting. When I walked out on that stage, it felt like a hand in a velvet glove. I wasn't scared; I wasn't even nervous. I just loved being the center of attention, just like I'd always known I would.

I performed in summer stock, and I acted in Clifford Odets's play *Golden Boy* exactly twice over a single weekend, but before I knew it I had been summoned to meet a studio executive at Universal Studios. It was the spring of 1948. I was excited, but I wasn't surprised. Going to Hollywood had been my life's plan since I could remember, and I was too naive to know it almost never works out that way.

I got myself out to New York's Idlewild Airport (now JFK) and boarded a TWA Super Constellation, a four-engine prop plane bound for Los Angeles. I had never been on a Super Constellation before, but I knew all about it from movies and magazines. I was served a little lunch. The stewardesses were real nice to me. One of them was very pretty, so I had a chance to flirt. I was just a kid, but already I loved flirting. Mostly I succeeded in sparking some kind of response, which was what I lived for.

On my first flight to LA, I sat in coach. In those days the sections weren't partitioned, so I could see into first class, where a man with a mustache and a herringbone suit was being tended to by what was clearly a personal assistant. The guy in the suit would whisper something to the other man, who would jump up and do his bidding.

To my surprise, a little while after we took off the assistant came over and asked me, "Could you join my friend in first class?"

"Sure," I said. I got up and walked forward

to Herringbone Suit. I had no idea who he was, but he was cordial and expressed interest in why I was going to LA.

"I'm going to be an actor."

"I figured you might be," he said.

"I've got a meeting at Universal," I said.

"Do you know anything about the other studios?" he asked.

I had heard the same Hollywood gossip as everyone else, but I had paid special attention to it, knowing that this was where I would work one day. So I said, "Warner Brothers is a tough studio to work for. Twentieth Century Fox makes action pictures. At MGM you have to sing and dance a little bit. RKO wants actors who are stable. And Universal wants young people. So that's where I'm going."

We talked for a few moments, and then I went back to my seat and fell asleep. After we landed, I went to pick up my luggage and there was Herringbone Suit, waiting for his assistant to fetch his bags. He saw me and said, "Can I offer you a ride?"

"That would be great, thanks. I'm staying at the Hollywood Knickerbocker Hotel."

He said, "My driver will take me home first, then he'll be happy to drop you off at your hotel."

We drove through the winding streets of

Beverly Hills for a while before finally pulling up to a big metal gate. Barely visible through the trees and groomed shrubbery was a tasteful mansion. After we pulled up to it and my benefactor's bags were unloaded, he reached over and shook my hand.

I said, "Well, it was a pleasure meeting you. And thanks for the ride. My name is Bernie Schwartz. What's yours?"

"Jack Warner," he said. "Let me tell you something, kid. If Universal ever drops you, come see me. I'll change your name to Tyrone Goldfarb and make you a star all over the world!"

We both laughed. Warner got out, and his limo driver took me to the Hollywood Knickerbocker Hotel, where I slept like a baby.

The next morning I walked from the hotel to a big intersection at Highland Avenue, where a trolley took me into the San Fernando Valley, up the middle of the street, ending up at Universal Studios. After I got off, I walked under a bridge with the freeway overhead until I came to the Universal lot.

I walked right up to the gate. Now it was starting to hit me. This was an absolutely thrilling experience for a twenty-two-year-old kid fresh from the streets of New York. My whole life I had dreamed of being an actor in a movie studio, and here I was about to walk through the entrance of Universal Pictures as a prospective employee. I pinched myself, but the dream continued. The gatekeeper told me to go to a door marked CASTING. I walked through it and up to a big, gleaming desk.

"I've been invited to come to the studio for a meeting," I said.

A girl behind the desk looked up at me and said, "What's your name?"

"Bernie Schwartz." Now I had my heart in my throat. I thought, *Suppose this is a big fucking joke?* I was pretty sure it had to be more than that because the studio had sent me a plane ticket. But what was a hundred and twelve dollars to a movie studio? So I held my breath for the long moment before she said, "Yes. Here you are on the list. Welcome to Universal Studios, Mr. Schwartz. You have an appointment this morning with Mr. Goldstein. To get to his office, turn right when you come out of the gate across from the barbershop, go up the path, and you'll see his name on the door."

I was amazed. Not only had she known my name, but she was sending me directly to the office of the man who ran things at Universal. As soon as I left her, though, I got completely lost, so I figured maybe this was an opportunity to make a spur-of-the-moment detour. In New York I had gone to see some filming of *The Naked City,* a Universal picture. Howard Duff was the star. While I stood there watching the location shoot, I struck up a conversation with the propman. We talked, and I told him I wanted to be in the movies.

He laughed, but not unkindly. "Don't break your heart," he said to me. "Just enjoy going to the pictures and don't even think about working in the business. It's just too tough. You have no chance at all."

So while I was wandering around lost on my way to see Mr. Goldstein, I decided to see if I could find my friend the propman. It turned out the props department was right nearby, and there he was.

He remembered me. "Hey, kid. How are you? How did you get in the lot?"

"I'm here to sign a contract," I said.

"No!"

"Yep."

He was genuinely happy to see me and took obvious pleasure in my good fortune. He gave me directions to Bob Goldstein's office, and not long after that I arrived at the studio's inner sanctum, where all the executives had bungalows interspersed with perfectly groomed lawns. I walked along the path to an office marked GOLDSTEIN, where a well-dressed woman looked me over coolly.

"Mr. Schwartz?" No one had *ever* called me Mr. Schwartz before.

"That's me," I said.

"Just a moment, please."

The door opened. Bob Goldstein was in town for a couple of days and was using his brother Leonard's office. Bob sat me down, and we talked. He showed me my contract and said it would be good for seven years, with options renewable every six months, at the studio's discretion. Each time they renewed I'd get a raise. My starting salary would be seventy-five dollars a week.

"I'll take it," I said. He laughed. I picked up the pen to sign the last page, and he said, "Never sign anything until you read it."

"There are a lot of pages," I said.

"I don't give a shit," he said. "Sit down and read it. I'll be back in an hour."

I didn't have the patience to read every page, but I flipped to the section that related to payment: if they were renewed, my six-month options would go from a starting salary of seventy-five dollars a week up to twelve hundred a week at the end of seven years. Other than that all I could make out was page after page of whereofs and wherefores. When Goldstein came back to his office I was reading magazines, having spent all of four minutes scanning the contract. I'm sure he knew that. I signed on June 2, 1948, one day before my twenty-third birthday. I was officially under contract. Bernie Schwartz was in the movies.

Now that I knew I was going to live in LA, at least for six months, the first thing I had to do was find a place to live. The studio had been picking up my tab at the Knickerbocker Hotel, but I didn't want to overstay my welcome. I had heard about a rooming house on Sycamore Street where five or six other Universal actors lived. I could get breakfast and a room there for thirty dollars a month, which I could swing on my seventy-five dollars a week and still have some money left over for a car.

I moved in with whatever I had in my suitcase: a toothbrush, a comb, and some clothes. My room contained just two pieces of furniture — a bed and a dresser — but the location was perfect. After a three-block walk to Highland Avenue, I could get on the trolley and ride twelve minutes into the San Fernando Valley to Universal Studios. The trolley also went to the Beverly Hills Hotel and from there to the Pacific Ocean. Along the way you could see big, beautiful homes in the pastel palette of Southern California, with their emerald expanses of manicured lawn.

I was required to join the Screen Actors Guild, so Bob Goldstein made me deduct twenty dollars a week from my paycheck until I paid my union dues. Bob didn't want me to wait until I got my first movie role and then be stuck having to pay a big lump sum. He was very kind to me. He made sure I was smart about my money, and I was grateful to him for that.

I got all dressed up for my first day of work at the studio, and I was sent with a photographer to meet various executives, including Wally Westmore, the famous makeup man, and the head of the props department. When I heard that Jimmy Stewart was going to be coming onto the lot, I walked down to the front gate and waited for him to arrive.

When he drove in, the guard at the gate greeted him: "Good morning, Mr. Stewart."

"How are you, Irving?"

"There's a new kid here who just signed with the studio. Would you like to meet him?"

"Sure," Stewart said. He got out of his station wagon, walked to the little kiosk where I was standing, and greeted me graciously while the studio photographer captured the moment. Then Jimmy Stewart got back in his car and went to work. This was my first photograph with a major star — and I had been signed with the studio for less than twenty-four hours!

I started attending acting classes provided by Universal. Richard Long, a young actor who would become a friend of mine, was in one of my classes, along with a half dozen other actors and actresses. The instructor was Abner Biberman, who had acted in a movie with Cary Grant. Abner kept making passes at all the pretty girls, but he seemed to take special pleasure in showing me up. It couldn't be that I was Jewish, because he was too; maybe it was just that I was young, good-looking, and under contract. But oh, did I catch hell from this guy! You could tell that he had it in for me, so he was doing what he could to make sure I'd get dropped by the studio.

After a few weeks of this, I went to Leonard Goldstein and told him what Biberman was up to. I was smart enough to know I needed the ear of somebody like Leonard, who had the clout that came from being Universal's most prolific producer. Leonard told me that he had received other complaints about what Biberman was doing and that he wasn't going to let anyone dump on me for any reason. A short time later, the studio fired Biberman and replaced him. And I stopped being singled out.

The best thing about moving to California was that I was enjoying total freedom for the very first time. Though I had been on my own in the service, Uncle Sam had still kept his watchful eye on me. Out here in sunny California, I was single, young, and being paid while I was training for a movie career. There were great-looking girls everywhere, so I decided it was time to start developing my knowledge of the opposite sex.

The trolley was no way to take a girl on a date, so I went out and bought a used pale green Buick convertible, with Dynaflow Drive, from Sailor Jack's on Lancashire Boulevard in the Valley. I paid very little for it, and it wasn't long before I discovered why. One day I pulled up the rubber mat on the driver's side and found a hole that had rusted right through the floorboard. I could see the street below, but I didn't care. I had wheels.

The girls I was meeting, actresses under contract at Universal, were completely different from the girls I had known back in

New York. These girls were beautiful, outgoing, and friendly, and they weren't bashful about sex. For girls in New York, sex was a big deal, and lots of girls were waiting until they found Mr. Right. The girls I was meeting in California had often tried sex at a much younger age, so they were more comfortable with themselves, and with men.

I remember some of those girls with great affection. Debbie from Iowa had an apartment in Beverly Hills, a pretty, little place. We'd go out for dinner, she'd invite me upstairs, and then we'd spend the night together. Her boyfriend happened to be an executive at one of Universal's distribution companies, and he had brought her to LA for a six-month tryout. I found out that this wasn't uncommon. Producers would bring these beautiful girls out from their hometowns, put them under contract for six months, give them bit parts in movies, and screw them the whole time. Then bim, bam, thank you ma'am, they'd go back to wherever they'd come from.

The Universal executive never found out about Debbie and me. I was very discreet. I respected the girls, so I kept my mouth shut, not wanting to get them into any kind of trouble.

In addition to aspiring actresses, I was surrounded by girls whom the studio hired to deliver the mail, beautiful young ladies who rode bicycles from stage to stage and office to office, bringing scripts and messages. There wasn't one I didn't find attractive. If a girl gave me a look, letting me know she was interested, I'd show my interest right back. I was still shy, but I was teaching myself to get over it.

I had lots of different experiences with these girls. Sometimes things would lead straight to sex, and other times we'd just neck. Whatever happened was fine with me. I was just happy that they seemed to like me. One of the girls lived in a house with a little porch, and we'd sit out there, kissing. We'd go to screenings at the studio and hold hands until her hands got sweaty. But that was it. If I had pushed a little harder, maybe we could have had a relationship, but I wasn't ready to do that. I didn't want to cut off the opportunity to go out with all those other girls.

I couldn't believe how much fun I was having. To make it seem a little more real I started to keep a romantic diary; when I went out with a girl I would take a Polaroid picture of her and put it in my book along with some cryptic notes that only I could decipher. This book was proof that I wasn't dreaming the whole thing up. Without it I might wake up one morning and find myself in my parents' apartment in New York!

One of the girls who came to Hollywood looking for a contract in the fall of 1948 was a very young actress who had recently changed her name to Marilyn Monroe. I first saw her at Universal just walking down the street. She was breathtakingly voluptuous in a see-through blouse that revealed her bra. Her beauty was intimidating, but there was something about her smile that made her seem approachable. She and I were about the same age.

When I walked by her I gave her my usual friendly greeting: "Hi-i-i." She smiled. I smiled back.

By this time I had more or less settled on a new name for myself. The one and only book that I had read while I was in the Navy was *Anthony Adverse,* by Hervey Allen, a historical novel set during the days of Napoleon. I had decided to call myself Anthony Adverse, but when I mentioned that one day to a casting director, he said, "There's already an actor in town with that name." So I kept the Anthony, and I added Curtis; I had a relative, Janush Kertiz, whom I liked very much, so I took his last name for mine. Kertiz is actually a very common Hungarian name.

What a perfect name that is, I thought to myself: Tony Curtis. I had wanted a name that was a little mysterious, and this seemed just right.

I said to this beautiful girl, "My name is Tony."

"My name is Marilyn," she said.

"I'm driving into town," I said. "Can I give you a lift somewhere?"

She paused, looked at me for a moment, and then said, "Okay."

We walked together to my car, and I held the door open for her. I got behind the wheel, drove out the gate at Universal, turned left, and then we were on the Hollywood Freeway, heading into the city.

I twisted the rearview mirror a little to the right so I could see a bit of Marilyn's face, and I caught her looking in the mirror at me. We both laughed. Nice. She had red hair then, pulled back in a ponytail. As we chatted I got a strong feeling of, well, *heat.* She gave off an extraordinary aura of warmth and kindness, of generosity and sexuality. I'd never experienced anything like it.

Both of us were aspiring to be famous, to be in the movies. I had gotten my first break, and this girl was still looking for hers. She was wearing a summer dress, and I could see her shape, her thighs, and her back. She didn't wear much makeup, just a little lipstick and mascara maybe. I know it sounds crazy, but I noticed she had beautiful arms.

We hardly spoke, but I was keenly aware of her. I drove down Highland to Sunset Boulevard and asked Marilyn where I could drop her off. She mentioned a street, and I drove to this little hotel where she was staying. The whole trip took maybe twenty-five minutes.

I said, "Here we are."

"Thanks," she said.

"Can I call you?"

"If you like."

She took a minute to write out a number. I wasn't sure whether the number was for the hotel or directly to her room. She left, and for two or three days I couldn't think of anything else. But I didn't dare call her. It was too soon. I figured a girl who looked like that had to be in a serious relationship. She may have been married, for all I knew, although she wasn't wearing a band. After a week, I figured enough time had passed, so I called her.

"Would you like to go out for dinner?"

She said that would be fine. A few nights later I picked her up in my car, and we drove to a popular restaurant on the Sunset Strip. The food was good and we talked, but not about anything serious. We laughed a lot and had a good time. We went for a drive down Sunset going toward Beverly Hills before I took her home.

On our next date we went to a club called the Mocambo. I picked Marilyn up at her hotel, but I never asked her any questions about her living there, which I think she appreciated. During the ride we talked about the movie business. She wanted to know everything about it — the people I'd met, the structure of my contract, my acting classes.

"Any good?" she asked about my class.

"My first teacher wasn't great, but he left and the class got better after that," I told her.

I could see how much she was interested in movies. She didn't talk much, but she listened closely. I told her a little about myself, but when I asked about her life she didn't offer much, so I didn't press her. I figured the way she looked, she must have had an interesting history.

It was more interesting than I could have ever imagined, as it turned out. If anyone had had a worse childhood than mine, it was Marilyn. She had been in foster care until the age of seven, and not long after her mother took her back, her mom ended up in a mental hospital. Marilyn spent the rest of her childhood bouncing from foster home to foster home until she got married at age sixteen just to get away.

That marriage had ended about two years before I met Marilyn. She had been discovered by a photographer who had seen her working in an airplane factory. Twentieth Century Fox signed her but let her contract expire. Then Harry Cohn signed Marilyn to a six-month contract at Columbia, and she had appeared in a movie called *Ladies of the Chorus,* which went nowhere. Harry had the reputation of demanding sex with his starlets before signing them, and I doubted that Marilyn escaped his clutches. But Columbia hadn't re-signed Marilyn, either. When I met her, Marilyn Monroe was unemployed and still looking for her first real break.

We went into the Mocambo, which had one wall lined with canaries in cages. When the two of us walked in, heads turned. Marilyn was wearing a flowered dress, nothing fancy, but she still looked fabulous. It was a weeknight, so the place wasn't crowded. I had the feeling that Marilyn was uncomfortable being seen in public, as if she didn't want to run into somebody who might see she was out on a date. What I didn't know was that Joe Schenck, the head of Twentieth Century Fox, had a place in LA where Marilyn stayed with him on weekends. Twentieth

Century Fox hadn't picked up her option, but Schenck sure had.

Schenck was married, so during the week he'd go home and Marilyn would stay at her hotel. At this point I didn't know about her arrangement with Schenck; I only pieced it together later.

There was a live band at the Mocambo playing great music. Marilyn and I were sitting there talking, teasing, and enjoying the eye contact. I was falling in love with her. I could tell she liked me too. It was really special getting to know her then, before the fame and craziness ruined her life. I wasn't thinking about bedding her, or perhaps I should say it wasn't foremost on my mind. I was just enjoying getting to know her and taking pleasure in how much fun it was spending time with her.

While we were talking, I looked at one of the canaries in its cage. It was sitting on this little perch, and while I was watching it just keeled over, fell to the bottom of the cage, and died. The place was heavy with smoke, and the poor canary must have suffocated. I looked over at Marilyn, but she hadn't noticed. I was about to tell her what had happened when a waiter came over, pulled out a fishnet from his pocket, opened the cage, scooped up the dead bird, put it under his coat, and walked past us. Another waiter came over, opened the cage, and put in a new bird. It fluttered around for a moment before settling on the empty perch.

That scene had a profound effect on me. I couldn't help but think about how tragically brief life can be. You're here and then you're gone, and is anyone really going to know the difference? I looked over at Marilyn. She was so — open. And I felt the same way with her. That evening I had a strong intuitive moment: *We're going to do really well in this town, you and I.* I didn't dare say that to her, though; you can't tell anybody you think you're going to be successful, but somehow I knew that given an equal chance, no one was going to stop me. And this amazing woman next to me was destined for great things as well.

Sure, some people in my acting classes had made some negative comments about my New York accent, but I knew how quickly I could learn things. I could fix my speech if I had to. And I loved the social side of this business, going to parties where you could meet the right people, which I knew would prove important. I was street-smart enough to know that the way to get ahead was to keep my mouth shut and my eyes and ears open.

We finished our dinner, and then we drove to the beach, where we watched the waves break over the shore. We necked a little, and then I dropped Marilyn off at her hotel.

One day I went to the gym to work out, and there was Burt Lancaster. Someone said, "Burt, this is Tony Curtis."

He said, "Where are you from?"

"New York," I said.

"Where?"

"Manhattan."

He said, "I'm from Manhattan. East Side or West?"

That did it. I knew we'd be friends.

"East," I said.

"West," he responded.

Burt and I hit it off from the moment we met. He told me where the parties were going to be held, and he introduced me to his agent, Mike Meshekoff, who agreed to take me on as a client too. Mike in turn introduced me to Howard Duff, an actor who had begun his career on radio in *The Adventures of Sam Spade.* Howard was starting to switch over to the movies when I arrived in town, and we became fast friends.

Howard had a house down the beach just outside of Malibu. He said to me, "Use the house whenever you want. I'm only down there on the weekends." I called Marilyn, and we agreed to go to the beach. I picked her up, and we had a nice dinner at a popular drive-in restaurant that served steaks and hamburgers. The sun was setting, and I was feeling a bit nervous; I thought it would look too obvious to her that I was taking her down to the beach to lie with her, and I didn't want to offend this girl. We put our blankets down, and we lay on the beach and talked. Again she asked about my life, so I told her more about myself.

I told Marilyn that a friend had lent us his house, so we went over to Howard's place, which was a wonderful little bungalow with a cozy fireplace. He had a little bar set up with whiskey, vodka, and scotch. I offered her a drink, and seeing my awkwardness, she helped me make us scotch and sodas. Then she began to tell me a little about herself.

She told me her mother had been sick when Marilyn was a child. I didn't find out until later that her mother was mentally ill and living in an institution. Marilyn didn't mention her father. She had a friend, Jeannie Carmen, a showgirl, who was very important to her, but on the whole Marilyn made it sound like she was very isolated. She lived in that hotel, and it didn't sound like she had much of a life. We started to kiss and fondle each other, but that was the extent of it that evening. About eleven o'clock I drove her back and then on to my place on Sycamore.

I liked Marilyn *very* much. I really enjoyed her company. She was a little odd, but I knew I was a little odd too. We both acted like we were outgoing, but down deep we weren't really at ease with ourselves. I didn't have self-confidence, or peace of mind, and neither did she. Her reluctance to open up about her own life just made me that much more interested in her. But the next few times I called to make a date, she told me she was busy.

Marilyn had been spending time at the Twentieth Century Fox studio. She was changing her style, her look, even her persona. When we first started going out, she spoke in a normal voice, plainly and directly. But she was learning what the public wanted, so by the end of our relationship she was beginning to talk with that breathy, sexy affectation that became her trademark. She had also changed her hair color from red to platinum blond. Her clothing had become, if not more revealing, a little more stylish.

On our next date we went for lunch at the Twentieth Century Fox commissary. If you were under contract at one studio, you were granted access to all the movie studio commissaries in town. I'd go to Twentieth Century, to MGM, and over to Columbia just to grab a bite and see and be seen, since actors, producers, and directors tended to congregate in their commissaries. On this day the commissary was teeming with actors, but even in this crowd Marilyn's beauty created a stir. What must it feel like to turn heads wherever you go?

That weekend I asked Howard Duff if I could use his house again, and he said, "Do it." I bought a couple of steaks from the market and picked Marilyn up at her hotel. Howard had a little grill in the garden, so I put some charcoal in it, poured on the lighter fluid, and lit it. I had never done this before, and I was stunned that I had succeeded in lighting the charcoal — and that it stayed lit. I cooked the steaks, opened a can of string beans, cut up some tomatoes, and uncorked a bottle of wine that Howard had in his bar. Howard was very generous. I didn't take advantage, though, and I made sure the house was always clean.

We ate our dinner leisurely. We had a drink and went outside to sit in the moonlight. I knew something was going to happen that night, and so did she.

Around two o'clock in the morning we went up into the bedroom, and I took off my shirt. Marilyn made herself comfortable by stripping down to her panties and bra and sat on the edge of the bed. She was magnificent. We started to kiss and hold each other, and I undid her bra. Her breasts were every teenage boy's fantasy come true. As we began to make love, I could tell that this was not her first time. She moved easily, and seemed comfortable, which made me comfortable too.

It was very satisfying. Something about it just seemed so right. I was bedding more than a few great-looking girls at this time in my life, but I liked Marilyn more than any of the others. She was different. She was very fragile and vulnerable, which attracted me greatly. We continued seeing each other for a while. I would arrange a place we could go, or she would. We would go to her friend Jeannie Carmen's place, or Howard's bungalow, and once we even went to Marilyn's hotel room. We almost never went out at night in public, though.

Marilyn was the first woman I felt truly close to. For the short time we were together we both depended on each other. We had real feelings for each other, although I wasn't ready for a serious relationship, and neither was she. Neither one of us was willing — or able — to take what we had between us to the next level.

Eventually our relationship began to take a backseat to our careers. I started making movies, and she did too. As her career took off I could sense Marilyn was looking for men who could move her up the ladder in Hollywood. She met Greg Bautzer, a big-shot entertainment attorney who represented Howard Hughes and was a good friend of Joe Schenck's. Greg was very handsome, and he knew everyone in the business. In *The Asphalt Jungle,* she played the girlfriend of Louis Calhern, a good character actor. Then Marilyn got a tiny part in *All About Eve,* which was nominated for fourteen Oscars and won six. You could see her developing as an actor with each role.

After Marilyn and I stopped seeing each other, we'd run into each other at various Hollywood parties. She'd say to me in that sweet way of hers, "Whatever happened to your Buick convertible with the Dynaflow Drive?" Her affection was obvious, and I felt the same for her. We just couldn't find any time to be together. We were both so busy. We were also both changing — and liking it. But as Marilyn's success grew, lots of people seemed to want something from her. That was one of the nice things about our relationship. Neither of us wanted anything but companionship and a little romance, and that's what we provided for each other.

Marilyn and I were together a relatively short time, but we both felt that time was something special. When fate put the two of us together there was bound to be a physical attraction, and there's nothing we would have done to change that. Nevertheless, I was very respectful of her, and we were both careful to put the emphasis on our friendship. In fact, we were both trying so hard to avoid a sexual relationship that it became the elephant in the room. So when we finally gave in to our desires, it was truly something unforgettable. No other woman I've known made me feel that way until I met my wife Jillie almost fifty years later.

My parents, Emanuel and Helen Schwartz, on their wedding day, 1922.

2
A Battered Childhood

When I was a little boy, two or three years old, my parents would go out for dinner and a dance at the First Hungarian Independent Lodge. Because I carried on so much about being left with anyone else, they had to take me along. While they were eating dinner, I sat by my mother on the floor, and when she got up to dance with my father, I would latch on to her and not let go. She'd be dancing with my father, and I'd be holding on to her leg for dear life.

Neither of my parents was very demonstrative with their affections. My father, Emanuel (Manny) Schwartz, was a first-rate tailor, and I can see him even now, hunched over his sewing machine, making alterations to people's clothes. As talented as he was, during my childhood he made very little money. I remember one time he had come home only to discover he had lost the little yellow envelope with his twenty-two-dollar salary in it.

He ran out of the house. I followed him down the street as he looked in the gutter and on the sidewalk for the entire twelve blocks back to his place of work. *How did the envelope fall out of his pocket? Did his pocket have a hole in it?* I felt terrible for him that day. My father was visibly shaken by the fact that he'd lost that money. It was one of the few times he expressed emotion of any kind, other than the frustration he regularly showed my mother during their constant bickering.

My father wasn't a fearful person; quite the contrary. And yet there was a kind of pathetic quality to him. When he was a young man, not long after he got married, my father came across an ad in the Hungarian newspaper that read DANCERS WANTED. It gave an address in Brooklyn. He took time off work and made the trip to the outer borough to pursue his dream of being in show business. When he got there, they told him to take off his shoes and roll up his trousers and go into an adjacent room. In the room was a vat of grapes, and he was told to step in it. They were making wine, and they needed grape crushers. That was his dancing career. He went there that once, and he never went back.

Victor Schwartz, my father's father, came to America around 1917 with his eldest son, Arthur, who joined the merchant marine, went off to sea, and never was heard from again. Grandpa Victor had arranged for his wife and four younger children in Hungary to join him in America once he was established. Soon after he opened a secondhand clothing store in New York, he wrote a letter to his wife, but she didn't hear from him after that.

Running out of patience, my grandmother got herself and her children on a boat in steerage to America. When she walked into my grandfather's store with my father and his three sisters in tow, Victor nearly fell over. He had had no idea his family was coming, and now he had five additional mouths to feed! My grandmother didn't make a big fuss over her husband's less-than-enthusiastic reception. She just got on with it. She found a cheap place to live, my grandfather moved in, and they were a family again.

I have only fleeting memories of my father's parents. I remember Victor Schwartz as a tough guy. Once, when I was young, I was in my father's tailor shop when my grandfather lost his temper over something and picked up an iron as if to strike my father with it. I was terrified, but my father just stood calmly and looked at him. My grandmother, a tall, forceful woman who ran my grandfather's life, stepped in and stopped him. The feeling I remember most from my grandparents is sadness: somewhere along the way they lost their love of life, and they died soon after.

My father, Manny, was originally going to become an electrician. When the family was still living in Hungary, Victor had arranged to pay an electrician in Budapest to teach my father the trade. After traveling five hours on the family donkey, Victor and Manny arrived in the city, but when they came to the electrician's shop, it was closed. After staying overnight at a nearby inn, they found the shop still closed the next morning.

My grandfather wasn't about to spend any more money on lodging, so he walked a few stores down to a tailor shop. He told the owner how good his son — my father — was with his hands, and he arranged for the tailor to take my father on as an apprentice. The tailor gave my father a room and a sewing machine, and after several months my father became very adept at his trade. He had a real aptitude for it.

Years later my father told me about a relative of his by the name of Katonah Hershul.

Katonah in Hungarian means *soldier,* and *Hershul* is *Harry.* Soldier Harry. Katonah Hershul stood over seven feet tall, and he was so strong he could pull a cannon out of the mud. When World War I began, my father wanted to enlist in the Hungarian army. He and some friends had hidden pistols in his bathroom in case the town was attacked, but my grandmother put her foot down about joining the army, so he never got his chance to fight.

One of my favorite things to do as a kid was to visit my father's three sisters, who lived with their families in the Bronx. My parents would dress me and my younger brother Julius up in our nice clothes, and we'd get on the subway to go to see my aunts: Irene, Helen, and Barbara.

Irene was a huge, obese woman who had married a man who was very thin, which struck me as funny. Aunt Irene would always greet us at the door with fresh-baked cookies or candy. Aunt Helen was also very generous. Her husband, Morris, owned a butcher shop, and every time I went to visit him there, Morris would cut up some meat for me, wrap it up, and say, "Take it home to the family." My third aunt we called Barbara, although her given name was Burish. She had married a man in the restaurant business, and they had a giant of a son, as big as Soldier Harry.

Among these three families, I had seven cousins, six girls and the young giant. I remember Cousin Stella best. One night when I was about ten, I was playing at Stella's house when she and her two girlfriends went into her mother's closet, took out lingerie and sleeping gowns, and played house. They took off their play clothes and put on these see-through garments. They were a year or so younger than I was, so watching these half-naked little girls prance around in their nighties didn't have as much effect on me as it might have later on, but still it was something I never forgot. I wasn't quite sure what sex was yet, but I knew it was something forbidden and exciting.

One of the cousins enjoyed driving me crazy. When she was sixteen she would wear summer dresses without underwear, and she would rub up against me. My other cousins were older, some much older, so I didn't have a chance to get to know them very well.

The Hungarian lodge that my father belonged to met on the East Side of Manhattan around 110th Street. Sometimes when he went, he'd bring me along. As president of the lodge my father ran the meetings, and whenever he announced a five-minute break, I can remember everyone running next door to grab a smoke. All those lodge members were heavy smokers, and my father was no exception. From the time I can remember, my father smoked two packs of Lucky Strike cigarettes a day.

The lodge members would light up and talk about sweet-looking girls they'd seen, how business was going, and how things were at home. After the five minutes were up, they'd stub out their cigarettes and drift back to the meeting room. My father would take up his mallet and rap the dais, and then they would discuss serious matters, like where they were going to hold the summer picnic.

I wasn't always a big fan of those lodge meetings, but I enjoyed that picnic the Hungarian lodge held every summer in Corona, Queens. The outdoor tables groaned under the weight of Hungarian salami, goulash, and stuffed cabbage — all the great Hungarian delicacies. Everybody had a good time. The women clustered together, gossiping and clucking good-naturedly at the children. The men sat around in their colorful, embroidered vests and long-sleeved shirts, smoking and telling stories about the old country. Going to those picnics was one of the few times I felt like I was part of a community, connected to something larger than myself.

The idea was that lodge members were supposed to help each other out during tough financial times, but after the Depression hit in 1929, there wasn't much anyone could do. They were all broke. Not long afterward my father lost interest in the lodge and in his Hungarian heritage. So did a lot of other men who were dragged down by poverty. Instead of pulling together, they left to go it alone.

My memories of my mother, Helen Schwartz, are dominated by how unhappy she seemed in a loveless marriage. All she ever seemed to talk to my father about was his lack of financial success. She rode him mercilessly about it. I don't really know why my father wasn't more successful. He was a talented tailor, and he was well liked in the neighborhood, but I guess he just wasn't much of a businessman. Unfortunately, my mother viewed his financial struggles with contempt. When she looked around and saw her own relatives thriving, it only made her feel worse about my father. And her tongue only grew more caustic.

The moment my father came through the

door after work, my parents started screaming at each other. It made me want to run away, but there was no place for me to go. One time I tried staying at my cousin Andrew's place, but that didn't last. I just couldn't make the adjustment. Not that I was nuts about living with my parents. Even in my own home I wrestled with feelings of loneliness and depression. But over time I learned to cope, mostly by realizing that I couldn't count on anyone else, which later on would have the unexpected benefit of making me resourceful and independent.

My father made so little money that at one point we lived in the back of my father's tailor shop in a building that had been condemned by the city. Not only was the place run-down and drafty, we were vulnerable to being robbed by anyone coming down the fire escape from the roof. Our windows didn't lock. One night my father heard sounds outside the window, so he grabbed the wooden stick he used to hold up the sleeves of the clothing he was sewing, pulled the window open, and scared off an intruder. There was no one to turn to for help. Except for our apartment the building was lifeless, abandoned. We were squatters, pure and simple, and left to our own devices.

Like lots of kids in those days, I escaped

the constant stress of poverty and unhappiness by going to the movies. I saw my first movie when I was all of two years old. I don't remember its title, but I recall a stuntman jumping over buildings and I remember horses. From that day on, I went to the movies as often as I could. If my mother couldn't take me, she would pay an older girl in the neighborhood a dime to go along.

Apart from the escape provided by Hollywood, the tension from the endless fighting between my parents was relentless. I can recall only one time when they weren't at each other's throats. I was fifteen or sixteen, and when I arrived home after school I was surprised to see my father wasn't in his shop. Both my parents were in the kitchen — kissing! I stopped and stood there, dumbstruck. They were laughing and talking as if they liked each other. I had never seen them like that.

My mother looked up and said to me, "We're going to be eating pretty soon. Go wash up and get ready for dinner." My father didn't take his eyes off her, and she was smiling at him. I went into my bedroom, where, to my astonishment, I broke down in tears. I hadn't realized what I was missing until that moment, when my parents were actually getting along. Unfortunately, the mood didn't last. By dinnertime my parents were at it again, screaming at each other or lapsing into the usual bitter silences.

My mother had been eighteen or nineteen when she came to America and learned to read and write English. After she met my father, she helped him in the tailor shop for a while, sewing sleeves and collars. But once they married she apparently decided her working days should come to an end. Now my mother seemed bitter when she worked part-time jobs and angry when she didn't. So although you could probably say that my parents did their best with us, it was a pretty joyless environment that my brother Julie and I grew up in.

As a kid I had a sense that there was something wrong with my mother, but I didn't know what it was. She always seemed to be mad at me, or at Julie. That was par for the course. But every once in a while she would look at me, and her face would become twisted in fright, as though something scary was chasing her. Her eyes would dart around and she would talk quickly, and then she'd just bury her head in her arms or leave the room. I'd think, *What the hell is going on here?* Looking back, I suspect those were the times when she was hearing voices, times when she couldn't control her illness. Years later she would be officially diagnosed as schizophrenic.

My mother was always much nicer to me and Julie when other people were around. We'd visit another family, and she would be telling jokes and patting me on the head. But once we got outside, she'd grab me roughly and say, "Go play with your brother, but keep an eye on him. And don't make any trouble."

The thing about my mother was that she never seemed to have any fun. She rarely laughed, or even smiled. The only time I can remember hearing her laughter was when she was with Olga, her older sister. Whenever they got together, they'd both giggle hysterically. My mother's father had had a wife who died young, and after he remarried, my mother was born. So my mother had three half-sisters from the first marriage, women who were educated and independent-minded. One worked as a secretary, and another was a businesswoman who sold bootleg whiskey. The third sister stayed in Europe, and was later murdered in the Holocaust.

Ethel, the bootlegger, owned a townhouse in the Bronx. During the Depression she made whiskey in her basement, and she made a very good living selling it. Our neighborhood was populated mostly by Jews like us, who usually weren't big drinkers, but she did a good business in the Irish and black neighborhoods nearby. With the proceeds she was able to send her two daughters to college and her son to dentistry school.

Looking back, what I wanted more than anything as a child was to feel like I was part of something. Until I was four or five, we spoke only Hungarian at home, but I never really felt connected to my Hungarian identity. And out in the streets, where people were speaking an English language I barely understood, I was treated like an outsider. I started to learn English in elementary school, but I spoke it with a thick Hungarian accent.

When I think of my childhood, I can feel the chill weather at night in the fall and winter. We never seemed to have enough heat. As I walked through my neighborhood on the way home from playing in the streets, I saw fathers coming home from work — tailors, icemen, milkmen, and shopkeepers. These were the lucky ones. I also saw a lot of fathers who were coming home after a day of trying unsuccessfully to find work — of any kind. The Depression made it hard for everyone, and we were no exception.

My parents were neither intellectual nor

artistic. They never read books, either to us or on their own, so Julie and I never got into the reading habit either. We had some toys, but I didn't play with them much. Our family did have a radio, though, and we boys would sit in the kitchen glued to the sounds of *The Lone Ranger* or *Superman.* It was almost as good as going to the movies.

When I came home in the evening, after playing outside, I always had to be quiet. My father would quit work at seven or eight, but because he had to get up early, he went to sleep right after dinner. We lived in a one-bedroom apartment, so any little noise would wake him up. When morning came, I had to be quiet all over again while my father got ready for work. My mother enforced the silence with lots of slaps and whispered threats. I don't think my parents intended to make us feel bad, but they gave Julie and me the feeling that we were mostly just in the way.

And so it was that I figured out early in life not to depend on my parents — or anyone else, for that matter. By the time I was twelve I was going out and earning my own money. I'd seen other kids selling newspapers, so I followed one of them to his supplier and started my own paper route. I also shined shoes. My father helped me by making me a shoeshine box. I bought shoe polish, black and brown, and I had a big brush and a small cloth that I would use to slather the polish onto the shoes. Then I had a big strap for taking off the excess polish and another strap to polish the shoes. I had to be careful to use the right polish for the right shoes.

My father gave me a whiskbroom and told me it would be a good idea to use it to brush the customer down after shining his shoes. One time a customer slapped my hand away and said, "Don't bring that thing near me." I felt demeaned, and not for the first time. It's an occupational hazard when you're poor, and I was particularly sensitive to it as a kid.

Every now and then my father would hand me a pile of secondhand clothes to take to Welfare Island, which was below the Fifty-ninth Street Bridge, which went over to Queens. I was supposed to deliver the clothes, get a ticket in return, and then take that ticket to a window where I'd hand it over and get fifty cents or a dollar. At times I'd feel so uncomfortable about this that I would come back home without it.

My father would ask me, "Where's the money?"

"I didn't hand in the paper."

"Where's the paper?"

I'd say, "I have it right here."

"Why didn't you give it to them?"

I'd shrug sheepishly.

He'd sit quietly for a moment. Then he'd say, "Next time don't forget."

"Okay, Dad." There was no discussion. I was incapable of telling him how I was feeling, so I couldn't share my humiliation. But he must have sensed it, because he never got after me for coming home empty-handed.

I delivered groceries, and I worked for a pharmacy in the neighborhood, delivering prescriptions to people. I enjoyed doing these jobs because I was making money. It was only nickels and dimes, but it meant I could buy myself hot dogs and doughnuts and go to the movies. I was never broke. I always had a few coins in my pocket.

Even as a kid I was always very picky about my relationships. I was like the Lone Ranger, only without a sidekick like Tonto, unless you counted my little brother. I didn't have a crowd of guys I regularly hung out with. I'd do stuff with whoever was around. There was no one I really considered to be my best friend.

I remember one childhood friend, Frank Vitucci. The few times I went to his home, his mother would take me into his bedroom and pull down the sheets to show me how

Frank had wet his bed. Right in front of him, she'd say to me, "Look what he's done. Look how he pisses in his bed." I would nod uncomfortably. Then the same thing would happen when Frank came over to my house. My mother would pull the sheets down to show him how I had peed in my bed, and Frank and I would look at each other. It went without saying. *We're both fuckups.*

My other, happier memory of going over to Frank's house was that his mother would make wonderful Italian bread. She'd take a fresh, hot loaf from the oven and spread garlic and butter on it, and I'd never tasted anything so good. I envied Frank because when I brought friends home, my mother didn't put any effort into making them feel welcome. She was very suspicious of people, especially strangers. She didn't trust anybody, a feeling that must have rubbed off on me.

The only person I can honestly say I liked was my brother Julius, who was four years younger than I was. When I was six or seven, my parents let me know I was responsible for Julie, and I took that very seriously. I knew I was his surrogate father. If he came home late from school, I would get angry, but it was because I was genuinely worried about him. When I saw him someplace where he wasn't supposed to be, I'd ask him, "Why are you hanging out with those guys?" It was my job to protect Julie.

Julie was a gentle boy, and very careful not to offend me. He was probably a little intimidated by me. I never laid a hand on him, but he knew I had a temper, so he was careful not to get me started. Despite my affection for Julie, I rarely took him with me when I went out to play. When you're twelve, a four-year difference in age is as wide as the Grand Canyon. Mostly when I went out, I went alone. I didn't want to be held back by anyone, including Julie, and he understood that.

The time Julie and I had the most fun together was when we went to bed. We'd be lying in our separate beds, close to each other, and we'd talk about whatever came to mind. Not that we talked about anything of substance. He was too young for me to share all of my feelings. Still, this was as close as I got to intimacy during my childhood, and it felt good.

When I was ten and Julius was six, things got so bad financially that my mother and father put Julie and me in the Sycamore House, a government-sponsored orphanage in Manhattan, down on Sixty-second Street. During that time, at the height of the Depression, a lot of parents were forced to take extraordinary steps like this, just to survive. My parents brought us to this institutional-looking building, but they didn't tell us it was an orphanage. They just looked at us, kissed us, and said, "We'll be back soon." And then they left.

I had no idea where they were going or why, and it frightened me to death. I had no way of knowing that they were broke and needed to park us somewhere safe while they figured out what to do next. To make things worse, Julie and I were separated that very first day.

When the people at the orphanage took Julie away from me, I went into a panic. It was terrible. *Where's Julie?* I didn't know where they had taken him, or what they had done to him, and I was really upset. I remember a kind woman coming over and talking to me, and after I told her what was bothering me, she explained that Julie had been put with the younger boys. Then she took me by the hand and brought me over to see him. It was very nice of her, and it calmed me down.

I didn't have much appetite at mealtime, and the counselors were worried about me. They weren't sure what my problem was. It didn't seem too hard to figure out, when I look back on it. My problem was that my parents had dropped me and my brother off in a strange institution, acting as if they'd be back in twenty minutes; here it was, four days later, and they still hadn't returned.

Besides not eating, I expressed my feelings by peeing. I'd wet my bed at night, and during the day I would urinate in my pants. I just pissed my way through that whole period. Julius also wet his bed. I remember they refused to give Julius and me hot chocolate at night, because they didn't want us wetting our beds. One more humiliation for a thin-skinned kid.

At the orphanage there were twelve to fifteen other boys who were approximately my age. We all slept in one big room. One of the kids would moan and groan when he slept — not just occasionally, but all night long. The rest of us had a hard time sleeping as a result, but nobody dared complain. Another kid was always coming over and touching us. He'd be sitting across from you, then without any warning he'd reach over and touch you on your arm or on your back. He just didn't have any sense of what was appropriate. Some kids ignored him. Others kids refused to let him near them.

To make matters worse, while Julie and I were in the orphanage, we were never allowed out of the building. I badly wanted my freedom. One of the things I missed most about it was not being able to play stickball. I was an avid stickball player. When I hit a Spaldeen solidly with a broom handle, I could almost drive it up to the roof. I also liked to take bottle caps, put wax on them, and then play a game where if you hit the other guy's bottle cap, you picked it up. We'd take cheese boxes and cut holes in the bottom, and try to shoot marbles in the holes. Some wise guys would make the holes too narrow to let the marble get in. Ah, chicanery! I was schooled in it at an early age.

In the wintertime, when the snowplows would push the neighborhood snow into tall piles by the side of the streets — five, six, even seven feet high sometimes — we would carve out passageways and make rooms inside the snow. One of the guys would stand guard in front, so nobody could come in except the four or five members of our little club.

Julie and I lived at the orphanage for about two weeks, but it seemed like an eternity. I'll never forget the day my parents finally came to get us. I was grateful they had come and got us out of there, but I was also absolutely furious that they hadn't told us what they were doing when they dropped us off. Talk about feeling conflicted!

Unfortunately, when Julie and I got back home, nothing had changed. My parents continued to fight, and we continued to be trapped by poverty. I sometimes had the feeling that my brother and I were like little lightning rods, waiting for some miraculous force to hit us and break open our lives. Meanwhile we just tried to keep it together.

At least we weren't alone. During the Depression the whole country was mired in hopelessness. One afternoon my father took me for a walk in Central Park. I saw a sea of canvas tents and corrugated huts, extending in all directions. My father told me this was called Hooverville, and that the people living here had once been stockbrokers, lawyers, and accountants, but now they were homeless, without jobs, completely broke. As a kid I couldn't figure out what had happened to them. How could you be rich one day and poor the next? I didn't know anything about the stock market or about investing. But I did get the message loud and clear that poverty could strike anyone, anywhere, anytime.

As a kid I thought a lot about death. When my grandparents died, I started to wonder how long it would be before my parents died too. They assured me that they had lots of good years left. Mostly I believed them, and it helped that the only people I knew who had died were old. As kids we never saw a young person die. It was always somebody's grandmother or grandfather.

I found reassurance in routine as well. My brother and I would get up in the morning and we'd eat whatever breakfast was available. We'd take our schoolbooks and our marbles, yo-yos, pencils — whatever we needed for the day's work plus what few coins we had — and then we'd tromp off to school. P.S. (Public School) 28 was four blocks from our home. Inside the school, one big room was divided into four classrooms using movable walls. Whenever there was an event for the whole school, we'd move back the walls. It was simple and economical.

I never studied at school or did my homework. I guess I just didn't see the point. I had no sense of the future, much less how schoolwork could possibly prepare me for it. And my parents didn't do anything to enlighten me. As far as they were concerned, school was just a place Julie and I went to every day where they didn't have to worry about us.

We lived in Manhattan for my first twelve years, moving from place to place when we got too far behind on the rent. In those days living in New York City meant living in ethnic neighborhoods — Italian, German, Spanish, Hungarian, and Jewish. If you had a name like Schwartz, Goldberg, Epstein, or Birnbaum, you were Jewish. Some of these names had been given to Jews when they first settled in Europe. If someone was Jewish and big, for example, they might be given the name Gross. My father's family originally came from the Middle East, and they must have been dark-skinned, because when they came through Germany, they were called Schwartz, which means "black."

When I was in elementary school, there was a nasty bully there named Frank Weber, who loved to curse at me. He'd see me and he'd yell, "You Jew cocksucker. You motherfucking Jew." He kept this up relentlessly. Whenever I walked past him on the sidewalk near school, he'd try to shove me into traffic.

Frank Weber was the enemy. He was tall and wiry, and he had a narrow face with piercing eyes that burned with hatred — at least when he turned them on me. Whenever my class rolled back the movable walls to make individual classrooms, I tried to make sure Weber wasn't around, because if he saw me he would walk by, slap me on the back of the head, and keep walking. I couldn't stop thinking about him. I became so distracted that I even lost interest in throwing spitballs and paper airplanes in class. I couldn't think of a way to keep Weber from coming after me, so I just waited for something to happen. Somehow I knew the situation couldn't last.

There was only one other Jewish kid in school, and he didn't help me. He was older, and either he didn't know what was going on or he didn't want to get involved. I didn't hold it against him, and later we even got to be friends.

One day things changed in a way that would affect me for the rest of my life. That morning on the way to school Frank Weber had screamed at me in front of everyone, "Hey, Jew. Hey, Jew. Hey, faggot Jew." Now we were walking into the main school auditorium, and there he was. He turned and glared at me, his eyes heavy with unspoken malice.

I had never even considered raising my hands to him, but suddenly I found myself filled with a fury I couldn't control. Weber turned away from me, and when he did, I ran over and leaped on him, grabbing him around the neck with my left arm and punching him in the head with my right fist. He struggled, and we fell down. As he started to get up, I kicked him in the ribs, really got him good, and then again, and then I found myself — all of a sudden — in a place I'd never known before. I had always thought of myself as sensitive and easygoing, not someone who would take pleasure in someone else's pain. But in that moment that I was punching Frank Weber and realized he had no appetite for fighting back, I felt a kind of joy that I can't adequately describe.

I was called into the principal's office for a lecture. Fortunately for me, the principal, Mr. Driscoll, seemed to understand what had happened and why. He said to me, "Bernard, I can appreciate how you feel, but I cannot tolerate fighting on school grounds. When you have a problem with one of your peers, you have to speak to a teacher or come to me. You cannot resolve it with your fists. Do you understand?"

The principal couldn't take sides, but he must have known what a bigot and a bully Weber was. I knew from Mr. Driscoll's tone of voice that I wasn't going to get into big trouble, and I was right. He didn't even call my parents.

Weber never came near me again. And from then on I was determined that if anyone gave me shit, I would be ready to battle it out. Once I made that decision, I learned how to defend myself, and I became an excellent boxer and wrestler. As I walked down the street I would skip and throw punches like the boxers I saw in the movies. A guy would call me a "dirty Jew," and I'd say, "Fuck you." He'd throw a punch at me, but by the time he threw it, my left hand was up to protect my face, and my right was counterpunching. Once I found out I could defend myself, no one ever beat me up again. I realized that if I was in a position where I had no choice but to fight, I should become the aggressor and try to end the fight quickly. It worked. And if the guy was too much bigger and older, I'd pick up my books and run.

I remember one fight I had over a girl named Gretchen. She was beautiful, and I was chatting her up when this burly kid came over and said, "Stay away from her." I stood my ground. Gretchen watched as he came at me. He threw a big roundhouse punch, and when I ducked, his momentum carried him past me. I stuck out my foot and gave him a little push that knocked him to the ground, hard. The fight was over, and I hadn't thrown a single punch.

Gretchen looked at me and smiled. I took it to mean that I hadn't done anything wrong, and that she was impressed. I remember walking away feeling very good about myself. It was a hell of a lot better than being taunted and punched and feeling helpless.

I learned to avoid the toughs who ran in gangs. Even if you won a fight with one of those guys, they could gang up on you later and hurt you very badly. I never picked a fight, either, but if somebody did me dirt, I was capable of biding my time and getting even.

When I was about twelve there was a big kid who used to pick on me because of my shabby clothes. On weekends I would go to the dances at the Central Jewish Institute on Madison Avenue and Eighty-fifth Street. This kid didn't badger me for being Jewish, because all of us at the dances were Jewish, but he kept after me for the way I dressed, for the worn secondhand clothes I wore. My father would give me a coat, and I'd just wear it, but after this kid started on me, if my parents gave me a piece of clothing, I would ask my father to tailor it. It's funny how life works sometimes. Just because this one kid baited me about my clothing, I would become very meticulous about how I dressed and take great pleasure in looking good.

After two years of listening to this kid go

on about my clothes, I got even. At this one dance he was all over the most beautiful girl in the room. But every time I turned around, she was looking at me. I don't know where I got the chutzpah, but at one point I just walked over, stepped between them, and started talking to her. He stood there dumbfounded, but he could see she was smiling at me. He reached out to grab me, but I ducked out of the way and gave him a quick shot in the balls. He let out a loud groan, and as he slumped to the floor, everyone in the place turned to look at him. He never said another word to me again.

The girl invited me to her home for a party. There were about ten kids there, five boys and five girls. I wasn't wearing any underwear, but I was wearing a jockstrap that I'd kept on since gym class, and in the middle of the party it started to itch me something terrible. I wanted to scratch, but I couldn't do that, so I excused myself, went to the bathroom, took off the jockstrap, and threw it under the tub. I was so relieved, I was a new man.

Fifteen minutes later her father came out of the bathroom holding up the jockstrap.

"Who does this belong to?" he wanted to know. I put on one of the great performances of all time, reassured by a hunch that he wasn't going to make us all take our pants off. I said, "What's that? Never saw it before," and I just kept on talking to the girls. I didn't know it then, but that was my start as an actor.

My clothes may not have looked like much, but I began to realize that I was considered handsome. I didn't understand the power my looks gave me until I was in my late teens, but I did notice that older women paid attention to me, and sometimes men as well. One time a guy sat next to me in the movie theater and tried to grab my hand. I moved away and he followed me, so I ran out of there. Another time when I took Julie to the zoo, this pervert came up behind us and started rubbing himself against me. We ran away from him as fast as we could.

I was almost thirteen, and with my confidence growing I was beginning to see some signs that things were looking up. But I had no idea what lay just up ahead.

In high school, 1942.

3
Fuck 'Em and Feed 'Em Fish

Until the fall of 1938, it seemed like I always had my brother Julius by my side, which was both gratifying and annoying. Even though Julie was four years younger than I, he was still a big part of my life. He looked up to me, and he loved me. At night we would wrestle and fool around, and Julie was the one dependable connection I had to the rest of humanity.

We were living on the Upper East Side of Manhattan at this time. I was thirteen years old, and my bar mitzvah wasn't too far off. Early that evening I had been watching the American Legion parade over on Second Avenue. Some kids and I were standing around behind the police barricades when Julie came over. I was embarrassed to have him pester me in front of my buddies, so I shooed him away. I said, "Go play with your own freakin' friends." We didn't need a nine-year-old hanging around, ruining our fun.

That night my father went to synagogue for Shabbat services, and by the time he came back, Julie still hadn't come home. My mother asked me, "Where's your brother?" I said, "I saw him a while ago, watching the parade." She replied, "Why didn't you stay with him?" I said, "I was playing with some of the guys." I could see she was getting worried. It wasn't like Julie to stay out without letting us know where he was.

My mother said, "I heard a boy was hurt on First Avenue up around Seventy-eighth Street." That was just five blocks away from the tailor shop, but there were so many kids out on the street that day that I didn't think much of it. Then, about an hour later, we heard a knock on the door. Two cops were standing there, and they asked if they could come inside. One of them wanted to verify our names, and then he asked my father if everyone in the family was home. When my father told him that his younger son hadn't come home yet, and we were starting to worry, the other cop said, "We think your son may have been hit by a truck a few blocks up on First Avenue." My mother grabbed her breast and started to cry. My father stood motionless.

The first cop said to them, "This boy is unconscious and isn't able to talk, so we'd like to ask you to come down to the hospital and see if you can identify him. We'll give you a ride over in the squad car." I had a terrible, sinking feeling that Julie was in big trouble.

My mother gave me a shove and I stumbled forward, and the two cops took me out to their car. I couldn't believe my parents weren't coming with me, but I guess they were too terrified by the thought of what might be waiting at the hospital. I turned to look back at them, still hoping they wouldn't send me into that police car alone, but they just stood there like statues. Tears were running down my mother's cheeks.

The cops were very nice, which only made me more nervous. The situation with Julie must be pretty bad if they were on such good behavior. Up to that point I had never seen anything but a stone face on a cop. Once I'd been coming out of the five-and-dime store with two friends when a cop barked at me: "Get over here." I stood spread-eagle against the building while he patted me down to see if I had stolen anything. When he came up empty, he just gave me that tough, expressionless cop stare and walked away. All the cops I'd ever met acted like that — like they were sure I was doing something wrong, and it was just a matter of time before they caught me at it.

The police cruiser took me to New York Hospital, which wasn't far from the tailor shop. When I got out of the car, a hospital attendant was waiting for me. He took me up in the elevator, and we walked down a hall that smelled of ammonia and into a simple room. I remember a glass filled with water with a straw in it, sitting on a nightstand. It hadn't been touched. A doctor was standing there, and my kid brother was lying in the bed, unconscious. His head was wrapped in bloody bandages, and his face was black and blue, swollen almost beyond recognition, but I knew it was Julie from his cracked front tooth, where a kid in school had hit him. Every once in a while the body on the bed would shudder, like it was having a seizure.

They asked me if it was my brother, and I said, "Yeah, that's Julie."

My voice shaking, I asked the doctor, "Is he going to be all right?"

The doctor said, "Don't worry. It's just a concussion." Then he added, "Even though he can't recognize you, he can still hear you." I wasn't sure what that meant, but I sat down on the edge of the bed and told Julie how bad I felt about telling him to go play with his own friends. "If I hadn't sent you away," I said, "you wouldn't have been on that corner where the truck hit you." Sitting there, dark thoughts ran through my mind. Maybe Julie had been so upset by my rejecting him that he ran in front of that truck on purpose. I wasn't being rational, but I was devastated, and these are the games the mind plays when we're most vulnerable.

A nurse asked me to sign a form, and then the two cops took me back home. "Don't worry, kid," one of the cops said. "It's going to be all right."

I sat down with my parents and told them what the doctor had said: Julie had a concussion, and he'd be all right. To which my mother replied, "I hope so." She asked me whom she could call at the hospital, and I gave her the doctor's business card. Everyone relaxed a little bit. At least we knew where Julie was, and that he was getting medical attention.

The next morning my parents got up early and went to the hospital, while I stayed home to keep an eye on the store. I sat outside on the stoop, its steps shiny from all the people who'd come in and out of the building over the years. Behind me was my dad's old sign that read SCHWARTZ DRY CLEANING AND PRESSING, and in little print ONE-DAY SERVICE. Looking out across the street, I could see the elevated trains going by. I couldn't understand why I wasn't feeling more upset, but I guess the doctor and the cops had convinced me Julie was going to be okay.

I sat there until about ten thirty in the morning. There were no customers. I didn't do much, just watched the trains and the pedestrians walking by. Then down the block, amid the pushcarts under the El, I spotted my mother. When she got to the middle of the street she screamed at me, "Julie's dead. Julie's dead."

My heart froze. I couldn't believe it. The doctor had said he was going to be all right. How could he be dead? And it was all my fault. If I had been doing my job, Julie would never have been run over. I felt like I was going to throw up. I put my head in my hands and wept.

That afternoon I went down to the East River to find a stone to throw into the river and to commune with Julie. When someone Jewish has died and you want to show them you miss them, you put a stone on their casket or grave. Why is that? I don't know, but that's what relatives did whenever I went to an unveiling — the Jewish ceremony at the gravesite one year after someone dies.

Now that Julie was dead, I wanted to do something to help him in the afterlife. He and I used to go over to Carl Schurz Park a lot, so it seemed appropriate to head over there. I got to the East River and looked around for a stone. When I found one, I held it up to show it to God. I walked down by the river, and as I stared into the murky, turbulent waters I knew I was in the right place to be thinking about my brother. I held the stone to my heart. I was sure that somehow this stone would help me see Julie again, or at least let me hear his voice.

I prayed. "God, please let me see Julie every now and then. If you do that for me, I promise I will never do anything bad for the rest of my life." And with that I threw the stone far out into the river. I think of that day a lot. I remember what the stone felt like. I guess it goes without saying, but I never got an answer to my prayer. I didn't see Julie again, not even once.

After my brother's death, my father and mother and I sat shiva in the tailor shop for a week. Lots of friends and relatives came by to offer their condolences, and we all sat on orange and apple crates we'd set out on the floor because we didn't have enough chairs for all our visitors. I was given a box to sit on, even though I hadn't yet had my bar mitzvah, so I wasn't technically deserving of an adult seat. I sat there on my crate, wearing a yarmulke, watching the men and women who came to express their sorrow to my parents and to try to find words that might ease the pain of my brother's death.

The funeral was held on Lexington Avenue, way uptown, just before you get to Harlem. They put my brother in a coffin on a little stage, and everyone prayed for him. When I looked at that coffin I remembered seeing his unrecognizable face and bloody bandages in the hospital. I was told the truck had run over his head.

After Julius was killed, I thought I'd never feel comfortable in my skin again. I was empty. Our little bedroom that we'd shared felt empty too. I just walked around like a zombie. At school I became an even worse discipline problem than I'd been before.

I do remember the kindness of my teacher, Miss Hopper, at P.S. 28. When I came in, she told the rest of the class, "Bernie has lost his brother in an automobile accident." She pulled me aside and told me she had lost a sister. For the first time I felt like someone really knew how I was feeling. My fellow students didn't come up and say, "We're sorry," but I could feel their compassion too.

My parents never let on how terribly Julie's death affected them, but they closed down the tailor shop and we moved to the Bronx, near the corner of Fox and Simpson Streets. I can't say for sure they moved because of Julie's death, because I never questioned where we lived. All I knew was that whenever they decided to move, I had to take all of my toys and goods and put them in a cardboard box and hope no one would steal them.

The Bronx wasn't as alien as it might have been, because my aunts and uncles lived in the neighborhood. I had hoped that Julie's death would have exempted me from having to study for my bar mitzvah, but no such luck. My parents signed me up at my aunt and uncle's temple, and I had to start going to Hebrew school there. I had a lot of studying to do before I would be ready to conduct a service in front of the whole congregation; this was the big day when, according to Jewish tradition, I would become a man. *Poor Julius,* I thought, *was never going to get that chance.*

I made it through Hebrew school and the bar mitzvah itself, including the speech that every kid makes. Mine was pretty generic: I talked about how much I loved my parents, how I was planning to devote myself to my religion, and how I was looking forward to a life of accomplishment. These were the things I knew everybody expected me to say, so I did, although to be honest I didn't believe a word of it.

To my surprise, it still turned out to be a very emotional day for me. It felt very strange to be up on that bimah without Julie in the audience. The experience shook me, and I felt that terrible sense of loss all over again.

My mother and father both seemed to be very happy, although they must have been feeling Julie's absence too. There were a lot of people in the synagogue that day. Some of them came over to me, hugged me, and slipped me envelopes. I slit them open and saw singles, five-dollar bills, and tens. It was the first time I had ever held paper money in my hands. Just when I was beginning to think that this was going to be a really good day, my father came over, took all the envelopes, and put them in his pocket. I never saw them again.

My parents had registered me for P.S. 80, the local public school, but I hardly ever went. When I did, the teachers would ask me, "Where have you been? You can't skip school." I would make up extraordinary stories. "My aunt got sick, and I had to help her with her pushcart, or she wouldn't be able to feed my cousins." I created a fantasy world populated by family members who needed me so much that I couldn't possibly go to school.

One time in spelling class my English teacher said, "Schwartz, come here." We had just been tested on ten spelling words, and I had spelled every one wrong. He said, "Not only did you get every word wrong, but you made a mistake in your own name." Sure enough, I had left out the *tz.* I thought that was kind of funny.

I'd get up in the morning, and if I went to school, I would always try to get the seat near the classroom door, so I could make a fast getaway. As it turned out, school wasn't a total waste; despite myself I was learning to read and write and learn a little arithmetic. But I couldn't help but feel that my life had absolutely nothing to do with algebra, or the Spanish-American War, or *Beowulf,* or whatever else I was being forced to study. I just didn't see the point.

In one class there was always so much turmoil that when the teacher's head was turned, I could sometimes sneak out altogether. I'd hide my knapsack full of schoolbooks in the stairwell, then I'd climb up the train trestles — that was quite a feat — and I'd sneak onto the Third Avenue El, making sure I didn't land on the tracks when I jumped over the top of the wall. That way I could skip the fare. I'd ride deep into the Bronx, and then I'd turn around and come all the way into Brooklyn, Coney Island, or Brighton Beach.

Sometimes my buddies would go with me. We'd be at school, hiding out in the stairwell, and I'd ask my friend Charlie, "Hey, what do you want to do?"

"Let's go to the nudie show."

"Okay." So we'd ride the train down to the sleazy theaters on Forty-second Street, where the burlesque nudes performed. We'd slip in a side door when one show was ending and everyone was leaving. Once inside the theater we'd duck down until the next show, and then we'd pop up from under our seats to see all those girls with their bare breasts jiggling.

Those dancing girls were exciting to look at, but even they weren't better than the movies. To survive life at home I'd invent roles for myself based on the movies I'd seen. I would sit in my room and imagine sword fighting alongside Errol Flynn, as the two of us rescued Olivia de Havilland. I'd reach over suavely and light a cigarette for Greta Garbo, or take Jean Harlow out for a romantic dinner. I'd picture myself riding horses with Norma Shearer, or swinging across the deck of a pirate vessel with Douglas Fairbanks Jr.

The big neon sign out front identified Loews Schooner Theater on Simpson Street, but I didn't need that sign to find it. After Julie died, I practically lived there. My shoes may have had holes in them, and at home my parents may have been squabbling, but when I was sitting in the movie theater, all of that disappeared. In my mind I was wearing a pin-striped suit with a .45 stuck in my belt. My hair was slicked back, and on my feet were the same expensive two-toned shoes Jimmy Cagney wore. My father was a tailor, and I knew clothes. I couldn't own suits like they wore in the movies, but I sure could pretend I did.

On days we skipped school and didn't go to the movies, we'd go over to the Hudson River, which was on the West Side of Manhattan, and we'd watch the big ships go by. There was a lot of traffic on the waterways, and sometimes we'd sneak onto the ferry going to Jersey. I became really good at it. As I walked toward the ticket taker, I would point and say, "Oh, look at that guy," and then I'd duck past him and run onto the ferry. It wasn't easy, but I could do it almost every time.

Not only did I climb up the trestles of the

El up to the subway platform, I would jump on the backs of trolley cars or taxis, holding on for dear life. People inside the cabs or the trolley cars would look out to see a kid hanging on the back, and sometimes they would scream. When the vehicle stopped, I would jump down and take off running. I figured I was becoming a self-taught movie stuntman, and in fact I was becoming a pretty good athlete — not because I was dedicated to a sport, but because I was preparing myself for the movies.

I became a child of the streets. That's where I lived — and I don't mean that in a negative way. When the weather was good, we played stickball. Or we'd climb into tenement houses that had been condemned. We played war on abandoned lots, using bricks as hand grenades. I was always fearless as a kid. I guess I just didn't feel like I had anything to lose.

As a teen I didn't eat much food at all. Once in a while we'd steal an apple off a pushcart, but on some level I knew that food wasn't what I needed. I needed to come to grips with who I was: with being a Jew, with being poor, with being raised in a household where the only feelings I could get in touch with were tension, anger, sadness, and humiliation.

■ ■ ■ ■

Not long after we moved to the Bronx, my father got a job with Shapiro and Sons, an important clothier in Manhattan's garment district. Soon after my father started they made him a supervisor and put twenty other tailors to work under him. He didn't want the job, even though it paid him a better salary, but they gave him no choice.

Given my mother's focus on success, my father's ascent to management tipped the balance of power, at least for a while. Now he was the boss at home, demanding his dinner, telling my mother what to do and where to get off. I often wonder: if he had gotten this job earlier, would he have left my mother? That was the only time I remember my father acting with confidence, even a little swagger.

Unfortunately, his new job didn't last long. He wasn't really suited to being a supervisor. He tried to take a humane approach to the workers, but they mistook his kindness for weakness and took advantage of him. And when they stopped producing clothes in the quantities the company demanded, my father was fired. He went back to working for himself — and to making very little money.

I'm not sure my father would agree with

this assessment, but I thought that he was happiest when he worked for himself. Maybe not quite so proud of himself, but happier. He didn't have to service the sewing machines. He didn't have to worry about other employees. He only had to do his job. He made thirty or forty bucks a week, enough to take care of the basics, and somewhere deep inside, I think he was satisfied. If only my mother had felt the same way.

To pass the hours I spent alone each day, I started to draw. My first drawings were made on the brown paper my father used to wrap his customers' clothes. He would pull off a three-foot length and give it to me, and I'd cut it into three pieces and draw on them using my father's tailor's chalk or pencils or crayons. I also drew on the sidewalk with different-colored chalk.

I found myself able to accurately copy things I saw, and then I found I could add things, and all of a sudden my artwork wasn't just copying anymore. It was something else again. In the movies I could fence with Errol Flynn, but with my art I could go even further. I liked drawing what I was thinking or seeing. It became a driving force in my life.

Art was also an antidote for the deep depressions that I suffered as a child. They would strike without warning, and all of a sudden I would just lose interest in everything around me. I loved playing stickball, but if depression hit, I'd just sit there in my bedroom, and I wouldn't move. I'd hear my friends calling me: "Bernie, come on, we're going to play ball." But I wouldn't go out. I wouldn't do anything. I would sit there like a zombie. Eventually something would snap me out of it, then I'd look around and realize that I was sitting in the bedroom, or on the floor, or lying under the bed, hiding.

I had had these spells while Julie was alive, but they got worse and came more frequently after he died. I was never sure when they'd strike. I'd be looking out the window, and I'd turn my head, and all of a sudden I would be overwhelmed by the feeling that I had to hide.

Now in my ninth decade of life, I still get overwhelmed by these deep depressions, this sense that despite how fortunate I've been, perhaps I haven't done as well as I should have, perhaps I haven't achieved enough success. It may not make sense, but when I'm in a funk there's no room for logical thoughts, only that heavy feeling of unbearable sadness.

Objectively, you might say I did just fine in

life, but when I'm feeling depressed that just doesn't seem good enough. And to be honest, I never was interested in just doing okay. All my adult life I wanted to be the best. Or at least to do my best. If you aren't doing your best, if you aren't trying as hard as you possibly can, why bother? I've never had much patience for people who were loaded with talent but didn't give it their all. I still don't understand that. If anything, I was an overachiever. I took the talent that I had and made the most of it. And even when the deep blues come over me, I take comfort in that thought.

One afternoon after I'd been playing stickball, I went into our apartment to clean up. I went into the kitchen and I could see that my mother was very agitated. I wasn't sure what the trouble was.

"Come with me," she said in a fury. I had no idea where she was going.

We went out of our house and over to Southern Boulevard, where there were three theaters, a Loews, an RKO, and another small art house. I didn't dare ask my mother where we were going or why. We walked to the front of the Loews and waited. All of a sudden, I saw my mother stiffen.

Coming out of the theater was my father,

and it looked like he was with a redheaded woman. Could have been, anyway. I didn't know who she was, and I was giving him the benefit of the doubt. But when my father saw my mother standing there, he went white. He saw I was there too, and maybe that embarrassed him even more. The girl stopped too, so I suppose they had been together.

My mother started to bawl out my father in Hungarian, calling him a "good-for-nothing bum." He didn't say anything. This beautiful red-haired woman stepped forward between my mother and father, and she said, "Don't hold your breath for a nickel's worth." With that, she turned around and walked briskly away. My mother didn't know what to do. She kept shouting at my father, and then she looked around, realized where she was, and stopped. To this day I don't know what the red-haired lady's comment meant, but I assume she was saying she wasn't going to be part of any marital showdown.

My father walked past her and came up to me, and both of us walked home. My mother came in about ten minutes later. I don't know what they said to each other, because I got the hell out of there. After that things were tense around the house, but not much worse than usual.

When I was in my early teens I used to take one of my roller skates and put an orange crate across it, and I'd sit in it and ride down hills in the Bronx. I could pick up a lot of speed, and I shifted my weight so I could steer it. I got very good at it. Then one day I dipped a little too close to the ground and I scraped the middle finger of my left hand. It didn't hurt much, but it created a blood blister, which became infected.

The next day it was festering, and a couple of days later it really hurt like crazy. My hand was swollen, I felt a lot of pain under my armpit, and I was dizzy. My mother took me the three blocks to East Bronx Hospital's free clinic. A young doctor looked at my finger, and without saying a word he pricked it with a needle. I didn't feel a thing.

He said to me, "You've got a serious infection here. Hey, you're a good-looking kid." That washed away my anxiety. He added, "Take advantage of it. Don't neglect your life like you've neglected your finger."

It was the first time anyone had told me that I was good-looking, or that I should make something of my life. But both thoughts stayed with me. I think I've always been vain, but this is when I first became fully aware of it. I soon grew very fond of my thick, luxuriant head of hair, which I could slick down on the sides and leave curly on top. I loved the way people looked at me. Underneath all that hair was a good-looking face. I've always been a little ashamed of acknowledging that I was handsome, but the truth is that I took real pleasure in looking good. I always kept that feeling inside me because I was afraid of the Schwartz curse, afraid something bad would happen to snatch that good feeling away.

When I was fifteen, a woman in the neighborhood called me over and asked if I could give her a hand lifting something in her apartment. As soon as I got inside the door she closed it, grabbed me, and kissed me so hard that my mouth started to bleed. She rubbed her body against me. After a few minutes I found myself back outside her building, with the feeling of her lips on my mouth, and her urgency, and at the same time feeling violated. I walked the half block to my house, went upstairs, and washed my face. I didn't know what to think.

It was an era when nobody wanted to stand out, to be unusual. If you were good-looking, you were likely to be called a homosexual, a fairy. But once I found out the effect I could have on girls, I didn't give a shit what anybody called me. Before puberty, I had no interest in girls, like most kids my age. Now that I was fifteen, I was starting to notice the way the wind would blow girls' summer dresses against their bodies, and how great their legs and breasts looked.

When I first started to go out with girls I quickly fell for them, but they didn't seem to care about me the same way. I could tell from their behavior that I didn't mean anything to them. The lesson I took from this was simple: be careful; protect yourself. As a result, I was hesitant to enter into any relationships.

I was fifteen when I met Alicia Allen, a beautiful girl with a love of acting that made us instant companions. I had never told anybody but Alicia that I wanted to be in pictures, because I was sure they'd have laughed me out of the room. I hadn't done any acting yet, but I was interested in giving it a try.

So I auditioned at the 92nd Street YMHA and played the lighthouse keeper's son in the play *Thunder Rock.* Early in the play I had to walk through a scene and then come back in and speak my one line. It was actually just one word: "Yes." I also had a part in another play at the 92nd Street Y, a Clifford Odets play. I can still remember that line too. I said, "They found Lefty in a car barn with a bullet in his head."

Having the name Schwartz helped me get parts in YMHA plays. What an irony. The truth was that I didn't feel Jewish in any way. As a kid all it meant to me was being taunted, being bullied, and not being treated as an equal.

One day Alicia said to me, "What are you doing Saturday? I'm going to a party. Want to come?"

"Sure."

Saturday I called Alicia on the phone and told her, "I'll be there at six to pick you up." I got dressed in my coolest clothes. I wore a dark blue jacket with gray slacks, with loafers and a tie. My father had fixed the jacket, and it looked really spiffy.

I went downtown to Twelfth Street where Alicia lived. She was older than I was, and she had her own place. From there we took a cab to a private residence in the theater district over on the West Side. It was an old mansion. I had never been inside anything like it. We walked through the gate, in the front door, and went upstairs. Alicia introduced me to lots of people, and then, before I knew it, she was introducing me to Ethel Merman. I couldn't believe it, and I'm sure

I looked as starstruck as I felt. But Ethel Merman was very gracious, and she put me at ease. "Hi, kid. Oh, what a nice-looking guy you are."

I loved being at this party with all these nicely dressed people, and I was pleased with the way I was able to mingle. I spoke well. I watched my language. We had a really nice evening, and Alicia was pretty happy with me for holding my own with this sophisticated crowd.

The next time I took Alicia out she invited me back to her tiny little apartment, and we necked in the living room. Things were hot and heavy for a while, and then she said, "Excuse me a minute," and went into the bathroom. When she came back out, she was wearing only her panties and her bra. I was stunned. She had an amazingly voluptuous body. I started to unbutton my shirt, and she sweetly took my hand and walked me over to her bed. This is what I had always imagined sex would be like, just like it was in the movies.

We began to touch each other, and after all these years I can still remember the smoothness of her skin and how great it smelled. I was worried about how I would perform the first time, but I made up for my inexperience with sheer enthusiasm. And Alicia made it easy for me. She was just so sweet and loving. I can't imagine how I could have had a better first experience. I found myself thinking. *I've got to grow up in a hurry, so I can have more of this.* Even then I knew I wasn't ready for a real relationship.

Unfortunately, I was right. Alicia and I continued to go out, but the time between dates got longer and longer. Alicia was kind to me, which is to say that she didn't dump me. But we both knew that what we had together wasn't going to go any distance. We never made love again, but that one time was truly unforgettable.

That same year, two years after Julie's death, my parents decided to have another child. I couldn't understand what they thought they were doing. Maybe they were looking for evidence that God wasn't punishing them. But as far as I was concerned, my parents had no business having another child. They had cared so little for the ones they had already had! But the next thing I knew, I had a baby brother, Robert.

My parents bought a carriage for Bobby, and I would push it up and down the street. One reason I enjoyed it was that the good-looking girls who sat across the street rocking their own baby carriages would look at me as I walked by. They were eighteen and nineteen, mothers already, and I kept hoping one of them would invite me into her apartment and have sex with me. It never happened.

If I felt remote from my family before Bobby was born, afterward I felt even more so. What little enthusiasm my parents had for child rearing went into Bobby, although I can't say they treated him any better than they had Julie and me. My parents had mellowed a bit, and money wasn't quite so tight, but I just don't think they were cut out for raising children.

I tried to feel close to my new baby brother, but I didn't have much success. I couldn't help but compare him with Julie. Julie and I would fight and laugh and scream and hug each other. Without him, I was flying solo. Bobby just couldn't begin to fill the hole that Julie's death left behind. I was going to school, but I didn't give a shit one way or the other. Fuck school. Fuck that whole system. I wasn't going to get involved with it, not one bit.

I couldn't wait until I could get out of the Bronx, even though I had no idea what my future would hold. What future? When I look back on those days, I wonder what might have happened if my parents had said to me,

"We see that you're interested in art and acting, so we're going to send you to a special school that will help you develop your talents and interests." My parents had no idea what my interests were. I try not to fault them for that, since they raised their kids much the way everyone else did in those days. But the bottom line was that I was lost, and the education I was getting was "fuck 'em and feed 'em fish," although that wasn't a line I'd understand until I was stationed in Guam during World War II.

When we were stationed there, the chief quartermaster was responsible for feeding all the sailors on the island. He oversaw the menus, and made sure they were followed and the meals were cooked properly. One day one of the men who acquired food rushed in and said, "Chief, we're in trouble. I went out to get chicken and there's not enough to feed the men." The chief didn't miss a beat, replying, "Fuck 'em, and feed 'em fish." Word got out, and from that time on, we used that as our mantra.

Looking back, I can see that poverty also played a damaging role in my childhood. Lots of kids never get to know who they are or get a real chance at success in life because they don't have the few advantages they need. Good things may still happen to you, but if they do, poverty tends to cancel them out. My mother was frustrated and bitter about the cards she'd been dealt in life. After she'd take some of that frustration out on me by slapping me around a bit, I wasn't going to go out into the street and find a quiet place to practice the violin. That just wasn't going to happen. It's far more likely in that situation that you're going to take that rage you feel and go push some other kid around. And if you're lucky, you'll stay out of jail.

After I graduated from the ninth grade, we moved back to Manhattan, near the corner where my father had had his old tailor shop. I was glad to be back in Manhattan, which was a much better place for me to live than the Bronx. I always liked the action there, so even when I lived in the Bronx, I would find my way to Manhattan. I liked the subways. There were always good-looking girls on them, and sometimes they would make eyes at me.

After we returned to Manhattan my father opened a new tailor shop. One time my father went a little nuts in the new store. Whether it was caused by alcohol or stress, I don't know. I doubt it was alcohol. He kept it in the house, and he would take a nip now and then, but I never once saw him drunk.

My father just couldn't handle stress. He did the sewing, and my mother ran the store. If there was a dispute with a customer, she handled it.

On this day it was hot and muggy, a typical summer afternoon. I was hanging around outside the shop, when my mother called for me: "Bernie! Bernie!" I opened the door, and there was my father under the stairwell, gripping a knife in his hand as though he was going to kill himself. My father's eyes were fixed in a blank stare; they didn't move, or even blink. It was like he was hypnotized. When my mother tried to get his attention he didn't seem to see her.

My mother asked me to go under the stairs to talk to him, and as I moved a little closer I could see him begin to come to grips with where he was. He looked genuinely surprised to find himself under the staircase with the knife. I sometimes think my father may have had some mental illness too. But maybe it was just that the pressure got to be too much sometimes, and he snapped.

The pressure in the larger world was building too. We started hearing stories about the way the Germans were persecuting Jews, about the Nazis' Jew baiting and discrimination. I hated the Nazis. Once I started to hear about what Hitler and the Nazis were doing to the Jews, I would have recurrent nightmares about it.

A little ways uptown from where we lived was the part of New York they called Germantown. Here Americans who sympathized with the Nazis would march down First Avenue to show their solidarity with Hitler. When we knew that one of these parades was under way, a gang of my friends and I would make our way onto the rooftops, jumping from roof to roof until we overlooked the parade.

A year earlier I had discovered the existence of condoms, which now we filled with anything that would splatter on the German marchers. We'd fill them with water or piss or colored dye or dog food and drop them from the roof. We also took women's nylons, filled them the same way, twirled them over our heads, and let them fly! We'd watch as our missiles struck the young kids and their parents marching in those stinking Nazi uniforms.

The first time we did it, we didn't realize how angry they would get. The Nazi sympathizers ran up into the building in a rage, so we had to escape over the roofs to Second Avenue, where we climbed down a fire escape and dropped down to the street. Even then we couldn't just nonchalantly walk away. We were a pretty ragged lot, so we drew some attention. Three tough-looking men cornered me, but I was able to dodge past the first one, and then I just took off like a bullet down Second Avenue. The men had bats in their hands, and it was one of the few times I felt really scared. Fortunately, I was able to outrun them. And so it was that I fought my own little war. Little did I know that in a short while our entire nation would be engulfed by the real thing.

Around this time I decided I didn't like my last name, Schwartz, because it was German. Changing my name was my way of telling the Germans to go fuck themselves. I began experimenting with different names, calling myself David Street, or David Sparrow, or David Sorrow. Meanwhile, my parents enrolled me at Seward Park High School, which was so far downtown that the streets didn't have numbers anymore. As it turned out, I never showed up there because I so desperately wanted to get away. I knew if I hung around much longer, I'd never escape. So I decided to join the Navy and see the world.

Performing in a musical while enlisted in the Navy, 1943.

4
ENSIGN SCHWARTZ

In the spring of 1942, I took the Lexington Avenue train from my home to downtown Manhattan. I walked over to Whitehall Street and entered a big red granite fortress of a building where you could enlist in the armed forces. I went in and asked, "Can I join the military?" Needless to say, they were only too delighted to help me.

There was a whole group of young guys signing up that day. A sergeant asked all of us to fill out a form indicating what branch of service we wanted to be in. I put down the Navy. After the sergeant collected our forms he said, "Sixty-five percent of you want to be in the Navy, thirty-five percent of you want to be in the Army, and just two of you want to be Marines. That means that except for you two, all of you other guys want to live forever." I almost took the bait and switched my request to the Marines, but then I took a moment to consider whether I wanted to survive the war or not. I decided I'd take my chances with the Navy.

Because I was only sixteen, I had to get one of my parents to sign a form saying they consented to my enlistment. I had absolutely no intention of letting my parents get in the way of my escape, so I took the form outside, forged my mother's signature, waited an hour, went back in, and gave it to the guy at the desk. He took the paper, glanced at the signature, and said, "Welcome to the Navy."

That afternoon I went back home and told my parents I had enlisted and was due to report the next day. I'd been right about their reaction; they weren't at all happy about what I'd done.

My mother said, "How did you get in?"

"I just went and signed up."

"But you're so young," she said. "Why do you have to go into the war? Where are you going to go?"

"Mom," I said, "it's a great thing to join the Navy. You see the world. They'll be sending me everywhere, and don't worry about me, I'll be fine."

"If you say so," she said.

I packed a few clothes and returned for my enlistment the next day. I had to take a physical to make sure I was healthy, and after I passed it, I was issued a duffel bag, some clothes, and some underwear. A group of us went into a big room, where a recruiter lectured us on what it meant to be a sailor and what was expected of us. Then they fed us.

I was filled with excitement. The way I saw it, people are like leaves that have fallen into a swift-moving stream. As the leaves get carried downstream, some are caught in rocks and never get any farther. Some are swept to shore. Others — the lucky ones — keep going, missing the stones, staying clear of the shore, staying afloat until they reach the river delta and break free into open water. I was that sort of leaf when I joined the Navy. It was the happiest day of my life.

The following day the Navy sent me to a recruiting station in the town of Samson in upper New York State. There we were given haircuts and started our training. We marched a lot, which I loved. Everyone was very friendly. I didn't run across any animosity. A couple of guys didn't seem to like me, but they didn't like anybody, so I avoided them just like everybody else did. I made friends with a couple of Puerto Rican guys.

We were there for six weeks, and even though we had a couple of weekends off, I never left the base. They showed us movies and held dances for us. For the first time in my life, I tasted the unbelievable freedom of being on my own. My mother wasn't screaming. My father wasn't sitting there looking morose. All around me were the eager young faces of guys like me, and we all became friends.

I enjoyed the Navy because our country looked after us — I don't know how else to put it. The Navy was my surrogate family. They gave us shots, fed us, and tried to make sure we were safe wherever we went. Some of us would get killed, but not for lack of effort on the Navy's part. I have to say that I totally enjoyed the Navy experience.

Because I wasn't yet eighteen, I couldn't go overseas, so when I finished basic training, the Navy sent me to school to learn a specialty. I didn't know how to do anything when I went into the service. I didn't know how to fix an engine. I didn't even know how to cook or sew, so they decided to send me to school to become a signalman.

The Navy signalman school was located on the Champaign-Urbana campus of the University of Illinois. I had a really good time there. I learned Morse code, and I learned how to wave semaphore flags so that if all else failed we could communicate messages on the open water.

There were a lot of guys in the Navy who had never seen a Jew before. One guy, Jack

Petapalitta, who came from the Deep South, wanted to see my horns. Where he grew up, everybody believed that Jews had horns on their heads. I pulled my hair back and told him, "Jack, you can look all day, but you ain't gonna find no horns." The nice part was, he had no real feeling about it either way, and we got to be friends. But my antennae were always up for anti-Semites.

There were lots of beautiful girls at the Champaign-Urbana campus. Since I intended to go into show business after I got out of the Navy, I decided to try out for a part in a musical the college music department was putting on for the Navy base on campus. Here was a chance to pursue my dream of acting and meet girls at the same time. They had a casting call for sailors, and out of the hundred guys who tried out, eight or nine were chosen, and one of those lucky guys was me. I was ecstatic when the director picked me. I had just gotten to school, and already I had a part in a play!

Once again I found that I wasn't intimidated at all by performing. I felt that being up on that stage was where I belonged. I danced. I sang. I even nuzzled a girl in one romantic scene. Nobody taught me how. I just did it, and it worked.

I don't remember my lines from that show,

but I do remember how much I loved showing off. I also know that the girls were just nuts about me, which caused one of the other guys in the play to really hate me. But by this time I was used to guys being jealous, and it didn't bother me. Taking shit from a couple of jealous guys was a small price to pay for the good time I was having.

I was in the Navy when they showed us the Cary Grant movie *Destination Tokyo* on base. Cary Grant was my idol. There was nobody in the movies like him. He was the personification of everything a man should be. Cary could be funny, sure, but he could also be smart, or tough. In *Gunga Din* he played a hard man who didn't take crap from anybody. He was like that in a lot of his movies. But Cary had manners, too. He would light a woman's cigarette for her, and his clothes were always impeccable. He wore double-breasted jackets, and I noticed how high his shirt collars were.

I must have gone to see every movie Cary Grant ever made. It was clear that when I was in that movie theater, Cary Grant was talking to me. He was saying, *All right, Bernie, when you're on a date and you get out of a cab, give the driver a five-dollar bill on a two-dollar ride and then get out and open the door on the other side and hold it while the lady gets out.* This was the priceless information I learned from him: how to behave when it mattered most. Cary Grant was talking to *me,* and I was doing my very best to take it all in.

After I saw *Destination Tokyo* with Cary Grant as the submarine commander, I was glad I'd made an unusual choice about what I wanted to do in the Navy. Only a handful of sailors picked the submarines. I was one of them.

When my time at Champaign-Urbana was up, I was promoted from Seaman First Class to Signalman Third Class. I'm not sure why I was promoted; maybe it was because for the first time in my life I had good grades. Or maybe it was because I got along with the girls running the place. As I was packing my clothes to leave, I can remember one of the other sailors saying to his buddy, "You can see why he got promoted."

He walked over to me and said, "Hey, gigolo, what about us?" Meaning, why hadn't *he* gotten promoted — as though it was somehow my fault. He was about my size, and he was looking to pick a fight. Before he could move, I pushed my hand into his face and shoved him, and he fell over backward. He got up, and we threw a couple of punches at each other. He hit me on the side of my head, and I hit him in the mouth a couple of times before the other guys came over and broke it up. Fortunately, no one reported us. That was the end of that, but I still remember the guy's face.

The Navy sent fifteen of us to New London, Connecticut, the main U.S. submarine base. They bunked us down in the barracks, and I went to all kinds of classes to qualify as part of a submarine crew. I couldn't believe they would trust me with that kind of responsibility, so I decided to take my new role seriously. I paid close attention to everything they taught us, and I tried hard to do well in my classes.

This felt very different from the days in New York when I had hated school. I had hated school because I had hated my life. But I liked my life in the Navy. They treated me well, and for the first time ever I felt like I had a purpose. I also found I had an aptitude for it. Before the Navy, I had some idea that I might be bright, but I hid the feeling. I didn't want to be even more different. Also, the Navy appealed to your sense of honor, which resonated with me. So once I decided I wanted to be in subs, I vowed I would do the best I could because my honor was at stake. The washout rate for sub school was pretty high, but I was determined to make it all the way through.

Three subs were tied up at the base in New London, huge, intimidating, steel-plated monsters. Two weeks after arriving in New London, I went into a submarine for the very first time, along with four other new recruits. As we climbed down the conning tower, my first thought was, *I wonder if I did the right thing.* It was so tight in there that I couldn't help but feel claustrophobic, especially after they locked down the watertight door to the outside world.

Once we were amidships I couldn't believe how little room there was. The inside of a submarine looks a lot bigger in the movies. The training officers took us into the control room, where we were told all about the submarine: what class it was, how much range it had, how deep it could go, etc. Then we went forward to the torpedo room. We saw the engine room, the mess hall, and where the sailors slept. I couldn't believe how tight everything was. To get into a bunk I had to grab the bar above it and pull my butt and legs onto the mattress. It felt like I was resting in a chest of drawers.

Our trainers told us that submarine duty wasn't for everyone, and that if we wanted to opt out, now was the time to say something.

I imagined myself spending long stretches of time at sea, sliding in and out of those tiny bunks, eating in a crowded little mess area, not to mention living with the danger of having the sub blown apart by depth charges. I admit it was daunting, but I was damned if I was going to be drummed out because I couldn't take the pressure. I owed it to myself to make this work.

Once you elected to stay, you still had to pass some rigorous physical tests before you qualified for sub duty. But I was ready. As it turned out, all those times I had climbed up the steel beams of the El to beat the fare would serve me well. The toughest test of all was a simulated escape from a submarine. In the middle of our training camp a ten-story tower had been constructed and completely filled with water. You had to start at the bottom with a Munson lung, the predecessor to the scuba tank. Your job was to make your way gradually up to the top, using a guide line. If you floated up too fast, you could get the bends. A lot of guys couldn't do it; they panicked, let the rope go, and would have to be rescued by divers. I had no trouble at all.

Those of us who passed the physical and written tests were crammed like cattle into old-fashioned rail cars. Then we rolled and rattled across the country for five long days until we got to San Diego, California. The Navy purposely kept the train moving slowly in order to stagger the arrival of sailors all around the country who were converging on San Diego. Sometimes the train was so slow we could get out and walk alongside it to get some exercise and relieve the boredom. Along the way girls from small towns would hop on the train and ride with us as far as they felt like going. We'd play cards or charades with them, or we'd kiss a little.

Finally we arrived in San Diego, where I was assigned to another base for more schooling. One weekend a group of us drove up from San Diego to Los Angeles, where we went to the famous Hollywood Canteen restaurant and nightclub. Movie stars came there to entertain the troops, and on this occasion the headliner was Gloria DeHaven. She was a real beauty. At one point our eyes locked; I was smiling, and she smiled back at me. I thought, if I wasn't in this sailor suit I could talk to her a bit, and we could have a drink, and who knows? Her hair was almost blond, and I was struck by the way her dress clung to her voluptuous body — to her full breasts, her tiny waist, and her curvaceous hips. Then it was back to San Diego, where I completed my training. Before I knew it, I was boarding a huge transport ship for the long journey to Pearl Harbor.

There was very little for us to do on board ship. We watched a war movie or two, and we played cards, talked, and somehow whiled away the endless hours. When we finally got to Hawaii, Pearl Harbor looked like a massive naval junkyard. We could see the towering wreckage left from the Japanese attack the year before. Oil was still leaking out of the sunken battleship *Arizona.* There was a tension in the air here at Pearl Harbor, where thousands of American sailors had died so recently, along with a sense of disgrace that America's Navy had been caught unprepared.

We trained intensively over the next year or more, and when my training finally came to an end, I felt I knew everything there was to know about submarines. As it turned out, however, I never did serve much on subs. One day my officer called me in and told me I was being assigned to the submarine tender *Proteus,* which supplied and maintained the sub fleet. It was a very large ship with two huge hooks on either side, which it used to pull a submarine out of the water. The *Proteus* carried tons of supplies, food, and ammunition — everything a submarine needed.

After I reported to the *Proteus,* we sailed to

Guam, where I bunked onshore in a Quonset hut. Guam had been captured from the Japanese in August 1944, but there were still Japanese soldiers in the middle of the island who had never given up. Every now and then they'd sneak into our encampment and steal food. Guam was a great place to wait to be called for duty. The base had a beautiful swimming pool carved out of coral, where I got a chance to swim almost every day.

I also had a chance to practice my signalman skills. I would go out on a submarine, and when it surfaced after its dive I'd go topside and signal to the sub tender. After one of those training missions, we came back to Guam to learn that the war was over. After all that training I hadn't seen a single shot fired in anger!

I did have an amazing moment on the *Proteus* when the U.S. fleet sailed into Tokyo Bay. The Japanese had surrendered, and on September 2, 1945, from the deck of my ship I was able to use my binoculars to watch General Douglas MacArthur, Admiral Chester Nimitz, and Admiral William "Bull" Halsey sign the treaty to end the war with Japan.

After the ceremony our ship docked for twelve hours, and we were allowed to go ashore. While walking around a sub base about four hours from Tokyo, I discovered a cave filled with Japanese provisions, blankets, machine guns, and all kinds of equipment. I signaled back to the *Proteus,* and they sent a detail to come and collect everything. The captain shook my hand and congratulated me.

The *Proteus* chugged back to Guam and picked up some sailors, then we returned to Pearl Harbor, where the local girls greeted us like war heroes. A group of us visited wounded soldiers in a nearby hospital. There wasn't much work to do during the day, so we figured we could use the time to do some good by going and keeping these guys company. Some of them had been sent here from other islands, and a few had been hurt in the original bombing of Pearl Harbor. Guys my age had arms and legs blown off. One guy named Steven had broken his back. We had a great conversation, so I went back to see him several more times while I was in Pearl Harbor.

Another, less selfless reason I kept going back to the hospital was a beautiful nurse from Wisconsin named Emma. She was older than I was, and she was both matter-of-fact and kind, in the way that good nurses often are. When she came on the ward and I saw her for the first time, I asked, "May I give you a hand?" She looked at me and said, "Come on." I followed her to her station, where she gave me a tray of medicine to carry. Then we walked together from ward to ward as she visited the patients, and I gave out medications.

An evening with her at her apartment was my last great moment of the war. Not long afterward I got my orders home. From Hawaii we traveled through the Panama Canal up to Norfolk, Virginia, where a lot of us debarked. The Navy took us by train to Samson, New York, where the rest of us were discharged.

I had spent more than three years in the Navy. I was handed a modest check and my discharge pin, and later the Navy sent me a piece of paper in the mail saying I had served my country honorably.

I was twenty, and it was time for me to get serious about finding a way to get into the movies.

In Guam during the war, 1944.

5
The Dramatic Workshop

Once the war ended, I began making plans. I figured once I got home I would spend the first couple of months getting acclimated to civilian life. I had some dough, about seven hundred dollars in Navy pay that I had accumulated, plus another two hundred they gave each of us on discharge. That was enough so that I wouldn't have to ask my parents for any money.

Once I was discharged in Upstate New York, I took a Greyhound down to New York City. After the bus pulled into the Midtown terminal, I called the house, and my mother got all excited when I told her I was in Manhattan and would be home soon. I hadn't been home in more than three years. I took the shuttle over to the Lexington Avenue subway, and while I was standing on the platform with my duffel bag waiting for a train, a short, stocky man came up to me and said, "Welcome home, sailor." I thanked him, and we started to talk. He said, "You know, you should be in the movies."

"Thank you," I said. "Maybe I will be one day."

He said, "Do you have an agent? You're gonna need one. I've got some connections in Hollywood. Would you like to come to my house for a drink?" Now I was starting to feel uncomfortable. It seemed pretty obvious that his interest in me was not purely professional, so I thanked him and took the train to my family's house.

When I arrived home, my mother was standing outside the apartment building waiting for me, and we hugged. A woman walked by and said to us, "This is the first homecoming I've seen! Welcome home." Being back felt very strange. My father was working downtown, and my little brother Bobby was now five years old. It didn't take me long to see that nothing had changed except me. Only a handful of guys within a ten-block radius had joined the service. The ones who had stayed behind seemed terribly immature to me. The returning servicemen weren't exactly sophisticated, but we were a lot more knowledgeable and worldly than our buddies who hadn't gone anywhere or done anything. Even my family members seemed to have shrunk somehow.

My mother said, "So how was Paris?"

"Mom, I didn't go to Paris," I told her. "I went to Asia."

My first day back I tried going out in my Navy uniform, but it didn't attract too much interest, so I put it away. Instead I dressed up really nicely and went downtown, and this became a regular trip for me. Over the next few years I saw lots of Broadway shows using the trick I'd learned as a kid to avoid the steep ticket prices: I'd wait until the second act, and then I'd sneak in. I saw Marlon Brando in *A Streetcar Named Desire* that way. On stage Marlon worked with extraordinary ease — or at least he made it seem that way. He brought incredible personality and individuality to the role, and I found his work enthralling.

Marlon and I were about the same age, so seeing him on stage got me thinking about my own dreams. While I was watching him up there, my mind raced with questions: *How do you get up there? What makes it happen? Do you have to have a natural talent, or special smarts, or can you go to school for this?*

When the play ended I went outside, where I heard people buzzing with enthusiasm about what they had seen. Suddenly I felt a wave of sadness come over me. When I looked around me at the people who had been in the audience, I could see they had sophistication and intelligence. But not me. I didn't know *nuttin.*

Back in the neighborhood I told everyone I knew that I was going to be in show business. Around this time I developed an obsessive interest in my appearance. I went to the pool regularly, and I worked hard on my physique. I was a good-looking kid, with my dark hair and light eyes. One day I found some peroxide and put it in my hair to lighten it, and my hair turned red. At the time a play on Broadway featured a cast of redheads, so when people asked me about my new hair color, I told them I was trying out for that play.

The consensus in the neighborhood was that I was a redheaded homosexual. Any guy who would dye his hair had to be peculiar. When the old women in the neighborhood who kept watch on everything saw me going out at night all dressed up, they started a rumor that I was working in a club where men dressed as women. How did that get started? What a bunch of *meshuggena yentas.*

Once I'd made my ambitions public, I had to deal with people in the neighborhood constantly asking me, "Well, how's it going? Have you seen anybody?" By this they meant talent scouts, or agents, or casting directors. Again and again, my answer was, "Well, no, not yet."

After a while I met a photographer who took some publicity photos of me and sent them to the Conover Modeling Agency. This was something that wasn't done. Usually you went for an interview and brought your pictures with you. When the photos arrived, the agency assumed I had already had an interview, so they called me to come in for a meeting. When I showed up, the agent asked me my name. I won't say he was anti-Semitic, but I thought the temperature of his voice dropped after I told him I was Bernie Schwartz. In those days, Jews weren't models, and models weren't Jews. But to my surprise I did score a couple of modeling jobs from him. I even got on the cover of a magazine, which earned me a hundred bucks for a day's work.

Those minor successes encouraged me, but they didn't make up for the constant insecurity I felt. No matter what I did, I never felt okay, I never felt like I was good enough or that I belonged. My looks set me apart, but that wasn't always good news. Sometimes I thought my mother had been so quick to beat the hell out of me — and not

Julie — because she couldn't understand why I didn't look anything like her. My worn clothes set me apart too, even though my father made them look good as only a master tailor can. Hard as he tried, I always felt there was something threadbare about them. Maybe it wasn't the clothes that were second class; maybe it was me.

After coming home from the war, I found that I still felt incomplete, which led me to behave strangely sometimes. On the one hand I was overly sensitive: I was always expecting to hear someone insult me for being a Jew, so I was quick to start a fight if I even suspected that someone was being rude to me. On the other hand, I found myself kissing up to people. I would laugh at jokes whether they were funny or not. I was always so attentive, hanging on the other person's every word. If some guy mentioned his mother, I might say, "No kidding. You mean your mother is still alive?" even though the guy was only forty-seven years old. Of course she was alive. But I would make a big *megillah* out of it. I wanted people to like me, so I wanted to show them that I cared about their lives.

Unfortunately, my behavior often had the opposite effect. People could tell I wasn't being genuine, and they were right. How could I be, when I felt so incomplete, like a pile of Legos that hadn't yet been put together?

It was painfully clear that one piece of the puzzle that was missing was my education. Simply put, I didn't have one. I knew I was smart; I had learned that in the Navy. But an education — knowledge that didn't have to do with the Navy or submarines or being a signalman — that was something I just didn't have. I hadn't attended school much in junior high, and by the time high school came around I had already enlisted in the Navy.

After I came home from the Navy, I re-enrolled in Seward Park High School so I could get my GED; but once again, my attendance suffered. This time I wasn't cutting class to climb the El trestles; now I was making the rounds of talent agents, trying to jump-start my show business career.

At first I'd just walk into a talent agency or a modeling agency and say to the girl at the desk, "May I speak to one of the agents?"

She'd reply, "Which one?"

"I don't know."

"Sorry, I can't help you."

After that happened a few times, I realized I needed to take a different tack, so I wrote to the big agencies and asked for a list of their agents. Once I had that list I could ask for a specific agent, which helped a lot; now I could ask specifically for "Mr. Lefkowitz" at the William Morris Agency, so I started getting in the door here and there. I made a point of spending six or seven hours each day looking for work. Then I'd head home, although some nights I'd stay downtown if I'd been invited to a party.

During this time I renewed my search for an alternative name to Schwartz. If I met a girl, I might tell her my name was David Street and see how she reacted. I was trying to find a name that would look good up on the silver screen.

Even though I went to class only occasionally, Seward Park gave me a GED, which made me eligible for two years of university, paid for by the GI Bill. The government gave you a list of schools you could attend, but when I went down the list I couldn't find a single acting school. I saw plenty of schools for auto mechanics, but nothing for actors. I was terribly disappointed.

One night I went to a theater downtown to see a play, and a guy there told me that the Dramatic Workshop, which was part of the New School of Social Research on the West Side of Manhattan, was accepting students on the GI Bill. The school had been founded in 1940 by Erwin Piscator, an exiled German Jew; after he died, the school had been taken over by his wife. Hearing this, I just about ran over there.

When I inquired about enrolling, they told me the GI Bill would indeed cover the cost of going to school, but I would have to try out and be selected in order to attend school there. To try out you picked any monologue you wanted and performed it for the school faculty. That was fine with me, and I came back the next day for my audition.

When you're trying out for a big-name acting school, of course you're going to think about performing Shakespeare, but how was a guy like me supposed to wrap his tongue around those soliloquies? I didn't want to do anything that would underscore my working-class Jewish background. In fact, I really didn't want to talk at all, if I could avoid it. So I hit upon the idea of enacting a scene from *Dr. Jekyll and Mr. Hyde* — in pantomime. If I didn't speak, there was no way they could reject me for my accent, right? In total silence I came through a door onto the stage, opened a cabinet, took out chemicals, took the tops off, combined them judiciously, and, when I had the right mix, poured the potion down my throat. It was immediately obvious that something had gone terribly wrong with my experiment! Step by step I walked through the scene, miming each character.

I was accepted to the Dramatic Workshop and enrolled in February of 1947. I don't think my skills at pantomime got me through the door. I think my audience saw just how badly I wanted to act and were compassionate. A lot of young GIs who went to that school were just scammers. They went through the motions so they could draw their GI Bill stipend of sixty bucks a month without having to get a job. Others came so they could learn a little diction or have some fun up on stage, but their hearts weren't really in it — not like mine was.

The school was excellent. It had a theater, the President, on Forty-eighth Street, over on the West Side. Classes took place on the second floor. You got a sense of what it was like to be an actor just from taking classes with other students who had already had some theatrical experience. Not everyone studying there had talent, but some were very impressive — Walter Matthau, Harry Belafonte, Rod Steiger, and Bea Arthur among them. Marlon Brando had studied at the Dramatic Workshop the year before, and already Marlon was getting raves for his starring role in *A Streetcar Named Desire,* and I knew from having seen him just how richly he deserved them.

While I was going to acting school, I was living at home and taking the subway. I would leave the apartment at midday, get off the train at Forty-second Street, and walk over to Eighth Avenue, where the school was. It was a schlep, but I loved the chance to see people from different neighborhoods. On my way home I might run into someone I knew and we'd hang out together, go to a candy store or a pool hall. I loved the fact that in one part of town I could get corned beef and cabbage, and in another I'd find spaghetti and meatballs, and if I went all the way to Canal Street, I could eat Chinese food, which back then seemed very exotic.

Sometimes when I'd come home late at night the train didn't seem like so much fun. The subway cars were empty and not always safe. Sometimes I'd see two or three tough-looking guys get on together and look hard in my direction. I knew that if they decided to mug me between stops, there wasn't much I could do about it. I was never attacked, but I was often very aware of the possibility.

I wasn't sure whether I'd made the right decision in coming back to New York and living at home with my parents. My mother and father were still fighting. My mother was still mentally ill, and it was starting to look like my younger brother Bobby had inherited some of her problems. As part of her illness, my mother was very paranoid. She would constantly question me: "Where were you? Where did you go last night? Is there really a school? Which school are you going to? What do you do at night?" She'd hear the local gossip, and it would bring out her worst fears.

After more than three years of living on my own in the service, I had become a lot better at handling my mother. When she started ranting, I just heard her out, nodded, and did whatever I wanted to. I wasn't around home that much anyway. But when I was around, she would try to pick fights with me. My father stayed out of it, but I could see that he hated seeing her go after me.

It wasn't long after I started acting classes that I was able to say to myself, *I can do this.* I was inspired by my own progress, and by the encouragement of my fellow actors, talented people such as Walter Matthau. I liked being in classes with Walter. He was a little older than I was, twenty-seven or twenty-eight, and he had already worked off-Broadway. He had some acting experience, and he was kind enough to share what he'd learned.

Bea Arthur was a magnificent woman, highly intelligent, charming, and also very generous to anybody and everybody. She was a natural. We put on a play called *Whistler's Father,* and she played Lysistrata, who arranged for all the women not to have sex with their husbands or boyfriends until they stopped the war. I played a married soldier, and Bea and I had a three- or four-minute scene where I tried to convince her that making love was the best thing to do, but she wouldn't have any part of it. In the show I wore a sort of kilt and laced-up boots, and I carried a shield. When I came out on that stage, I could hear the girls in the audience go "Ooooh." Hearing that sound helped boost my confidence.

Harry Belafonte was about my age. He had had a lot of additional hurdles to overcome simply because he was black. He wasn't sure how much of a future he could have as an actor since there weren't many good parts being written for black men, so he also maintained a career as a singer. Harry and I were very much alike — we were both outsiders. He was like a brother to me. We had a wonderful relationship. We'd hang out together and go to pubs down in the Bowery, where we were less likely to run into racial discrimination. Harry knew where he could go and where he couldn't, so I just followed his lead.

We used to have dinner at one of the several Horn & Hardart's Automats in New York. This was a chain of cafeterias where you put your money in a slot, a little window would open, and you took your food. Horn & Hardart's cafeterias were safe for blacks because there was no maître d' to tell you to get out. After dinner, Harry and I would go down into the subway, and while we were waiting on the platform for the train, he'd beat out a rhythm and sing. When we were with other guys, some of them would hum while he sang, "Daylight come and me wanna go home." Even then he sounded great.

When people invited me to parties, I'd say, "Can I bring my friend Harry?" The place would be crowded with good-looking girls, and we'd work the room like nobody's business. I'd be with this one girl, and I'd look across the room and he'd be with another one, and we'd nod to each other. I loved sharing that moment with him.

Another thing I had in common with Harry was a tendency to get depressed. Knowing that feeling only too well, I could recognize it when Harry had a bad case of the blues. I'd sit down next to him and say,

"Come on, Harry. I know what you're dealing with, and I'm here for you. Come on. Pull out of it." I knew how he was suffering, and I knew he appreciated my support.

One evening we were putting on a performance at the school when a group of toughs from the surrounding neighborhood came in to harass us. How they got in, I don't know. They were fifteen or sixteen years old, a gang of young hoodlums. When I came out on stage, I could hear them rustling in the back seats. One guy screamed out, "Hey faggot! Fairy! Yoo-hoo!" We didn't have any security, so I stopped in the middle of my line and said, "Fuck off, get out of here," in the toughest voice I could muster. Then Harry and Walter and a couple of teachers walked over and told them they had called the cops, so the kids took off.

I was still standing on stage, so I said to the audience, "Excuse me, please." I calmly turned around to the girl I was in the scene with and gave the next line in the play, like I imagined a real pro would do it. Slowly, surely, I was learning.

I was also becoming more experienced with the ladies. One afternoon I met this beautiful girl on the street. I chatted with her, and we went up to her apartment. She was a few years older than I was and a real stunner. After we made love, she told me her boyfriend was Bobby Thomson, the outfielder for the New York Giants. I was still in bed with her when the phone rang. She answered and said, "Hi, Bobby, how are you?" She talked to this great ballplayer while I was snuggling next to her in bed!

As the spring semester was coming to a close, I saw a notice on the bulletin board that there was an opening for an actor with the Stanley Wolf Players. It was a nonunion job, which made it possible for me to apply. Wolf had been a Broadway producer, but he had fallen out of favor with the powers that be in the New York theater world, so he created a drama troupe that played the Borscht Belt resorts in the Catskill Mountains. I went to meet Stanley in his office in Manhattan, and he hired me on the spot. We would be going out on the road for the whole summer. My pay was to be forty bucks a week.

To make a stage for us, the hotels would clear away the dining room tables and set up folding chairs for the audience. We did the same play everywhere we went. It was *This Too Shall Pass,* a play about anti-Semitism and the Jewish experience in America. The audiences always seemed to like it, so we played it every night: three nights in one hotel, four nights in another.

There were five of us in the cast, three guys and two girls, and we all got very close. That was what being on the road in the Catskills was all about. We'd play the hotels at night, and during the day we were expected to circulate among the hotel guests, so that's what I did. To me the Catskills was female guests in bathing suits and all the food you could eat. In the evenings, we put on the play. It was a great experience, heightened by the knowledge that it wouldn't last beyond the end of the summer.

In smaller hotels, we slept in cots in the corridors near the kitchen. There was usually a bathroom down the hall, and the strong smell of food all through the night. At the bigger hotels, sometimes we'd be lucky enough to get our own rooms. I'll never forget one night when I got lucky, and I do mean lucky. I'd been given my own room, right next to one that was being shared by my two fellow actresses. A door with locks on both sides separated us. I was twenty-two, and they were a little older than I was, but not by much. At the time we were all a little crazy.

After the performance that night, I knocked on the door between the rooms. The girls unlocked their side and invited me in. As I entered, one of the girls left to go into my room. The girl who stayed behind started to undress and made it clear she wanted me to do the same. We got in bed together and had sex, and after we were done, I went back in my room and did it with the other one! Incredible! I was able to have great sex on both sides of that door! We shared those adjoining rooms for only two nights, but it was sweet while it lasted.

I liked my part in *This Too Shall Pass.* Stanley also put on *The Jazz Singer,* and I had the Al Jolson role, although I didn't have to do much singing. It was a cut-down version of the full play, which moved from one scene to the next without the musical number in between. I was disappointed that I wasn't allowed to do more, but I was glad they didn't ask me to do the full play. Not only would that have been taxing, but I was probably the wrong guy for the part. Wolf knew what he was doing. He had been in the business for a long time.

While I was performing in *This Too Shall Pass,* Oscar Oskeroff, who ran the Yiddish Theater in Chicago, came to see the play. *This Too Shall Pass* was very Jewish, and he loved me in it, so he asked me to come to Chicago and perform in his company. He said he'd bump my salary to sixty-five dollars a week, so I took the job.

He also wanted me to change my name. He said, "If I put you on the stage as Bernie Schwartz, everybody is going to think I got an Italian boy from the neighborhood and changed his name to Bernie Schwartz. So I'm going to call you Bernie White." I didn't understand his logic, but it was his nickel, so I agreed. After I arrived in Chicago, Oscar also said he wanted me to marry Henreyetta Jacobsen, an actress in the company, so we could become the reigning couple of Jewish theater. He offered to increase my salary to a hundred and fifty dollars a week if I'd do it. At first I wasn't sure he was serious, but to my astonishment it turned out that he was.

Henreyetta was a nice enough young woman, but certainly not someone I wanted to marry. She didn't exactly remind me of my mother, but she was much too close for comfort. Throughout my whole life I've had one overriding philosophy: Don't marry someone who reminds you of your mother. And I'm happy to report that I never did. So to Oscar's great disappointment, I turned him down.

Oscar's play opened with me, playing a kid, running into the house. I'm dressed in short pants and a cap so I look about twelve years old. My father in the play, acted by

Menachim Rubin, is eating dinner. Rubin was a real character in real life. He would carry around a little cotton bag with his gall-stones in it. He loved to show them off. In the play, I would say, "Look what I made, Dad. I earned a quarter cleaning someone's basement." With that, Rubin slaps me in the face, taking altogether too much pleasure in the job. Every night this guy almost knocks my head off, and there's nothing I can do about it. Then he says to me, "Listen, you'll never have to work like that. I want you going to college. I want you to become an attorney or a doctor — no cleaning anybody's house."

The curtain closes, and when it opens again I'm lying in my pajamas on a couch reading the funnies. My mother, played by Gertrude Berg, says to me, "Listen, things are tough for your father. I thought maybe you could go get a job." I say, "No way. I'm going to go to college, just like Dad wants me to."

Then my father enters. He says, "A funny thing happened to me today on the way home from work. I told somebody I worked for the Metropolitan Insurance Company, and they thought I said, 'The Metropolitan Opera.'" Then someone in the audience would scream, "Menachim, sing for us what you sang for them!" And he'd stop and sing an aria from *Figaro.*

At the end of the play, he and my mother come over to where I'm lying on the couch in my pajamas, and my father says to me, "Son, things are not too good lately. I don't have that much work anymore."

"No, Menachim, *oy,*" the people in the audience are screaming.

Finally he says to me, "Son, I think you're going to have to go to work."

I get up from the couch, fold the comics, and walk straight down to the edge of the stage. I look at the audience, and I say in Yiddish, "I would rather die."

The audience starts to boo, and then I begin to ad-lib in Yiddish and say, "I would rather be in the movies!" It wasn't part of the play, and the audience didn't quite know what to make of that, but I got a kick out of saying that line every night.

Oskeroff had promised me good parts, but the snooty kid who was too good for his parents wasn't an auspicious start. In the second play, I played a boy selling newspapers; that's all I did. So after the first performance of that play, I wrote Oscar a letter: "Dear Mr. Oskeroff: This part is something I cannot play. It's too complicated." I signed the letter and left it for him. Then I went to the house where I was renting a room and threw everything I had into a sheet. I tied the sheet up, threw it over my shoulder, and left. After hitchhiking to see some relatives in Cleveland, I eventually made my way home.

I returned to the Dramatic Workshop to find my buddies Walter Matthau and Harry Belafonte still there, much to their chagrin. Walter and I starred in a production of *Twelfth Night,* where I played Sebastian, the brother of Viola. I had been taking speech lessons, which made it possible for me to do Shakespeare, hitting each one of the words properly. Another play we put on was Clifford Odets's *Golden Boy,* about a boxer named Joe Bonaparte who plays the violin. At one point in the play, Joe goes out and gets himself a fight to make some money. When his father finds out, he goes nuts. The play was somewhat like *This Too Shall Pass* and *The Jazz Singer.*

The Cherry Lane Theater, a professional theater connected to the New School, had scheduled the production of a play for the coming weekend, but it fell through, so they asked the staff at the Dramatic Workshop if they had something that might take its place. The teachers said they had this kid, Bernie Schwartz, who was playing Joe Bonaparte in *Golden Boy* and doing a good job of it. The

Cherry Lane was thrilled. What they didn't know was that we'd worked on only the first two-thirds of the play. The next thing I knew, my teachers came to me and said, "We're going to open *Golden Boy* at the Cherry Lane Theater for a weekend, and you've got five days to learn the rest of it."

But I didn't mind. "I'm ready," I said. And I was. By this time I had enough experience to know what I could and couldn't do. Besides, I loved the play, and the role was perfect for me. It allowed me to play a tough, pugnacious kid who had an artistic side. (Sound familiar?) For five days we rehearsed six to eight hours a day at the school. We'd go to Central Park for a lunch break, and I would sit in the grass and learn my lines. I loved learning lines. It didn't come naturally to me, but I loved doing it anyway, and eventually I got pretty good at it.

By the time the play opened on Friday night, I had it down well enough so that when I hit the stage, I wasn't nervous at all. I was enjoying the atmosphere and getting into the part. Everything went off like a charm. We did our weekend of performances; then it was over, and I went back to school.

On that first Monday after *Golden Boy* finished its run at the Cherry Lane, I went to see a theatrical agent named Joyce Selznick, who worked for one of the smaller talent agencies. It turned out she was the niece of David Selznick, the legendary producer of *Gone With the Wind.*

When I went to see Joyce, I wanted to seem taller, so I took a deck of cards, cut it in half, and put half in one shoe and half in the other. I also wore high-backed shoes so I wouldn't look strange from behind. When I asked Joyce if there was any way I could get into the movies, she said she'd call me if something came up. I'd heard that a lot, but at least she actually wrote down my number, which was something.

The very next morning Joyce called me and asked me to come back to her office. When I got there, she told me she thought I was very handsome and that I would be great in the movies. Then she took me to see David Selznick. I went into his office, and we talked briefly before he said to Joyce, "He's a handsome boy, but he walks funny." That deck of cards was making me lean forward. I gave him credit for noticing.

Then Joyce said to me, "I'm going to take you over to the New York offices of Universal Pictures. Bob Goldstein's in town, and Bob is the talent scout for Universal. His brother, Leonard, runs the Universal studio in LA."

I went down to Bob Goldstein's office to meet him. We talked for a minute or two, and then I left. I didn't think much of it, because Goldstein didn't seem terribly interested.

A couple of days later, I got a call at home. A woman named Eleanor was calling from the Universal Pictures offices in Manhattan, asking me to come back down there right away. I was startled, but I hopped on the subway. When I got to the office, Eleanor ushered me into Bob Goldstein's office. He said, "Somebody from our office saw you in *Golden Boy.*"

"That was this past weekend," I replied.

"Yes," he said, "and he thought you were excellent. I'd like to send you to California for a screen test."

I was stunned. I called Joyce Selznick to see if she'd represent me in my negotiations with Universal if I passed my screen test. But Joyce said, "I can't afford to go to California and set up shop to look after you. Maybe later, but not right now. But don't worry about it, kid, you'll have no trouble finding an agent when you get to LA." Joyce never did represent me, but I was always deeply indebted to her.

This was 1948, and most of the actors in

the movies at that time were in their thirties, forties, and fifties. There were no young people in the movies, so when the war ended, the studios needed to hire some fresh talent. In the past, most actors started making movies in their thirties and had short careers, but the studios were coming to realize that if they hired very young actors and signed them to long-term contracts, they could both replenish their talent and get it more cheaply. It was during this postwar period that the studios signed such actors as Robert Wagner, Piper Laurie, Janet Leigh, and Natalie Wood, who had started as a kid actor. Marlon Brando, of course, was part of the new generation as well. Marilyn Monroe was also on the verge of becoming America's favorite pinup girl.

And now it was my turn. I took the screen test and was offered a seven-year contract with six-month options starting at seventy-five dollars a week. I knew Universal Studios was a low-budget operation, but I didn't care. I just wanted to get into the movies.

An hour before I had to board the flight, I grabbed my piece of luggage and took a trolley car over the bridge to Queens. Glancing over my shoulder at Manhattan, I suddenly felt a pang to be leaving that I hadn't felt when I had gone into the Navy.

When I got to the airport I bought my ticket and sat quietly in the lounge, eyeing all the pretty girls, wondering which ones I could get to smile back at me. Then I stared out the window at the ground crew working on our airplane. To me, its big, gleaming body looked like the future.

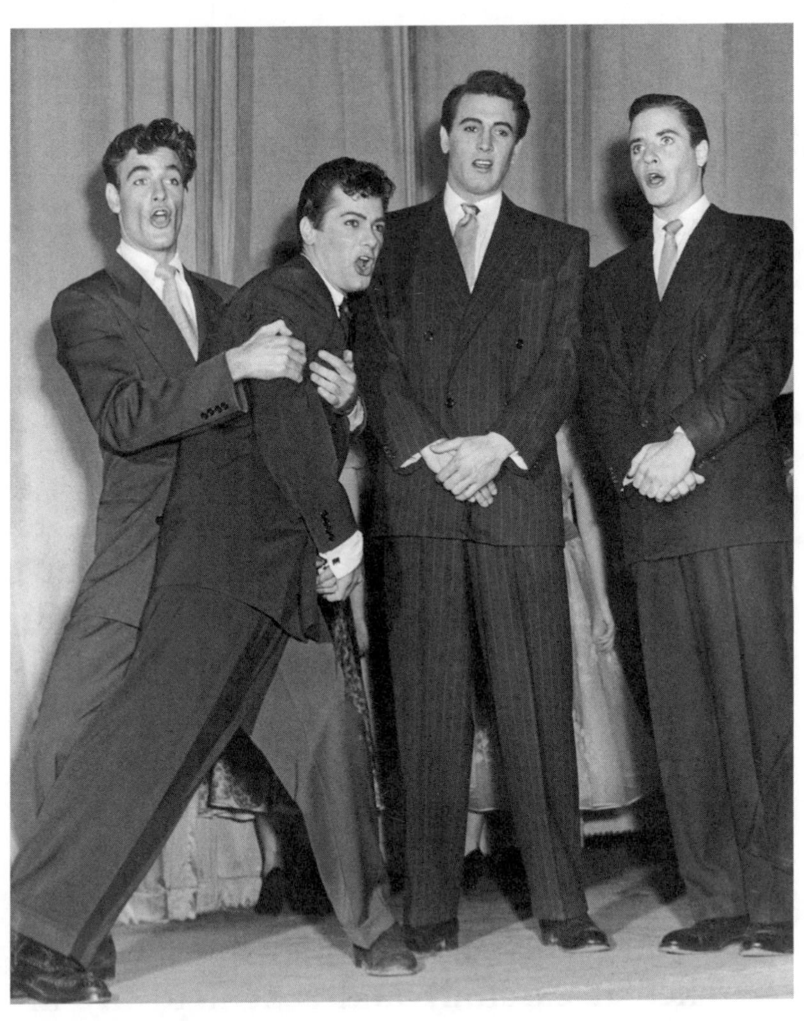

Jim Best, me, Rock Hudson, and Richard Long, 1949.

6
DANCING WITH YVONNE DE CARLO

Soon after I signed with Universal, the casting department worked out a deal with a speech instructor over at MGM Studios to take me on as one of her students. The studio wanted me to improve my diction and to soften my New York accent, so I went to speech class. I didn't go for very long, but I enjoyed the experience. We'd have to recite sentences like "The rain in Spain falls mainly on the plain," the way Eliza Doolittle did in *My Fair Lady.* Our instructor even gave me marbles to put in my mouth, to make me more aware of my tongue and its movements. I swallowed one of the marbles by accident, and when it came out a few days later I washed it carefully and sent it to my instructor in a little box. She had no idea of the trip it had taken.

I loved going to the MGM lot for my speech class. I had seen a lot of MGM's great movies as a kid, and on the lot I could even pick out certain streets and connect them to specific films. MGM was founded in the 1920s, and its first great epic film had been *Ben-Hur.* Among its roster of stars were Greta Garbo, William Powell, Buster Keaton, Norma Shearer, Joan Crawford, and Clark Gable. MGM would go on to make wonderful musicals starring Judy Garland, Fred Astaire, Gene Kelly, and Frank Sinatra.

After my very first speech lesson, I went to get some lunch at the MGM commissary. I sat down in an empty spot at the counter next to a couple of girls who were eating together and chatting. One of the girls greeted me in a friendly way, so I struck up a conversation.

"I've never been here before," I said.

"You'll love the food," she replied, and we chatted for a minute. She was a pretty, articulate young woman who seemed very intelligent and sure of herself. I wondered if she was an actress. I asked her if she worked at MGM, and she said she did.

"I'm going to be coming out here again for class. Can we have coffee?" I asked her.

"Sure," she said. She took out a pen and a piece of paper, and when I saw the name she wrote out — *Judy Garland* — I nearly *plotzed.* I took her number, but I never called her. To this day I'm sorry I passed up a chance to become friends with the woman who'd been so phenomenal in *The Wizard of Oz.* But Judy Garland was a *big* star, and I didn't have a lot of confidence at that point.

Those first few months in Hollywood I met a number of other young actors who were making names for themselves, including Debbie Reynolds, Rock Hudson, and Marlon Brando. At the studio various actors would get together and talk about what they were doing over the upcoming weekend. After a while we all knew each other, either from parties or from working together. Rock Hudson was signed shortly after I was. The two of us hit it off, became friends, and went on to become mainstays at Universal Pictures. Marlon Brando and I also developed a friendship from spending time together at parties, but he was always the odd one. He'd come to a party late, or he would show up but insist on not coming inside, or he'd bring some weird girl with him as his date. He was always pushing the envelope.

I loved going out, but I didn't have a lot of money to spend. After paying my rent and the installment on my membership in the Screen Actors Guild, I had about twenty-five bucks a week to live on, which was enough to get by but didn't allow for any luxuries. I was netting roughly the same amount I had been receiving from the GI Bill of Rights when I was studying drama in New York City. Back then my dad would slip me a few bucks here and there, which helped, but I didn't have his help here in Hollywood. Still, I loved being on my own. I just had to be frugal to make it work.

The important thing was that I had enough money to take girls out on dates now and then. There were so many beautiful women in Hollywood, and I was meeting more of them all the time. One girl I went out with had competed as Miss Sweden in the Miss Universe contest. She didn't win, but as one of six finalists she was given a contract with Universal. She was a breathtaking natural beauty, a tall, eighteen-year-old blonde with a spectacular figure. Her name was Anita Ekberg.

The first time I picked up Anita to take her out, she threw her arms around me and we never got any further than her couch. At least she had a couch! I was fortunate enough to have a number of romantic moments with Anita, but we ran into the same problem I'd had with Marilyn Monroe: we were too young and too busy with our careers to make time for a serious relationship. Like Marilyn, Anita's evenings were often taken up by big-shot film executives, and it was tough for me to compete with that. Anita ended up dating a string of movie stars, including Errol Flynn, Yul Brynner, and Frank Sinatra.

I went out with another actress, Betty Thatcher, who was also a knockout. I took her to a club in downtown LA owned by Benny Leonard, the Jewish prizefighter. Dean Martin and Jerry Lewis were working there weekends, doing their show. That's when I met Jerry — and that's when Jerry met Betty. It was obvious right away that he had big eyes for her. I had just met her, and we weren't emotionally involved, so I stepped out of the way.

When I first met him, Jerry Lewis seemed very gregarious and open, just the way he was on stage. As I got to know him better, I saw another side to his personality. He could be very domineering, even mean, and sometimes acted like everybody worked for him. But at the same time, Jerry was absolutely hilarious to be around. He loved being outrageous. We'd be walking down the street together and he'd start skipping, just like a little kid. When we went out to eat, he'd stick his fingers in everybody else's food. If you were driving a car with him in the passenger seat, he'd grab the wheel and force you onto the sidewalk. Jerry always had candy in his pocket, and if we were at a party, he would walk over to a girl, drop a piece of candy down her blouse, and go after it. I'm telling you, he was crazy, a helluva lot of fun, and completely impossible.

One day I was walking down a Universal Studios street when some guy stopped me and asked, "Can you dance?"

What, are you kidding me? Here I am, working to get my big break, so what am I going to say? "Of course," I replied. "There's nothing I can't do."

He smiled, and we made our introductions. He was Robert Siodmak, the director who had made *The Killers* with Burt Lancaster and Ava Gardner. Now he was making a movie called *Criss Cross* for Universal. He said someone from casting would call me. I was excited, but by now I knew enough about Hollywood to take a wait-and-see attitude.

Later that afternoon a girl from the mail department knocked on my dressing room door and handed me a note: *Call Bob Palmer.* Bob Palmer was the head of casting. When I called he said, "The director of *Criss Cross* just called and wants you in his film. Burt Lancaster is in it, too. The director wants you to dance with Yvonne De Carlo.

Can you really dance?"

"Sure I can dance," I said.

"He's expecting you first thing tomorrow," Palmer replied.

Most fans know Yvonne De Carlo as the TV character Lily Munster from *The Munsters,* but in 1945 she played Salome in *Salome Where She Danced,* a role that made her a star. Two years later she played the lead in *Slave Girl,* and audiences could almost feel the heat from her sultry sensuality. When I met Yvonne, her career was soaring, and now she was starring in a picture with Burt Lancaster, who was also a big star.

The premise of *Criss Cross* was that Burt and Yvonne were in a relationship, but had been divorced and he had left town for a year. While he was away, she worked as a dancer and a prostitute, and in this one scene she was dancing with me. I was on the screen for about two minutes. I was supposed to do the rumba, whatever that was. I just shook my body like crazy, and everyone loved it. When Yvonne's character and I are dancing, Burt walks in and sees us. She goes over to him, and I'm left standing there, but I decided not to let that bother me. I was going to dance, dammit, girl or no girl. So I kept on going. They liked that too.

I was very attracted to Yvonne, and she

took a liking to me as well. We started going out, and after a few dates we went to bed. The excitement of slowly taking off Yvonne De Carlo's clothes was indescribable. Having her undressed *with me* in a bed on Mulholland Drive overlooking LA was like winning first prize in the lottery. It was like a sweet, sexy Hollywood romance, only it was real.

The picture was released a few months later. My family still lived in New York, and I had told my mother all about the film, so all my relatives and friends were waiting for *Criss Cross* to come out. My parents reported that when I appeared on the big screen in my bit part, the theater in our neighborhood exploded with cheers and applause. And my friends and family weren't the only ones who liked seeing me up on screen. Fans mailed in hundreds of letters asking: *Who was that guy who danced with Yvonne De Carlo?* The studio was so impressed by all that mail that it renewed my contract right away and bumped up my salary to a hundred and twenty-five dollars a week. I'd been on screen exactly two minutes, but they turned out to be the most important two minutes of my life.

As soon as I started getting fan mail, I knew I was on the right track too. And when

I watched myself in the picture, I liked the way I looked and moved on screen. I'd already been working hard at learning my craft, but now I poured everything I had into it. I paid close attention to every last detail. Now I was in a hurry to be a movie star. I didn't want to have to wait until I was thirty; I *needed* it to happen *now.* I needed it to counteract all the negative stuff in my head that I had heard all my life from my mother, from relatives, and from people in the neighborhood. *You're good for nuttin. You're gonna end up a homosexual dancer in some lousy club. You'll never make a living as an actor.*

I didn't deny any of this crap, because I didn't want to dignify it with a response. Still, I could feel it all around me. I could feel it in my own family. But when I signed my contract with Universal, all of a sudden I could sense that things had changed. People from back home treated me a little differently. I was accorded a little more respect those days when I went home to visit. But I could see in some people's eyes that they were thinking I must have been shacking up with some gay studio exec, that someone powerful must be promoting me in exchange for favors. And there were people working at Universal who probably felt the same way. I didn't have any film experience. How else could I have gotten into a movie so quickly? I could hardly blame anyone for their cynicism when I was having difficulty believing things were going so well myself. So I played it cool and didn't let on when I felt insulted. I never became angry, mean, or frustrated. Even in those first few months I knew that success would be the best revenge.

My parents were also having a hard time seeing me as a successful actor. It seemed so implausible. They'd been going to the movies their whole lives, and for them to go to the movies and see me up on that screen — it was a major thrill for them. They were so excited they didn't even get upset when they saw my new name, Tony Curtis.

My next movie, *City Across the River,* was about street gangs. Based on my fan mail for *Criss Cross,* the studio wanted me to have the lead role, but the director, Maxwell Shane, got cold feet and refused to give it to me. I suspect Shane didn't take the chance because I had so little film experience: he had absolutely nothing to go on except one scene in *Criss Cross* when I was faking the rumba. I had some experience in the Yiddish theater, but no movie directors had seen me in those plays. Plenty of people like me got two minutes on screen in one film, and that was it; six months later their contract was allowed to expire, and they went back home. I didn't want that to happen to me, which was why I wanted this lead so bad. But at least I got a supporting role that gave me some lines. I was making progress.

In *City Across the River* I played Mitch, one of the gang members. Peter Fernandez played the lead, and Stephen McNally was the star of the film. McNally was a good-looking man in his mid-thirties who was a very versatile actor. Steve was good enough to play nuanced parts but usually not quite good enough to get the lead. Looking back, I remember that he did a perfectly fine job, but there was no bite to his performance.

So I played Mitch, a lesser role, and Joshua Shelley, a comedian and a solid character actor, played Crazy, a gruff guy from the streets. In the movie I watched over Crazy, took care of him, and made sure he was all right. He fell in love with the girl lead, so when she started going out with Peter Fernandez, Crazy wanted to kill himself. I talked him out of it.

I had a few lines, none of which was particularly memorable, but it was a nice part for a novice. And since we were filming some of the scenes from *City Across the River* in Manhattan, I was able to fly to New York with the rest of the cast. We shot in a downtown tenement area near the Bowery, and I *loved* being in front of the camera in public. I got a kick out of how people in real life responded to me working as an actor. There was a rope separating us from the spectators, and there were all these girls on the other side of that rope batting their eyelashes and jumping with joy whenever I looked in their direction. Steve McNally was pretty well known, but I signed more autographs than anyone else in the cast.

I stayed at the Sherry-Netherland Hotel with the rest of the actors, although every once in a while I would go home and spend an evening with my parents. I did it out of a sense of obligation rather than any real desire to be under their roof. I didn't want to go back home anymore; I was making my own life now. My parents came to watch me work a few times, and my mother liked to come down with one of her sisters. My mother just loved being around show business.

While we were there shooting *City Across the River,* Dean Martin and Jerry Lewis were working at the Loews Theater in Manhattan. Jerry invited me up to their dressing room, where he was clowning around as usual. Their fans were lined up around the block before their performance, so Jerry and Dean opened up the second-floor dressing room window and yelled down to the throng below. Jerry grabbed me and made me stick my head out, so I waved, and the girls squealed. I always enjoyed the fame that came with acting. As a kid I'd dreamed of getting this kind of response, if only I got my chance. And here I was, living it.

After we finished filming one afternoon, the studio limo took some of the actors back to the Sherry-Netherland Hotel. After they got out, I asked the driver if he would take over me to the President Theater at the New School. It was during school hours on a weekday, so I knew the students at the Dramatic Workshop would be there.

As we drove up, there was Walter Matthau, standing on the sidewalk. On a crazy impulse I said to the driver, "See that guy over there? Pull right up next to him, and then stop."

Walter was standing there, immersed in a newspaper that might have been *The Racing Form.* He loved betting on the ponies. It was kind of a gloomy day, and although Walter was only about twenty-nine years old, he looked fifty-nine — he always looked older than he was. We pulled up, and Walter peered at the big car, trying to look through the dark glass to see who was inside.

I rolled the window down. Before he could say anything, I said, "I fucked Yvonne De Carlo."

I rolled up the window and ordered the driver to speed off.

For me, that moment captured all the giddy craziness of Hollywood in those days, and how hungry one young person could be to make his mark.

With Cary Grant, 1952.

7
Getting Shot by Audie Murphy

Universal had a dozen or so young actors and actresses in its stable all starting out at about the same time I was. We all had our various strengths and weaknesses, but I had a weapon in my arsenal that no one else had: my hair. This was a time in America when men had crew cuts. That was the all-American way. In high schools and colleges, the Big Men On Campus all had short hair. Everyone who came back from the war had short hair, and so did politicians, businessmen, you name it. But I thought I looked better with a lot of hair, so I grew it long and twirled it on my forehead so it would look curlier, and on the nape of my neck I combed it into a DA (duck's ass). I had styled my hair to please myself, but soon after I danced the rumba with Yvonne De Carlo in *Criss Cross,* I discovered that my hair had made me a hero with practically every white teenager in America.

From 1949 to 1951, I became famous for my hair. I was mentioned in Ed Sullivan's column, which appeared all over the country, as "the kid with the haircut." Before I knew it, I was being featured in movie magazines. A newspaper cartoon from back then shows a guy in a factory operating a big machine; the guy has long hair combed back, and the caption says, "Those of you who have Tony Curtis haircuts, stay away from the machinery. Danger." I loved it. You can't imagine the publicity my hair generated. The studio didn't have enough money to pay for that kind of publicity. My hair took on a life of its own. In fact, for a while my haircut was more famous than I was. I felt like introducing myself to people as "the guy with Tony Curtis's hair."

It wasn't long before young guys all across the country started growing their hair long like mine. Elvis Presley was fourteen when *Criss Cross* came out, and it's not unlikely that he copied my look, as did countless other kids his age. That hair of mine was important, in its own way. What it did was reach out to kids and say, *We can be our own people. We don't have to wait until we're adults before we can have our own identities.* The youth of America responded. And as the fan letters kept rolling in, Universal decided to give me bigger and bigger parts.

The next movie I appeared in, later that same year, was called *The Lady Gambles,* starring Barbara Stanwyck, a big-time movie star near the end of her career. Her best roles, like the one she played in *Double Indemnity,* were behind her now, although she was still a very talented actress. This movie was about a woman hooked on gambling who gets beaten up by thugs. I had a scene where I played a bellhop who delivers a telegram to her.

On the day my scene was being shot, I had unfortunately developed a stye in one eye. I went to the director, Michael Gordon, and told him, "My eye is a little swollen."

He said, "Listen, kid, you're better looking with one eye than anybody I've seen with two. So not to worry." That reassured me, so I began to think I'd be okay. The direction was: *You're off camera, facing the room. You look through the door and see Barbara and Steve McNally, and you come into the room. Then you say your line.* My line was "It looks like it's followed you halfway across the country."

As I stood outside that door in my bellhop uniform, I kept running that line over and over in my head, trying to say it with different words emphasized to see what sounded best: "It *looks* like it's followed you halfway across the country. It looks like it's *followed* you halfway across the country. It looks like it's followed *you* halfway across the country."

Michael Gordon was watching me. By the door was a red light. When the light went on, that was my cue to knock. I was standing there, getting ready for the shot, thrilled and a little nervous about my big moment. I heard, "Quiet," while I was standing there muttering, "It looks like it's followed you *halfway* across the country." I kept looking at the light by the door. When that red light went on, that was my cue to knock and go on stage. I wanted to be sure I was ready when it turned red, so I wouldn't waste any precious time while the camera was rolling.

I looked to my right, and I saw Michael walking toward me. I thought, *What's he doing back here? Is he going to walk on with me?*

He looked at me and said, "How are you feeling, kid?"

"Oh, great," I said.

He looked at me searchingly and said, "All you want is a tip." Then he turned around and walked away.

Now, Michael couldn't have known I had

delivered groceries and shined shoes as a boy. But when I worked those jobs, that was exactly how I felt: all I wanted was a tip. So I knew just what he meant. How he nailed me with that, I will never know, but it was perfect.

The red light went on, and I knocked on the door and entered, and when I entered the room I was smiling, looking friendly and helpful. How I said the line no longer mattered as much as turning on the charm while I was delivering that telegram. I was doing my best to get that tip. I said my line, and Barbara Stanwyck reached into her purse and gave me some money. The director yelled cut. My scene was over.

"Excellent," Barbara said. That meant a lot to me, coming from her.

Michael Gordon had given me the best direction I'd ever gotten up to that point in my career, and believe it or not, I went on to apply it during every movie I made! I never forgot that I wanted my tip — the money they were paying me to make the movie. I wanted to behave professionally, and save the studio money. I wanted good reviews. And, just as important, I wanted everyone to like working with me. After the movie was in the can, I wanted everyone involved to say, "This guy is great. Let's use him again."

All you want is the tip. Neat, huh?

My role in *The Lady Gambles* was tiny, but I felt good about it. I was learning, which was what really mattered to me. And appearing in a movie with Barbara Stanwyck was going to raise my profile further. I was also starting to get publicity about all the girls I was going out with. Hedda Hopper mentioned me in her column, and in New York, columnist Dorothy Kilgallen wrote, "A lot of people in Hollywood are turning their heads when they see Tony Curtis." Mike Connelly, another gossip columnist, printed a phony story about me going out with Barbara Whiting, the younger sister of singer Margaret Whiting. I didn't care that the story got the facts wrong, as long as it was a girl they were writing about. It meant I was getting noticed.

In my next movie, *Take One False Step,* I played a race-car driver. For me the big thrill of that movie was getting to meet William Powell, whom I had seen in *The Thin Man* when I was a kid. I spent two or three days on the picture, enough to see what a pain in the ass Shelley Winters could be. She was about five years older than I was, and she had been dating Burt Lancaster, along with a lot of other actors. Shelley looked nice enough, but she was a real yenta, a big-mouthed busybody. Whatever she did, she made sure the press knew about it. She had never really made it to the top tier of stardom, which really pissed her off. As a result she could be very demanding — even dictatorial — on the set.

At one point during the shoot I was standing by a desk, waiting for my scene; I was sketching on a piece of paper, just killing time. Shelley grabbed the paper.

"What are you doing?" she growled. "Why don't you pay more attention to the scene?"

"Well, excuuuse me," I said. I felt like I was back in school, being tongue-lashed by the teacher. What a bitch!

Moviemaking at Universal gave me some insight into how quirky actors could be off-camera as well. Lou Costello, of Abbott and Costello fame, liked to take props from the sets and bring them home. If he saw something he liked — a bookcase, a vase, a writing desk — he would tell his stand-in to take it once the scene had finished shooting. The stand-in would put whatever it was under his arm or inside his sweater, carry it outside, and put it in the trunk of Lou's car.

It didn't take long for the propman to notice that things were missing, and if Lou was on the set, the propman knew who the culprit was. But it was a ticklish situation; no one wanted to blow the whistle on Lou because he was such a big star. Eventually the propman would go to the head of the department, and they'd confront Lou together.

"Lou, we need that table for tomorrow," the head of the department would say.

"What table?"

"The one that's in the trunk of your car."

"Who put it in the trunk?"

"We don't know, Lou, but we know it's there."

"How do you know that?"

"We just know."

They'd march out to Lou's car and open the trunk, and not only would the table be there, but also three or four other items that had disappeared during the week. Lou was contrite and tried to be funny about it, but no one laughed until after he left. Then everyone had a lot of fun at his expense.

I didn't have a speaking part in my next movie, which was called *Johnny Stool Pigeon.* I played a deaf and dumb druggie who gets killed and whose body is shipped from Mexico to LA in a coffin along with a massive amount of cocaine. I have to say that even though I was dead, I looked sharp. I was wearing a beautiful pin-striped suit as I lay there in my coffin.

Shooting a film could get really tedious, so to relieve the boredom, the crew would play practical jokes on me, the new guy, the green kid who didn't know the ropes. For instance, they sent me out to get left-handed cans of film. That one didn't work, but another one did. We were getting ready to shoot the scene with me in the coffin, and I was sitting up in the felt-lined box when the assistant to the director, Marshall Green, shouted to me, "Are you ready?" I said I was. He said, "Okay," and he called over the nurse who was always available if there was an injury on the set.

"What's she doing here?" I asked.

"She's going to be the one who gives you the shot," he said.

"What shot?"

"Well, you have to be convincing in this scene, and that's how we do it," Marshall said. "But maybe we won't need the nurse's help this time. Tell you what. You lie back, close your eyes, and act like you're dead. See if you can convince me." I did as I was told. Marshall said, "See, you can't do it." I sat up, and the nurse came over with a very long hypodermic needle in her hand.

"This shot will relax you," Marshall said. "You ready?"

"No, no, no," I said, my heart racing.

"You're not giving me any shot. I'm sorry. I'm not going to do it." I didn't care what it meant for my career; I'd reached my limit. That needle was so enormous that my heart was racing just from looking at it. As I started to get out of the coffin, everybody on the set cracked up. That was when I knew it was a setup. They were trying to scare the shit out of me, and it worked. Beautifully. I laughed right along with them, knowing their teasing was a sign of affection.

I lay back in that box, and they shot the scene. Deaf, dumb, and dead: no needle, but I was convincing.

I had been in Hollywood barely a year when my parents and my younger brother Robert ambushed me by moving out to Hollywood. I was still living in a rooming house, and they arrived without even telling me they were coming, much the same way my grandmother and her children had left Hungary and showed up in New York to join my grandfather. There was no discussion; their arrival was a fait accompli. My mother had told me they were coming just for a visit, but they abandoned that pretext as soon as they arrived. My mother knew that if they came out, I'd have no choice but to take care of them.

Their arrival totally upset my equilibrium. I thought I had left my poverty-stricken Jewish background behind, along with my given name, Bernie Schwartz. I was Tony Curtis now. This was supposed to be *my* time. I was dedicated to succeeding in the movies, and that was hard work. I kept odd hours. And I had little room in my life for distractions. Now, all of a sudden, I had to find a place for my parents and brother to live. I had to pay their rent. I also had to help them find a special school for my brother, who was already acting far more strangely than my mother ever had. Robert would look up at the sky distractedly for long periods of time. Or he would blink obsessively and display all sorts of other odd tics and say nonsensical things. As he grew older, he acted out more and more, and we all worried that he might become a danger to himself or to others. He needed serious care, beyond what my parents and I could give him.

My parents sent Robert to special doctors who cost me three hundred dollars a visit. I couldn't keep that up for long. Fortunately, a friend of mine suggested that I call the governor of California to see if he could help me get some state assistance for my brother. The governor connected me with the people at the state agency who handled this sort of thing. They arranged to have Bobby tested, which resulted in his diagnosis of schizophrenia. That diagnosis made Bobby eligible to become a ward of the state. It was hardly an ideal solution, but the truth was that we really had no choice. Given the possibilities, it was the best possible outcome, both for Bobby and for the family. Meanwhile, my mother, who was only too skilled at ignoring reality, kept pushing me to put Bobby in the movies.

"Give him a part," she would plead. "Let him play you as a boy."

I tried to let her down as gently as I could, but my mother was not an easy person to dissuade, especially when one of her precious children was involved.

Later in 1949 I made a movie called *Francis,* which was the name of the now-famous talking mule. Donald O'Connor, a child star who would go on to become Gene Kelly's sidekick in *Singin' in the Rain,* played a schlubby soldier who talked with Francis. This was Donald's first major role since he'd returned home from the war, and it probably ruined his career, because the studio went on to make a Francis the Talking Mule picture every year for the next five years, and Donald got typecast.

I played a lieutenant who was Donald's friend. In real life Donald was a hilarious guy, and we got along great. He used to love to use his film projector to secretly project porno films onto his next-door neighbor's garage door. A car would drive by at night, and you'd hear the tires squeal as the driver slammed on the brakes. Then Donald would shut the film off.

On the set, Donald and I would fool around between shots to entertain the cast and crew. Donald would talk in the voice of Francis the mule, and I would play Donald.

"How are you doing?" I'd say.

"Fine. How are you?" he'd say.

"I'm great," I'd say. "What are you doing?"

"Making a movie."

"Who's the star of the movie?"

"That fucking idiot Donald O'Connor," he'd say. The cast and crew would scream with laughter.

Most of the actors in the *Francis* cast were young, and we were always pulling practical jokes on each other. In one prank, someone would come up behind me with a stick and tap my shoe from behind. Then a crew member would come over to me and say, "Are you getting electric shocks in your foot? These soundstages are so old that the electricity jumps around like crazy." And just as he was saying it, another guy would tap my shoe from behind.

"Hey, there it went, I felt it," I said.

"Yeah," the crew member said, "it happens to all of us. Just be careful."

The one old-timer in the cast of *Francis* was Zasu Pitts, who had starred in the movie *Greed* in 1924. In that movie she had been slinky and beautiful; I remember one scene where she had sat in bed wearing very little, throwing gold coins around. While she was making *Francis* I went over and talked to her a little before she went on the set. I didn't tell her how much I loved her when I was a kid. Age was a sensitive subject in Hollywood, given the premium the industry placed on youth and beauty.

In my next movie, *I Was a Shoplifter,* Universal decided to showcase two of their young up-and-comers: Rock Hudson and me. Rock's real name was Roy Scherer. After spending several years in the Navy during World War II, Rock was discovered by agent Henry Wilson, who combined the Rock of Gibraltar and the Hudson River to create his screen name. Rock and I were the same age, but he looked ten years older than I did. He was a tall, handsome man who played against women in their mid-thirties, while I would play a younger role, like their son. As a result, Rock and I never competed against each other for parts, which was a good thing for me.

In *I Was a Shoplifter,* I played a fence who bought stolen goods from the girl who did the shoplifting, and Rock played the detective trying to catch her. This was not a movie that could be dignified by the designation Grade B; it was a Grade Z movie. Already I was beginning to see what people meant when they said Universal was a nickel-and-dime outfit. I could see why Universal actors got the itch to make pictures outside the studio, and it didn't take Rock long to start feeling the same way.

Rock used to invite me to parties at his house, and he and I would go out to the clubs every now and then. Even then word was getting out that he was a homosexual. I surmised it because Henry Wilson was his agent, and Henry was a very swishy man with a stable of gay clients, including Tab Hunter. Henry got wind that a gossip tabloid was going to run a story about Rock being gay, so Henry arranged for his secretary to go out with Rock and later marry him to keep the rumormongers away. Rock liked women, and he had a good time with them, but he liked the other team even better.

My next big break came near the end of 1949, when I was given one of the leads in *Sierra,* a western. Audie Murphy, the most decorated U.S. combat soldier in World War II, played the starring role of a horse breaker who's wanted for a murder he didn't commit. Murphy wasn't more than five feet five inches tall, but he was as tough as any man I ever met. I've been told that he killed two hundred and fifty Germans while fighting in Europe and blew up five or six tanks. I don't doubt it for a moment. If you want to know what heroism is, see *To Hell and Back,* the movie they made about his life. Murphy plays himself, and it's quite a role.

Once again, the crew had lots of fun playing practical jokes. One day one of them came up to me with a rectangle of black velvet cloth, about the size of a diaper, and pinned it on my belt, above my backside.

I said, "What's that for?"

"Get on your horse," the crew member said. I obliged him, and then he took the lower edge of the cloth and attached it to the saddle. He said, "You can tell an amateur horseman because he bounces up and down in the saddle a lot when he rides. When you're riding across the frame, we can see daylight between your ass and the saddle, and we can't have that. So you've got to wear this black cloth on your ass." When I started to sputter, everyone started laughing. You never knew when the next gag was coming your way, but it was a great way to pass the endless downtime between shoots. There's lots of that when you're making a movie, but I never minded. I would read the trade papers, hang out in my dressing room, or take a nap. I always made myself available, no matter how long the day was. I never complained. *All I wanted was the tip,* which meant being professional at all times.

I knew I was on my way in 1950 when the studio asked me to help publicize *Sierra.* Audie Murphy and Burl Ives were the big names in the picture, but when we held the premiere in San Francisco, I was the one who created a furor. Even though I hadn't yet starred in a picture, a lot of teenage boys had seen me in my minor roles and had started to wear their hair like I did. Young girls would show up at the movie theater if they heard I was going to be there. Universal got to the point where they started sending me out to talk about pictures I wasn't even in. I was the first of their young generation of actors to be used that way.

One of the first things the studio wanted from you was an attractive eight-by-ten glossy photo. When you signed a contract, the studio didn't see you as a long-term investment. All the brass cared about was money, and with that eight-by-ten glossy, they were able to judge how attractive you were to the fans who bought movie tickets. As I went out on tour to promote *Sierra,* I began to realize how important that photograph really was: it had as much impact as your work in the film! It helped you become an icon for your fans, who wanted that photograph to hang up in their rooms.

I received direct confirmation of this from Kelly LeBrock, the actress and model who said the famous line "Don't hate me because I'm beautiful" in Pantene commercials. Kelly told me that when she was a kid, she had a poster of me in her bedroom, and before she came out of the bathroom, she would always put something on. She said she didn't want me to see her nude.

At the premiere of *Sierra* in San Francisco, I was right there, standing in the theater lobby signing autographs. There were so many young girls carrying on in there that the owner of the place pleaded, "Get them out of here. They're peeing on my carpet." After they hustled me outside, hundreds of girls surrounded me, screaming like I was Frank Sinatra. And I didn't even sing! I signed autographs in a frenzy, and then the PR people and I jumped in the limousine and made our getaway.

When we first got to San Francisco, the publicity department came up with a promotion where I would randomly knock on the doors of twelve houses, wait for the door to open, and then surprise the owner by saying, "Hi, I'm Tony Curtis. I'm starring in the movie *Sierra,* and you're invited to the premiere. Here are a couple of tickets to the movie at the Loews San Francisco. Come enjoy the movie and join us for treats at the end of the show."

I went to three houses without incident. I knocked on the door, and when someone answered, the PR guys and the photographer would jump out from behind the bushes and take pictures. When I went up to the porch of the fourth house, it was about eleven in the morning. I knocked on the door, and a beautiful woman in her forties, wearing a long silk gown, answered it.

She looked me up and down and said, "Hello. What have we here?"

I said, "My name is Tony Curtis."

"I know who you are. Come on in."

So I did, leaving the photographer and the

PR guys still hidden behind me. I said, "We're having a premiere of my movie, and I want to give you two tickets. You can bring a friend, and there'll be refreshments."

She said, "Come with me." I followed her into a sitting room where there were three young women — one wearing a robe, another in a short dress, and the third wearing a smock. "Sit down," the older woman said.

"I have my friends waiting at the door," I said.

The woman said, "I'll take care of them." She left the room. The girl in the short dress asked me, "What are you doing here?"

"I'm on tour, promoting this picture that I'm in."

She said, "What a handsome kid you are."

"Thank you very much," I said. Then she sat down next to me, took my hand, and kissed me. The older woman returned and said, "How was that? Did you enjoy that?" I said I did. She said, "She'll keep you busy for a little while. I have some things I have to do."

The girl in the short dress led me into a little bedroom down the hall. Then she took all her clothes off and lay down on the bed. Against my better judgment (I was supposed to be working, after all), I joined her. Who could resist? I never thought movie promotion could be so stimulating!

After we finished, I went back out to the sitting room, and one of the other girls started to take my hand, but I thought about my colleagues waiting outside and my conscience got the better of me. I said, "Listen, there are some more houses I have to go to now. Why don't all of you come to the screening tonight?"

The girl in the robe said, "We're working tonight." I turned to the older woman and said, "Why don't you call in sick?" I figured I'd boost morale by introducing my new lady friends to the other guys promoting the movie. After the premiere, I chose three other lucky PR guys, and we all went back to the women's house. Everyone had a great time — just like I had that afternoon. And we added the cost of the champagne to Universal's promotion expenses!

Winchester '73 was the first big-budget picture Universal put me in. The movie, starring Jimmy Stewart, was about a rifleman whose stolen gun passes through many hands. I had only two lines, but I was thrilled to play in a picture with Jimmy Stewart, and to work under a fine director like Anthony Mann. By this time Jimmy had starred in a long list of great pictures, including *The*

Philadelphia Story, Mr. Smith Goes to Washington, and *It's a Wonderful Life.* Jimmy and Mann were a great team, and they had made some first-rate films together.

Jimmy was an incredibly nice person; in his case there was no difference between his lovable film persona and the man himself. When he showed up on the set for *Winchester '73,* he came right over to me and said, "Hi, Tony, how are you?" You could almost hear the other guys standing around wondering, *Why would Jimmy Stewart know this guy?* They weren't aware that I'd met Jimmy on my second day on the Universal lot, when I asked him if I could have my picture taken with him. Most guys would have forgotten all about a minor moment like that, but not Jimmy Stewart. He was a class act all the way.

The movie was shot mostly on the Universal lot and on some hilly property that Universal owned. Rock Hudson was in the film too, and we had a scene together up on top of a hill at the rear of a big country estate. Rock played the Indian carrying the gun of the movie title when he gets shot by actor Jay C. Flippen. I played a cavalry officer, and my job was to run up the hill, only to find Rock with the rifle in his hand, stone dead.

Shelley Winters was also in the movie.

There had been no change in her manner since last we'd met, meaning that she was very unfriendly to everybody, including me. I observed how negatively people reacted to her, which was a very useful lesson for me. When I was on the set, I was determined to enjoy every minute of what I was doing and to make it fun for everyone else too. I felt that my success depended on it. This was how I expressed my insecurity. But Shelley had a different take on it; she preferred to act high and mighty, always looking for an opportunity to push her career. This was how she expressed her insecurity. Unfortunately, Shelley had no idea how she was shooting herself in the foot. But I never complained about her. And the studio rewarded my efforts with a raise to two hundred and twenty-five dollars a week, which made taking care of my parents a little less stressful for me.

In my next movie, *Kansas Raiders,* I again played alongside war hero Audie Murphy. We shot most of our scenes on a back lot. I had very few lines, but I did a lot of horseback riding. I played a member of the Dalton gang, and Audie played Jesse James. Everybody — including me — was afraid of Audie. I didn't feel that way about many people, but Audie was different. At the time, he was dating an actress named Peggy Castle, a girl I didn't particularly like. One day I was walking down a corridor at Universal, and Audie grabbed me by the lapel and pulled my face down to his. He snarled, "Did you say anything bad about Peggy Castle? She told me you were talking bad about her."

"No," I said. "Believe me, Audie, I don't know what you're talking about." I didn't like the way he was yanking me around, but I couldn't help but think of all those Germans he had killed. Thankfully, he accepted my answer and walked away.

Audie was known to be temperamental and had a special reputation for being jealous. Less than two years earlier, he'd gotten married to the actress Wanda Hendrix, but their tempestuous marriage had ended in divorce. Audie once flew into a jealous rage that ended with him holding Wanda captive at gunpoint. It later came out that he was suffering from post-traumatic stress disorder as a result of everything he'd been through in the war, but we didn't even have a term for it then. All Wanda knew was that she wanted out.

As luck would have it, I started taking her out at around the same time that I was making *Kansas Raiders* with Audie. Wanda was a beautiful woman. She was petite, and she had a great figure and an exotic-looking face. She lived in the San Fernando Valley, so I picked her up in my green Buick convertible and drove her to a restaurant on the strip called Ciro's. The windows were curved, and they gave you a great view of Sunset Boulevard. We had a wonderful dinner, but Wanda had an early call, so after dinner I drove her back home. We kissed some outside her door, but nothing more than that. It wasn't the least bit serious. In the back of my mind, I wondered if Audie would be jealous if he found out, but I tried not to worry about it.

A couple of days after my date with Wanda, Audie and I were practicing our quick-draw technique for the film. We were working on an exercise called the handkerchief draw, where you and the person you're drawing against each hold a bandana between your teeth. Whoever drops his bandana first can draw his gun first. In twenty tries I never once beat him. I would let my bandana go, and as I would go to pull my gun from its holster, his gun would already be in my stomach. On the twenty-first try, I dropped my handkerchief, he pulled his gun out and stuck it in my stomach — and then I heard a muffled explosion.

I looked down at myself and saw smoke; I smelled it too. I couldn't believe it; Audie had found out about my date with Wanda, and he'd gut-shot me for it. I thought, *Well, if I'm going to die, I might as well die making a movie.* I fainted dead away.

The next thing I knew, I was under a tent with people gathered all around me. Audie was there too, apologizing for the prank he'd just pulled. He explained that he'd had a cap gun stuck in his belt behind his back. When he stuck his six-gun in my stomach, he'd used his free hand to reach behind and fire the cap gun, giving me the scare of my life. From then on, Audie was really nice to me, and we even became friends. But I never went out with Wanda Hendrix again.

With Piper Laurie, 1952.

8
JANET AND PIPER

In 1950, Universal wanted me to attend classes at the Actors Studio in LA. I went to one class and paid no attention. I was looking for girls. I had learned a lot from the Dramatic Workshop and my class at MGM, but I wasn't a big fan of Method acting. As far as I was concerned, you didn't need to make this more complicated than it was: you memorize your lines, you learn the subtleties of the part and what the director wants from you, and then you show up and act. You don't have to think about your mother punching you in the mouth in order to bring anger into your performance. You've got to be able to turn it on and let it go, just like that.

The irony was that right after I took that class and ignored it completely, I became housemates with Marlon Brando, the poster boy for the Actors Studio. Marlon's mother had been an actress in community theater in

Chicago, and his older sister Jocelyn had gone to New York to work in the theater, so he had been exposed to acting and drama from a very early age. Marlon's father sent him to military school, and that was where he took his first acting classes. Kicked out of military school because he couldn't stand the regimentation, Marlon followed his sister to New York and studied at the New School and the Actors Studio. Then he began his own career on Broadway, impressing critics and audiences in *I Remember Mama.* Next he wowed everyone — including me — as Stanley Kowalski in *A Streetcar Named Desire.*

Then, early in 1950, Marlon was cast in *The Men* for Warner Bros., his first movie role. He played a paraplegic war veteran. During the time when he was filming *The Men,* he and I lived together in a house on Barham Boulevard. He was a big Broadway star who was fast becoming a movie star, and I was still a player of bit parts, but Marlon enjoyed my company and treated me as an equal, which meant a lot to me.

I loved living in that house with him, and I even enjoyed Marlon's eccentricities. I knew he was really happy when he'd pull out a pan from the drawer and beat a rhythm on it. If we were the Odd Couple, I was Felix and Marlon was Oscar. He'd come in and throw his coat down, grab a beer from the fridge, and lie down on the couch. He acted like he was the boss, but for some reason that never bothered me. If he didn't clean up or take out the garbage, I'd do it. No big deal. Marlon didn't like to drive, so he'd tell girls he didn't know how, and every now and then one of them would come by to pick him up.

Marlon was into yoga long before it became popular. He spent time every day doing yoga exercises out by our swimming pool. But he was into alcohol, too; he would drink and that led to trouble. Marlon would start drinking, get distracted, forget about the time, and disappear for half a day — even if the studio had a meeting or photo shoot scheduled. They never could keep track of him. And if something didn't go his way, Marlon would blow up like a Hawaiian volcano.

Marlon was being represented by Jay Kanter, an important agent at MCA, Lew Wasserman's talent agency. One day Jay came by to take Marlon to the Racquet Club in Palm Springs, and Jay asked me to come along. Jay wanted Marlon out of LA for a few days because he was trying to get Marlon to relax and lay low for a little bit; that was how Jay and the studio tried to manage him. Marlon liked the idea that I was coming along, and he was fun to hang around with, so I said okay.

One night when we walked into the bar at the Racquet Club, we both noticed this great-looking girl sitting on a barstool, nursing a drink. As we walked over, she looked from Marlon to me, and never looked back at Marlon. I didn't think much of it, but it must have left an impression on Marlon. Years later we were at a Hollywood party together, and when Marlon saw me, he raised his hand. The room fell silent. Marlon pointed to me and said, "There's the only guy who ever took a girl away from me."

Marlon was a monumental talent, a truly gifted actor. Much as I tried not to compare my career with his, it was difficult sometimes. In a weak moment I'd tell myself that if Universal had put me in classic movies instead of westerns or desert adventures, maybe I could have become a legendary actor too. But Marlon was unique. Instead of comparing myself with him, I was better off focusing on my own strengths — my exuberance for acting and my boyish charm — and overcoming my liabilities: I was insecure about my upbringing, my being Jewish, and my lack of education. I needed a big boost of confidence, and Marlon's kindness to me helped with that. Of all the actors Marlon could have chosen to pal around with, he chose me, even though he was well on his way to becoming a legend and I was just that crazy kid with a lot of hair trying to make it in the movies.

When I was starting out I also got to be friends with another struggling actor by the name of James Dean. Not many people know that James Dean's first speaking role was in *Sailor Beware,* a Martin and Lewis movie. Jerry Lewis played a boxer, and James Dean was his corner man. Soon after we became friends, Jimmy flew to New York to study acting with Lee Strasberg at the Actors Studio. His first starring role was in *East of Eden.* The director, Elia Kazan, wanted Marlon, but the screenwriter, Paul Osborn, wanted Jimmy, and so did John Steinbeck, who wrote the book. When the movie came out in 1955, Jimmy became a star.

Jimmy and I used to go out to dinner together at a tropical-themed restaurant in Beverly Hills, and we'd sit there drinking mai tais and discussing our careers. We never spoke too much about his childhood. I knew he came out of the Midwest and that his early life was difficult and insular. He didn't use his upbringing as a crutch or let it hold him back in any way, though; neither did Marlon. Unfortunately I did, and so did a lot of other actors. I wanted to be able to emulate Jimmy and Marlon in that way, but I didn't know how.

Jimmy Dean had a kind of boyishness about him, as did I. The difference between us was that I never could get rid of my boyishness, but he could. He could become very tough and hard-bitten on screen. I liked that about him. I said to myself, *If I could find a way of tuning in to Jimmy's attitude, it would make acting a lot easier.*

I was devastated when Jimmy died. I needed friends like Marlon and Jimmy, guys I admired who also liked me back. It was so rare for me to run into guys my age who didn't treat me like shit. Everyone knew I enjoyed the ladies, and a lot of guys were jealous of me for my successes in that department, but not Marlon or Jimmy.

In my second year at Universal I was dating a lot of actresses, one after another, but they were just dates, not relationships. Then in 1950 I met the actress Janet Leigh. Janet, who was born Jeanette Morrison, was so bright that she had finished high school at age fifteen. Even though she was only twenty-three when I met her, she had already been married — not once but twice. The first time came at the end of high school, when she and her boyfriend ran off together. When they returned home, her father had the marriage annulled. Then she married another young man when she was eighteen, but that marriage lasted only a couple of years.

Everything changed for Janet when she was twenty. That was the year that Norma Shearer, the wife of the late Irving Thalberg, the great movie producer, saw Janet's picture in a magazine at a ski lodge. Norma got in touch with Janet and set her up with a contact at MGM, and the studio put Janet under contract. That was approximately the same time MGM signed Elizabeth Taylor, June Allyson, and a few other very talented young women. Janet was the embodiment of the high school sweetheart — so beautiful you couldn't even imagine you'd ever be worthy of dating her; she looked like an impossible dream. Of course, Janet and the other girls didn't have an easy time competing with Elizabeth Taylor, who had incredible allure. It wasn't long before Elizabeth Taylor was getting any star role she wanted, which made it hard on the other young actresses at MGM.

To Janet's credit, she did manage to get some good parts, despite dwelling in Elizabeth Taylor's shadow. When I met Janet, she was making the movie *Jet Pilot* for Howard Hughes. We met at a party thrown by RKO that was open to any contract player in Hollywood. The idea was to attract as many actors as possible so that fan magazines would show up, take pictures, and do stories about the stars and RKO — and of course, the movie.

In *Jet Pilot,* Janet was playing a Russian fighter pilot, and she came to the party straight from shooting on the set. She had her hair pulled back, making her look sweet and vulnerable, and, boy, was I stunned by the way she looked. Although she had hardly any makeup on, she was very beautiful and seemed quite nice and pleasant. I was instantly drawn to her. I wasn't sure how I would get her to notice me, but I had never let that stop me before. This time I decide on a direct approach: I walked right up to her and introduced myself.

At the time, Janet was living off Sunset Boulevard in a little house with her parents. Her father was also her business manager, which was often a tricky business. Word around town had it that Janet was going out with Arthur Loews Jr., of the Loews theater family. Arthur was a good-looking college boy with a ton of money, so I figured that if I even came up to bat, Arthur would be leading by a score of twenty to nothing.

Even worse, I soon found out that Janet was being pursued by Howard Hughes, who was not only Janet's producer for *Jet Pilot* but was also just about the richest man in America. Howard had a reputation for going out of his way to have sex with many of Hollywood's most famous actresses. The lengths he would go to were legendary.

According to one story, Howard became enamored of the star violinist of the Paris Symphony Orchestra, so to get her to come to Hollywood, he arranged for the Paris Symphony to perform the score for a movie he was producing. He flew the entire eighty-piece orchestra to Hollywood to record the music. Once the violinist got to Hollywood, Greg Bautzer, Hughes's attorney, warned her not to sleep with Hughes, but she didn't listen. The day after they went to bed, Hughes canceled the orchestra's contract for the movie and flew the entire orchestra back to France. He had satisfied his desire, and that was the end of that.

This was the man who had set his sights on Janet Leigh. He wanted her in *Jet Pilot* so badly that he reportedly gave her father the right to act as an insurance broker in a deal in which Hughes took out a two-hundred-thousand-dollar policy. Janet's father got some dough, Janet got to be in Hughes's movie, and Hughes got what he wanted: a chance to be with Janet.

At the party where I met Janet, I also saw Hughes, although I didn't realize it at the time. I remember seeing an odd-looking man wearing tennis shoes. Back then no one wore tennis shoes unless they were playing tennis, but Howard Hughes was different. He did what he wanted. And what he wanted now was to be with Janet. He'd already been with so many other famous, talented, beautiful women; who was Janet to turn him down? But when I asked her for her number, for some reason she gave it to me. I don't know why. I suppose I sounded sincere in my interest, which I most certainly was.

So, against all odds, Janet and I started going out, but as long as she was working on *Jet Pilot,* I couldn't shake the feeling she was still dating Hughes. One night at about nine thirty I drove to the RKO studios to pick her up after work. She had said she had some dubbing to do that evening. When I pulled up at the spot where we'd arranged to meet, I saw a tall guy standing in the shadows, wearing tennis shoes. Who else could it be but Hughes? The guy was like a ghost — a rich, powerful ghost, that is. He had the clout to get Universal to drop me with a single phone call, if he wanted to. That was the least of it. He had such a reputation for ruthlessness that I was actually concerned he might have me bumped off. I decided to give Janet some room until I knew for certain that the road was clear (although I don't really think I had a choice in the matter). After she was through with *Jet Pilot,* I guess she was through with him — or he with her — and we started going out regularly.

It didn't take me long to fall in love with Janet. We had a wonderful time together, although from the beginning she was the one who dictated all the moves. She, like most people I met in Hollywood, had more self-confidence than I did. I didn't dare initiate anything. I was happy just to be with her. Unfortunately, not everyone was so pleased about it. I had earlier dated an actress named Suzan Ball, a beautiful girl under contract to Universal who was Lucille Ball's second cousin. We went out a few times, but it didn't really go anywhere, which was the norm for me before I got together with Janet. Then, one night after I started dating Janet, Suzan saw me across the Universal lot and yelled to me, "Hi, Mr. Leigh, how's it going?"

I suppose she could have meant a lot of different things by that, but to me it sounded as if she was accusing me of going out with Janet for the publicity, or perhaps insinuating that Janet wore the pants in our relationship. The former certainly wasn't true, but there might have been some truth in the latter — at least at first. Sadly, that was the last time I saw Suzan. Later she was injured while filming a dancing scene in the movie *East of Sumatra.* When the doctors examined her injured knee, they were surprised to find cancer, and the leg had to be amputated. Not long after that she married my friend, the actor Richard Long, but she died soon afterward at the tragically young age of twenty-one.

Soon after I started dating Janet, Universal finally decided to give me my first starring role. The movie was a swashbuckler called *The Prince Who Was a Thief,* a sand-and-tits movie where they dressed me up in tights, gave me a scimitar, and asked me to run through harems of scantily clad girls. The studio had decided to promote me as the new Douglas Fairbanks, an idea that thrilled me. I could ride a horse or swing on a rope, and I could fence with the best of them.

However, it soon became obvious that the studio didn't just want me to be a swashbuckler like Fairbanks; they wanted to pair me with my female lead as a boy-girl team, both off and on screen, much the way Fairbanks had been paired with Mary Pickford. For the female lead in *The Prince Who Was a Thief,* Universal cast Piper Laurie, an eighteen-year-old actress who had just signed a contract with the studio the year before. She'd caught the eye of Bob Goldstein, the head of casting, and they had started dating; her contract soon followed.

Once Piper and I had been cast, the studio kept arranging for us to go out on dates. They wanted us to be seen going to parties together so that when they announced the making of the film, we would generate more publicity.

Even if Piper and I had been attracted to each other, there was little chance that anything would have come of it, because they never left us alone. But I didn't find her attractive at all. I never understood what Bob Goldstein saw in her. She was an unpleasant person, very suspicious of everybody. She reminded me of some of the girls I knew back in New York. She was a willful, headstrong person who did things her own way, regardless of the outcome. For instance, after the makeup artist finished getting Piper ready for her shots for the day, she'd go to the set, duck behind a bookcase or a dresser, open up her own makeup box, and completely redo her face.

When the crew looked at the rushes the next day, the head of the camera department would ask, "What is that dark shading over her eyes? That looks terrible." They'd look at the scene again and again, wondering what was wrong, until they figured out what Piper was up to. She was a piece of work.

I loved making *The Prince Who Was a Thief.* My role was physically demanding, requiring me to do a fair amount of stunt work, including horseback riding and fencing. One month before we started shooting, I took lessons in saber, foil, and épée, and I found that I had an affinity for it. I liked my costumes, and while I may not have been attracted to Piper, she was a very pretty girl, so we made a striking couple onscreen.

The movie cost four hundred thousand dollars to make, which made it a low-budget film. When it went on to gross more than two million dollars, Universal's executives figured that all they had to do to make a successful movie was put Piper and me in it. My buzz was building, and the studio had its own ideas about how to capitalize on it. The studio's casting director, Bob Laze, came to see me and said, "If you marry Piper, I can get you a big, fat envelope." I was confused; wasn't she Bob Goldstein's girl? Was this guy going behind Bob's back? But soon afterward another intermediary, a guy who was close to the casting department, offered me thirty thousand dollars to marry Piper. I couldn't figure out what was going on. Was this Bob's way of getting rid of her?

The studio kept up the pressure on me to marry Piper. In 1951, thirty thousand dollars was a fortune, and I badly needed the dough. But I was getting more and more serious with Janet. I didn't know where things were headed between us, but I wasn't going to walk away from what we had just because someone offered me a big payday.

I was also worried about getting typecast as Piper Laurie's costar. I could see that the studio was trying to groom me to be the next great screen lover. But what kind of lover was I really? I was a twenty-five-year-old kid just starting out in the movies. The studio pressure, the publicity, and the focus on my personal life — all this craziness really unsettled me, and I didn't know how to deal with it. And what I really wanted was to be in serious films like Marlon and Jimmy Dean. I didn't want to be stuck forever doing silly romances that no one would remember a year later.

I have to admit that had I not met Janet, I might have taken the money to marry Piper.

It certainly was tempting. And truth be told, I was so broke that if someone had actually riffled the cash money right under my nose, I might have taken it, Janet or no Janet. But no one ever did. And I'm glad they didn't. I cared more for Janet than I had ever cared for a woman before. I had gotten in pretty deep with Marilyn Monroe, but neither of us had any intention of marrying. We were too young, and too ambitious.

Janet was someone I admired greatly, and I badly wanted her to admire me back. She was better educated than I was, and I was honored that she wanted to spend time with me. I knew that if she married me, it would be for myself, because she was already an established star; it wasn't as if marrying me was going to do anything for her career. So I turned down Piper and the cash, and I held out for Janet.

Still, I had never felt so pushed and pulled in my life: dating Janet, being on tour, seeing those screaming girls night after night, and turning down wads of cash to marry Piper. Only one choice seemed to make any sense in all this madness — to marry Janet Leigh. In the middle of the tour, I decided to do it. I knew I was bucking the studio, but I reminded myself that I'd been able to make it past all of Janet's former suitors, including

Arthur Loews Jr. and Howard Hughes, and that made me feel superhuman.

I called Janet and proposed to her over the phone. She said yes, and we arranged for her to come and meet me in New York City, where we would get married. The evening before the wedding, Jerry Lewis cornered me. He and Dean were in New York doing their act. Jerry said, "What are you doing? Are you nuts? Getting married will kill your career. Don't do that." I liked Jerry, but I ignored his advice.

Then Leonard Goldstein — Bob's brother, and the head of Universal — called me later that evening and told me that as far as Universal was concerned, they thought it would be best if Janet and I didn't get married. "You have a *big* career in front of you," Leonard said. "Don't blow it." He'd slightly changed his tune, from "Marry Piper" to "Don't marry Janet," but as far as I was concerned it was still bullshit. Why didn't they want me to marry Janet? Because she was under contract to a rival studio, MGM. Meanwhile, Janet was getting the same kind of pressure from MGM and from her father, who didn't want to lose his meal ticket.

That night I called Janet, which was probably a mistake because I was angry and confused by the pressure I was getting. She was staying at another hotel in New York, getting ready for the wedding the next day. While we were talking, I said, "Maybe we shouldn't get married," and Janet said, "That's fine, because I don't want to marry you either."

"Wait a minute," I said, but the line had already gone dead. A few minutes later I got her back on the phone, apologized, and begged her to marry me. We talked for an hour and patched things up, regaining the perspective we'd lost when so many obstacles were set in our way.

Despite all the warnings and the naysayers, Janet and I were married one day after my birthday, on June 4, 1951, in the country outside New York City. Jerry Lewis was the best man (he'd quickly come around after that phone call), and our wedding was a lot of fun. We had a wonderful dinner at Danny's Hideaway, a trendy New York restaurant.

Shortly afterward, the studio sent Piper and me on a promotional tour for *The Prince Who Was a Thief,* which included Cleveland, Chicago, Philadelphia, New York, and Boston. I would walk out onto the stage, and the girls in the audience would scream. It happened in every city. It was nuts. I couldn't believe that I could generate that kind of response after nothing but bit parts and one starring role. Sometimes, when my success seemed overwhelming, I found some sanity by asking myself, *What is it about me that creates this kind of reaction?* It could only be my looks. None of those screaming girls knew anything about my personality, that was for sure. What they were infatuated by had very little to do with me.

Piper was unhappy because the publicity about my wedding was eclipsing news about the movie. For the remainder of the tour there was a lot of friction between Piper and me. She may also have resented my refusal to marry her, although I don't know whether she even knew about the studio's proposal to me.

After the tour I flew back to LA, to my new home with Janet. I loved the idea of being married to her, although married life itself took some getting used to.

I would be lying on the couch at home, and she would ask me, "Can I get you something?"

I'd say, "Please, may I have a glass of water?" She'd bring it, and I'd say, "Thank you, my darling girl."

"You're welcome, you wonderful man."

I'd take a sip and put the glass down on the coffee table, and then Janet would come back, take the glass away, and pour it out in the kitchen sink.

"Sweetheart," I'd say a few minutes later, "why did you take my water away?"

"I thought you were done, darling." That's how I found out how compulsively neat Janet was. Nothing could be out of place when she was around. Whenever she had to travel somewhere I would marvel at how she was able to fit so many items into one suitcase, every item fitting snugly into its compartment; and she always knew exactly where everything was!

I once asked her mother, "Where did Janet learn to pack like that?"

"She has always packed like that," her mother said. "She packs like the inside of a body." I looked, and sure enough, there was the stomach, there was the liver, there were the lungs, everything touching each other, stockings rolled up, nothing out of place. At home, not only was the laundry done, it was always ironed, folded, and put away. The house was impeccable. It was an attractive environment to live in, although sometimes Janet's insistence that everything be in its place made me a little edgy.

Piper and I had been a sensation in *The Prince Who Was a Thief,* and Universal wanted more of a good thing, so we costarred in the next two movies we made. The first one was called *No Room for the Groom.* Perhaps Universal had this movie in mind when they offered me that envelope full of cash, because the plot revolved around our getting married, my going into the Army, and my coming back to find my wife had filled our home with all her relatives. My problem now (in the movie) was to find a way to get the relatives out of the house so I could enjoy some conjugal relations instead. Things worked out okay on screen, but off screen I still didn't enjoy dealing with Piper's resentment. If anything, it had gotten worse, so making this movie was just torture.

To capitalize further on *The Prince Who Was a Thief,* Universal put us in another sand-and-tits movie called *Son of Ali Baba.* Piper played an escaped slave who took shelter under my roof. This movie provided another opportunity for me to run around bare-chested in pajama bottoms with a turban around my head. Part of the fun of working on that movie was getting to spend a lot of time with Davy Sharpe, the stuntman who was my stand-in. Over his career, Davy appeared in more than forty-five hundred films — no one knows the exact number — which means he may have appeared in more films than anyone else in U.S. film history. His first film appearance was as a double to Douglas Fairbanks in the movie *The Thief of Bagdad,* when Davy was only fourteen. In this movie, Davy and I would go out onto the back lot almost every day so he could spend some time training me in horseback riding, fencing, jumping, and tumbling. He taught me how to fall so my shoulders and upper body cushioned the blow, rather than landing directly on my feet, which could cause permanent damage.

Davy was twenty years older than I was, in his forties, but he was a superb athlete. He could take off his hat and fling it up in the air without looking at it, and it would always land on his head. When Davy was rehearsing, he always had a cigar in his mouth, and he could throw the cigar up in the air and catch that between his teeth. One time early in his career, a director filmed a rehearsal scene without telling him, and Davy vowed never to let that happen again. That was why he always kept a cigar in his mouth during rehearsal. He knew the director would ask him to take the cigar out when it was time to roll film. Davy was always upbeat, and a joy to be around. His signature line was "I greet you with cordiality and good cheer."

Son of Ali Baba was the movie where I gave a line that people unjustly made fun of for years afterward. There's a scene where I'm on horseback and Piper is sitting next to me, and I say to her, "Yonder in the valley of the sun is my father's castle." After the film came out, Debbie Reynolds, who would later marry Eddie Fisher, went on television and said, "Did you see the new guy in the movies? They call him Tony Curtis, but that's not his real name. In his new movie he's got a hilarious line where he says, 'Yonder lies the castle of my *fodda.*'"

You could chalk her ridicule up to my New York accent, but when she mentioned the issue of my real name on television, I began to wonder if there was something anti-Semitic going on there. I'm probably just hypersensitive on that topic. But either way, she got the line wrong! Unfortunately, her version stuck with the public, and for a while it became popular for people to quote the incorrect line in a ridiculous New York accent.

Years later, Hugh Hefner came up to me at a party and said, "Yonder lies the castle of my *fodda.*"

I looked at him coolly. "Hef, I never said that."

"Then don't tell anybody," he said. "It

makes a great movie story."

After starring in *No Room for the Groom* and *Son of Ali Baba,* I was on the cover of all the movie magazines, but even that didn't lead to the big break I was looking for. Being in those desert movies gave me my first leading roles, but it also reinforced a certain impression of me that I couldn't shake for a long time.

In the fall of 1952 I met the producer/director George Pal, who was Hungarian, like me; his real name was Julius György Märczincsák. George offered me the lead role in the movie *Houdini.* I absolutely loved the idea. A Hungarian Jew as an escape artist! What an incredible role. And George really wanted me. "Tony," he said, "I'm not going to make the picture without you." But we had a problem: this was a Paramount picture, and I was under contract to Universal. Actors sometimes got their studios to let them do "outside pictures," as they were called, but to get the studio to do you this favor, you had to be able to pull some big strings, and I just didn't have enough leverage to make that happen.

Then Lew Wasserman, the head of the MCA talent agency, interceded. I had met Lew through Jay Kanter, Marlon's agent, who also worked at MCA. Jay and I were great friends, so when I told Jay my situation with George, he said, "Let me introduce you to Lew." I had heard all about Lew; he was legendary, a man who could do more than just put picture deals together. When Jimmy Stewart signed to star in *Winchester '73,* Lew had made a deal that gave Jimmy a chunk of the profits rather than a flat salary. It was a deal that would change the balance of power in Hollywood, making actors the most important players in the movie business instead of just paid employees.

Jay took me to Palm Springs to meet Lew. I didn't have an agent at the time, so I asked him, "Will you handle me?" He said yes, so I signed an agency contract with MCA, and in that moment everything changed for me. With Lew Wasserman as my mentor, doors opened at the slightest touch. In those days, Lew was the most intelligent man in the movie industry; it wasn't even close. Lew Wasserman was so good that MGM wanted him to sell his agency and take over the studio. They sent him a blank piece of paper and said, "This is your contract. You write in whatever numbers you want. Just run the studio." But he turned the studio down. He said he couldn't just walk out on all the actors who depended on him for a living. He was the most honorable guy I ever knew.

Lew and I became great friends. I spent a lot of time with him, and Janet and I were invited over for dinners at his home in Palm Springs.

One day Lew said to me, "I've got something for you, Tony, but you'll have to pay for it." I couldn't imagine what it was, but he certainly had my full attention. Lew took me down to the basement of a private parking garage, and there was a gleaming, new, silver Rolls-Royce convertible with black upholstery. I had told Lew about my love of cars, especially how much I loved the Rolls-Royce, and Lew had gone out and bought the car for me. His partner owned a big car dealership in St. Louis, so Lew was able to get the car for a terrific price: seven thousand dollars. That was a lot of money in those days, but the list price was more than three times that much.

Janet was also one of Lew's clients. Aware of how well my career was going, Lew decided to pair Janet up with me in the Houdini movie. If the studio wanted me (and Lew knew they did), they had to take Janet. For this deal, we were a matched pair. I was thrilled for Janet and happy to have her play my wife in the picture, but I wasn't so sure this was the best thing for my own career.

My concern was that I was running into a Douglas Fairbanks–Mary Pickford pairing all over again, only this time with Janet instead of Piper. I loved Janet, and I wanted the best for her, but I hoped that somewhere down the line I could make an important picture of my own.

Preparations for *Houdini* proceeded. When I told the people in the Paramount wardrobe department that my father was a tailor, they told me he could have a job there if he wanted it. My father had already gotten a job clipping articles for Warren Cowet, who was handling my press, but here was a chance for him to work as a tailor again. When Paramount gave me the good news, I immediately ran for the phone to tell my father. But as I was crossing the soundstage, I slipped on a cable and tore all the ligaments in my right knee. The pain was unbelievable, but I just had the knee taped, and we forged ahead. I didn't even think about holding up production while I recovered. (By the way, if you watch *Houdini* closely, you can see me limping a bit.)

To prepare for the role of Houdini, I had learned how to do magic tricks. The studio hired George Boston, a magician who never had a big career but who was a wonderful teacher, to work with me and show me what magic was all about. I spent four months studying with George before we started shooting. I would drive my Rolls-Royce to work at Paramount, holding the wheel with one hand and doing one-handed cuts with a deck of cards in the other. I wanted my hands to have a feel for the cards the way a musician had a feel for his instruments. After a while I could do great card tricks for people, which made me a popular fixture at Hollywood parties. People were fascinated by how I did my tricks, and I wanted to bring that quality of fascination to the movie.

I'm very proud of the fact that I did all my own stunts for that film. In one scene Houdini is dropped into the Hudson River during wintertime, chained and handcuffed in a big box. Ice freezes over the hole where he's supposed to come out, and for a moment in the movie it looks like I'm going to drown under the ice. The "ice" we used was really a sheet of wax, suspended a couple of inches above the water. I knew that if I came up under the wax, I'd be able to breathe. I did all the swimming scenes myself too. All that work in the pool was really paying off now, not to mention those years of climbing the El trestles, boxing, and wrestling. Sometimes studio execs came on the set just to see what was going on; making this movie was as much fun as I'd ever had.

At the end of the movie Houdini was handcuffed and immersed upside down in a tank of water. For this scene I had to learn how to get out of handcuffs in a hurry. It wasn't that difficult, really; there was a certain way of twisting them that freed you. Still, for this shot I had to hold my breath while I escaped the handcuffs and then I had to maneuver my body in a very tight space so I was right side up. There was barely enough room to do it, and honestly, the stunt was a little dangerous. But I pulled it off just fine. In fact, I was feeling so much in control that I started acting like I was choking and running out of air, just to make the scene more exciting. Then I heard thud, thud, and the next thing I knew all the water was running out onto the floor, and I was spilling out along with it. The propmen were standing there with axes, looking scared and very worried.

I scrambled to my feet and said to George Pal, "Why the hell did they do that?"

George said calmly, "Because they thought you were in trouble, Tony. Why else?"

It turned out that my acting was a little too good that time. But the cameraman had filmed the entire sequence and had some good footage, so thankfully we didn't have to film it again.

No one expected *Houdini* to be a big hit, but it was very successful. My secret hope, however, was that *Houdini* was going to propel me into a whole new kind of filmmaking, where I would be recognized as the serious actor I had always wanted to be. When that didn't happen, I was terribly disappointed.

Me, Rock Hudson, and Robert Wagner, in a photo shoot for Life magazine, March 1, 1954. © GETTY IMAGES/TIME & LIFE PICTURES, SHARLAND

9
The Hollywood Scene

After I married Janet, I sensed some antagonism from people in Hollywood, perhaps because this Jewish kid had married a shiksa screen idol. It's possible that I was misreading the signs, but that's the way I felt. At the same time, marrying Janet also gave me instant entrée to an important Hollywood crowd, the WASP actors and actresses whose axis seemed to be Debbie Reynolds, the popular film and singing star. That group included Gene Kelly and his wife, Henry Fonda and his wife, and George Sidney and his wife. If Debbie liked you, her crowd would put up with you; but if for any reason she didn't like you, you'd have a lot of trouble in Hollywood. Because of Janet, Debbie and her friends accepted me.

Debbie was a real firecracker — a talented, compassionate person with many good qualities. She had the smash hit "Aba Daba Honeymoon," and she sang the song

"Tammy" and played the title role in the movie *Tammy and the Bachelor.* She also starred in *Singin' in the Rain* with Gene Kelly. For a long time she was America's sweetheart, and she still performs on TV. Debbie's a dynamo.

After Janet and I got married, Janet took me around to all the MGM studio parties, which was all part of working in Hollywood. We'd go to two or three studio parties a week, even if I had to go on the set the next day. I'd drink at a party, I'd go home wasted, and I'd still have to get up at six in the morning to go to work. I didn't know the ropes well enough yet to ask for a driver, so I drove myself to the studio. And I was never late. I wouldn't say I followed every studio rule, but when I was working on a film, I showed up on time.

Janet introduced me to all her chums. They were curious to meet me because I had had an impact very quickly, and they wanted to see what this shooting star was all about. For my part, I couldn't believe that this brash kid from New York was getting to know people like Gene Kelly. I got close to Gene because he had seen some of my work and was impressed that I was such a good fencer. Gene, a major jewel in the MGM crown, starred in a string of Hollywood musicals in the 1940s and 1950s, including *Cover Girl,* with Rita Hayworth, and *Anchors Aweigh,* in which he designed his own dance routines. In 1951 he starred in *An American in Paris,* and of course he was a sensation in *Singin' in the Rain* in 1952.

Not only was Gene a great dancer, he was one of the most extraordinary athletes I'd ever seen. He could do anything a stuntman could do, which gave us something in common. He also showed himself to be a very generous man when he started inviting me to his house on weekends so he could teach me some of the secrets of performing stunts. I'll always be grateful to him for that. Gene Kelly was one of the truly outstanding people in the movie profession. He could never have understood the great impact his kindness had on me. To be taught by Gene Kelly was to be taught by the best.

Around this time Janet and I began spending a lot more time with Jerry Lewis. She and I were among the few friends who didn't succumb to Jerry's powerful ego — or weren't put off by it. He liked to make amateur movies at home with a 16mm camera, and we had fun acting in them, along with Sammy Davis Jr. and Jerry's two little boys, Gary and Ronnie. Jerry put a lot of work into those amateur films, but his photography was not terrific, so his homemade movies were always either underexposed or overexposed.

I didn't think much of Jerry's cinematography, but I thoroughly enjoyed the camaraderie at his house. Knowing that the door was always open, Janet and I went to Jerry's almost every night. I saw very little of Dean Martin during that time, because at that time you had to choose one man or the other. The public didn't know it, but although Dean and Jerry were partners, they weren't close friends off stage.

Jerry and Dean had met in New York City and decided to form an act. For their first time on stage together, at a club in Atlantic City, they worked from a prepared script of jokes and songs. They absolutely bombed. The club owner told them that if they didn't do a better job with the next show that evening, they were through. So they threw out the script and decided to ad-lib the whole thing. While Dean sang, Jerry came out in a busboy's uniform and dropped plates and generally drove Dean crazy while he tried to perform. The audience loved it, and that was the start of Martin and Lewis. After headlining at the Copacabana in New York, they signed a contract with Paramount. Whenever Jerry and Dean would open their show someplace new, we'd all go to see them to show our support. They were the funniest. Jerry played a buffoon with uncanny skill, and Dean smoothly played off whatever Jerry wanted to do.

One of the reasons Jerry embraced Janet and me was because we had become part of the Hollywood establishment. I didn't know it at the time, but I learned later that Jerry badly wanted to be a part of that firmament. Jerry was very insecure, and sometimes his insecurity made him mean, even nasty. He would say the most awful things about people, sometimes right to their faces. He could turn to me and say, "You think you're going to be a star? You'll never be bigger than me." He treated Dean the same way. Somehow I found a way to just accept this about Jerry and still enjoy him as a friend.

After I'd hung out with Jerry for a while, I got curious about what kind of person Dean was, so I started to seek him out. I soon discovered what a wonderful man he was. After Dean and Jerry broke up in 1956, Dean became a serious dramatic actor. He never stopped singing, of course, and his song "Everybody Loves Somebody" knocked the Beatles song "A Hard Day's Night" out of the number-one slot on the charts in 1964. In Las Vegas, Dean became a megastar.

Dean introduced me to Frank Sinatra. Frank was from New Jersey, so he liked the fact that I was from New York. We hit it off right away. One night Frank called up and asked Janet and me to come to party he was holding at his house on Carrolwood Drive, high up on a mountain. Ciro's, the fancy restaurant in town, catered all of Frank's parties. At dinnertime a van would come up the hill, and two men would unload mountains of food into Frank's kitchen. When we went to Frank's we knew we could count on an amazing Italian dinner.

I ended up going up there a lot. By meeting Frank and Dean, all of a sudden I had a new circle of friends, guys I really liked, although they were usually eight or nine years older than I was. I became an honorary member of Frank's Rat Pack; I never went on stage with Frank, Dean, Sammy, Joey Bishop, or Peter Lawford, but anytime they had a get-together, I was invited. Whenever those guys got up to any kind of mischief, I was there. They treated me like a kid brother, which brought out the best in everyone.

Frank Sinatra was a very important player in the Hollywood game. He was like the sun, with a lot of people revolving around him. Frank represented much of what I admired in a person. He was independent, a free spirit who never spent time worrying about what other people thought of him. When Frank was living in Beverly Hills he wanted to get a license so he could land a helicopter in his backyard. When he was off traveling around the world somewhere, he wanted to fly from wherever he was to the Los Angeles airport, hop in his helicopter at the airport, and fly home. But the neighbors didn't want the noise, so they blocked the license. Frank was mad as hell, but even he was powerless to do anything about it.

As engaging and interesting as Frank was, he could also be antagonistic, quick-tempered, and dictatorial. He knew that when politically savvy people in Hollywood said, "Don't worry about that now," what they really meant was, *Don't worry about it now because one day you'll be in a position to fuck 'em.* But Frank didn't think like that; he wasn't one to bide his time if he didn't have to. If Frank got screwed by someone, he would get right on the phone and tell that person how he felt. And that was the end of it. If you screwed Frank, he took your name out of his address book. Forever. You didn't get a second chance.

When Frank asked you to do him a favor, you didn't want to say no, so when he asked me if I'd make a cameo appearance as a member of the audience in the movie *Meet Danny Wilson,* naturally I agreed to it. In the movie Frank played a hard-nosed, jaded singer in a club that attracted a lot of celebrities, so the actor Jeff Chandler and I sat there in the club audience, playing ourselves, listening to Frank while he sang.

Frank could be difficult, but I loved being around him. Sometimes it would be eleven thirty at night when he'd call and say, "Get over here." He'd add, "And don't bring Janet." I'd tell Janet, "Frank called, and he wants me to come up to the house. Boys only, he said." She'd say fine.

I'd arrive, and Frank would say, "We're going to run a movie." He had a beautiful screening room at his place where he showed movies whenever he felt like it. He liked action movies, and he particularly liked Gregory Peck. So I'd get up there after midnight, get a drink or two in me, and then once the movie started, often I would fall asleep in one of his comfortable chairs. When it was over, the lights would come up, I'd wake from my slumber, and Frank would serve food while I flirted a little with a couple of the pretty girls who were always part of the scene. Then I'd make my way home about four in the morning. I'd take a shower, go to bed, and a few hours later get up and go to work. It was tiring, but it was always fun.

As a boy, Frank had desperately wanted a set of electric trains, but he never got one; so after he became rich and famous, he decided to make up for what he had missed as a kid. He bought himself an incredibly elaborate set of Lionel trains and had them set up in his house in Palm Springs. The tracks ran through almost every room. You'd come in the front door, step over some train tracks, and go sit in the living room.

"Let me show you my trains," Frank would shout from the kitchen.

I'd sit down on the couch and yell, "I'm sitting, Frank. Let her roll."

While I sat there, in came the train, complete with steam whistle, running under my feet, under a table, through a tunnel, then out of the room.

"It's gone," I'd yell.

"It'll be back," he'd shout.

Then he'd come running in, jump over tracks, and sit down next to me. We'd both sit there, marveling at his fabulous electric trains.

When I met Frank, he was on Hollywood's shit list because he had left his wife for Ava Gardner, one of the sexiest women in the history of Hollywood. Ava was the one who saw to it that Harry Cohn gave Frank the Oscar-winning role in *From Here to Eternity.* Ava was incredibly beautiful, and anyone who looked at her could see why Frank — and a lot of other people — wanted her. She had married and divorced Mickey Rooney and Artie Shaw before she met Frank. All the studio execs had the hots for Ava, including my friend Howard Duff. Ava also went with Howard Hughes, but she dumped him. Frank, of course, had bedded a whole roster of Hollywood stars himself. His appetite for women was well known. He was relentless. But when he and Ava saw each other, that was it, and they got married in 1951.

Unfortunately, Ava's temper was almost as bad as Frank's, so the two of them had a very stormy marriage. It lasted six years, though, which wasn't bad by Hollywood standards. After Ava left Frank, he moved into an apartment in Beverly Hills with a beautiful actress named Jeannie Carmen. But Frank became chronically depressed after he and Ava got divorced. When I met Jeannie, she told me that all Frank did was sit around and play his own music.

Jeannie told me that one night they had been up late talking when she had asked him who his favorite movie star was. He said,

"Tony Curtis." She asked him why. "Because he beat the fucking odds," Frank said. Hearing that only made me love Frank more. Now I understood why Frank liked me so much. He could relate; he'd beaten the odds too.

You had to know how to handle Frank, and not everyone did. One night Frank invited Nat "King" Cole and me over to see his new hi-fi set. It was huge, about seven feet wide, floor to ceiling. Frank was going with Lauren Bacall then (her husband, Humphrey Bogart, had died about a year before) and they were throwing a dinner party. The food, as always, was catered by Frank's buddy who owned Ciro's restaurant in Hollywood.

While Frank was talking to Nat and me, describing the features of the hi-fi set, Lauren Bacall came over.

"Frank, dear, time to eat," she said.

"We'll be there in a minute," Frank said, and continued talking about the hi-fi.

Lauren went over and filled a plate with food, and then she came back and handed the plate to Frank.

"You've got to eat, Frank," she said.

Frank looked at her. While she stood there holding Frank's silverware and napkin, he turned the plate upside down, dumped the food onto the floor, and gave the plate back to her. Nat and I just looked at each other. I think Lauren made the right decision when she turned down Frank's proposal of marriage. They just didn't bring out the best in each other.

After Houdini came the film *All American.* I played a college quarterback whose parents are killed in a car crash on their way to watch him play in a game. My character comes from an Italian family and goes to a fancy college. He has long hair, and everybody plays a number on him because of his hair, just the way they did to me in real life. Dick Long, my buddy who would go on to TV stardom in such shows as *The Big Valley, Nanny and the Professor, 77 Sunset Strip,* and *Maverick,* was in the film, as was Mamie Van Doren, another of Howard Hughes's big-busted discoveries.

It was a typical low-budget Universal movie. We went out to UCLA, which had agreed to let us use their football field. As the star quarterback I threw touchdown passes and got tackled by Frank Gifford, the all-American football player.

Mamie Van Doren was another version of Marilyn, only even more voluptuous. She was another actress trying to climb her way up, but I didn't think she was smart enough to make it. Nobody was really that interested in her. She didn't really have any style; she just had this incredible body, she was sweet and kind, and she wanted a career in film. To my surprise, she was wonderful in *All American.* She played a villainous character who was fooling around with Dick Long, who came from a very high-class family. I still wasn't convinced Mamie had what it took to get into the big time, though. Hollywood was a tough nut to crack in those days. (I think it's even tougher now.)

My next forgettable movie was called *Forbidden,* which ostensibly took place in Macao, China, but was actually shot on Universal's back lot. This was a low-budget knockoff of *Casablanca,* with me playing the Bogart role. In the movie I owned a casino, and Joanne Dru played my love interest. Joanne had starred in a lot of westerns in the '40s. How she got this particular part, I'll never know. She must have had a studio connection, because she was too old for the part — or, I should say, she was too old for me. We didn't have any chemistry, but I made a great effort, and we did okay. This was another typical Universal penny-ante film. Eight days after they got the idea they had a treatment, and nine days later they had a script. That was the way Universal did it back then. My job was to do the pictures they put me in, and I always got them done, which was all they wanted from me.

In 1954 I made the movie *Beachhead,* a very intense film about two American soldiers on a Japanese-occupied island during World War II. The movie was shot in Hawaii, and I had to go out there alone, which I didn't like, but Janet was working too: she was filming the movie *Prince Valiant.* While I was in Hawaii, I got a phone call saying Janet had had a miscarriage. She was in the hospital and wanted me to fly back to LA.

The news of her miscarriage was devastating, and not just for the obvious reason. I hadn't even known Janet was pregnant! As I thought about it, my insecurity and my overactive imagination started wreaking havoc. Why hadn't she told me she was pregnant? It was possible that she herself hadn't known, but I couldn't help but wonder if she was keeping it secret for some reason of her own.

Our marriage wasn't thriving by this point, as you may have guessed. Neither Janet nor I was the best of spouses, so we'd gotten pretty distant. All I knew was that I had finally attained my dream of being in the movies, but I kept being distracted by my personal life. I couldn't believe how flimsy our relationship had become, but I stayed in it.

After receiving news of the miscarriage, I had a decision to make: fly home or stay in Hawaii and keep filming. I wanted to fly home, but this particular movie was very low-budget, and I had to act in most of the remaining scenes. This meant that if I left, the studio would just shelve the movie rather than eating the extra production costs caused by the delay. Also, they told me there were only three or four more days of shooting. Once we were done, I could get on the first plane home.

I talked to my agent, Jerry Gershwin of MCA, and he told me he was in touch with Janet and everything was under control. I still wasn't sure what to do, so I called Janet in the hospital and told her my dilemma; she told me not to worry, that she'd be fine. I decided to stay and finish the movie, but I couldn't help but be distracted by the thought of Janet in a hospital room.

My costar in *Beachhead* was Frank Lovejoy, who played my lieutenant. Our job was to help a scientist and his daughter get safely across the occupied island, where a ship was waiting to take them to safety. The movie had lots of action. In it Frank's character stops my character from having an affair with the scientist's daughter, played by Mary Murphy. Mary was a very beautiful young woman who was dating Curt Fringes, a big-time agent who was about twenty years older than she was. Curt intended to divorce his wife Katy, a very powerful screenwriter, and marry Mary. Meantime, he was hell-bent on making Mary a star. While we were in Hawaii, Mary told me that she and Fringes were having problems; among other things, he wasn't happy about the fact that another agent had gotten Mary her role in *Beachhead,* and that before Fringes even knew about it, she was on her way to Hawaii.

Once Mary and I started talking, I became extremely attracted to her. She was very attentive and wanted to know all about me. While we were shooting the picture, we had fun connecting with each other with just a knowing glance or a shrug of the shoulders, and sometimes by stopping to talk. Though we both realized what was happening, neither one of us wanted to consummate the relationship. I didn't want to do anything I would regret later; I didn't want to jeopardize my already fragile marriage. It was a case of my eyes saying yes but the rest of me saying no. This was difficult for me, because saying yes was a helluva lot more fun. But it didn't happen this time.

■ ■ ■ ■

The next picture offered to me was *Johnny Dark,* in which I played a brilliant but underappreciated car designer who designs a prototype that meets with disapproval from the owner of the car company (Sidney Blackmer). Don Taylor, who played Elizabeth Taylor's husband in *Father of the Bride,* and I steal the car, aided and abetted by the company owner's daughter (Piper Laurie) and we race it from Canada to Mexico. *Johnny Dark* wasn't a bad movie, but by now I was looking forward to the day when my Universal contract would be satisfied and I would be free to pursue other possibilities.

My next movie, *The Black Shield of Falworth,* starred Janet and me. I played a peasant who was really a king. It was reminiscent of my sand-and-tits movies, but this time we were decked out in armor instead of pantaloons, turbans, and scimitars. There was a lot of action for me in this picture. I learned to ride a horse really well, and I loved walking around in my shiny armor, which was actually made of plastic. I did some jousting and a lot of swordplay. Janet was upset because she, as a female, didn't get to do anything physical. She played a lady-in-waiting, and she got so impatient with all that waiting that sometimes she'd jump on one of the horses and ride around to let off steam.

Her unhappiness wasn't due solely to the movie. Janet's friend Barbara Rush was in the movie with us, and one day Barbara came up to me and asked, "Are you and Janet doing all right?" I had a feeling Janet had told Barbara we weren't, and that Barbara had come to me to confirm it. I just said, "Janet's not feeling well." When the movie ended and Janet and I went home, I tried harder to behave in a way that didn't anger her, and she made the same effort for me. We settled into a functional but unromantic marriage, the kind of life that was less unusual in Hollywood than you might think.

We threw huge parties at our big, beautiful house on Summit Drive. Janet invited the Debbie Reynolds crowd, and friends such as Danny Kaye. Danny was a major talent. He was born in Brooklyn, and after coming to Hollywood he starred in roles where he could act, sing, and play the comedian, movies like *The Court Jester, Merry Andrew,* and *Hans Christian Andersen.* I didn't care for Danny at all, but Janet and I had agreed that each of us could invite whomever we wanted.

To my way of thinking, Danny was a very

mean and bitter man, and most everybody seemed to agree with me. When we first met, he would belittle me all the time. He once asked me, "Where did you learn how to fence — the Bronx?" Another time he said to me, "How do you act in those high heels?" I said, "I don't wear high heels." Then I took a step closer to him, looked in his eyes, and smiled while I said, "Fuck you, Danny." I don't know why Danny had it in for me. Maybe it was because we both came from New York. Maybe it was because we were both Jewish, and he struggled with that in himself. Or it might have been some complicated sexual feeling.

It was widely rumored that Danny went with both men and women. One of the people Danny was believed to have had a relationship with was Sir Laurence Olivier. There had always been rumors about Larry's sexuality, but he was nothing like Danny. As it happened, I acted in one of Larry's most famous scenes, in the movie *Spartacus.* The irony is that this famous — or infamous — scene didn't see the light of day for thirty years after it was filmed, because it was deemed too racy for audiences at the time of the film's release in 1960. In the scene, Larry plays a Roman general, and I'm his slave, and he's sitting naked in a tub.

The general is trying to get the slave to have sex with him, so Larry says to me, "Do you like oysters and snails?"

I say, "I like oysters."

He says, "What about snails?"

"No, I don't like snails."

He says, "Well, I like both oysters *and* snails."

Live and let live. I don't look down on gays; it's just not my thing. George Cukor, one of the great directors, was part of the Hollywood gay crowd. George would throw a big, formal dinner party at his house. Then, after the party was over, George and his friends would go cruise Sunset Boulevard, looking for young men; they called them "after-dinner mints." To each his own.

When Janet and I threw our parties, her friends invariably outnumbered mine. That was fair. She had a lot more friends than I did. Sometimes Frank Sinatra would come join us, but you had to be careful not to push him. He never wanted to be forced into anything. You could ask him, and he might come, and he might not.

To tell you the truth, I wasn't that nuts about parties, but I realized that Janet's social networking was good for both of us. At that point our faces were on every magazine cover in the country. When Janet and I hit, we became the undisputed darlings of the Hollywood media. Richard Burton and Elizabeth Taylor? Forget it. Debbie Reynolds and Eddie Fisher? Not a chance.

The public liked me because I was rough around the edges, not only in my acting but in my life. I was different from Cliff Robertson or Robert Wagner, who were always so polished and cool. I was untamed, with an animal magnetism that immediately attracted young fans of both sexes. At the same time, I was always very decent to people, and they liked that too.

In Hollywood, working for the "right" studio gave you status. Actors like Janet, who were signed by MGM, had more status than anyone else. That was one reason Suzan Ball called me "Mr. Leigh"; Janet worked at glitzy MGM, while I was employed by low-rent Universal. And it was also true I was a Jew, which in those days was a strike against you in Hollywood — as it was in most places. So I had two strikes against me when I started. Despite those obstacles, I still managed to become a legitimate Hollywood phenomenon, which was fine with some people but made others unhappy; still others could go either way, depending on the situation. Debbie Reynolds was one of those people who seemed to blow cold, then hot, and then cold again.

To be fair to Debbie, she started to treat me badly when she and Eddie Fisher started having problems in their marriage. It was a time when Debbie was very hostile toward men, sparking rumors that she was gay, but I never saw any evidence of that. People wondered about her sexuality because she never did settle down with a man other than Eddie. While they were married, I felt bad for Eddie. Debbie was a lot like Jerry Lewis, very demanding and always wanting to be in control.

Debbie and Eddie had a daughter, Carrie Fisher (who became famous playing Princess Leia in *Star Wars*). Years after Eddie and Debbie divorced, Carrie would blame Eddie for her parents' split, putting him in the category of "difficult Jewish fathers." She put me in that class too. Carrie was angry at her father, much the way my daughter, Jamie Lee, would later be angry at me. According to Carrie, it was the fault of Jewish fathers when our marriages blew up.

After Eddie and Debbie separated, his romantic life took a surprising turn. Liz Taylor had been married to producer Mike Todd, who died in a plane crash. Eddie was a good friend of Mike's, and after Mike died, he started taking care of Elizabeth. One thing led to another. I found it strange that Elizabeth would allow Eddie to look after her, since I got the feeling she didn't really care for him. Besides, she and Debbie were good friends. It was a strange time for all of us in our profession. You never knew who was going to end up with whom, or who would make it and who would fall by the wayside, personally and professionally.

Janet, meanwhile, was becoming very critical of my behavior in public. We'd go to a party, and she'd watch me very carefully wherever we were. From a distance of fifteen feet, she would nod her head yes or no to approve or criticize the way I held my glass. She'd point to her own glass, and she'd mouth the words, *Hold it like this.* She was trying to teach me etiquette, and I began to resent it.

One night Janet and I were invited to have dinner with Cole Porter at his New York City apartment. I had never met Cole, so I was looking forward to getting to know him. Ethel Merman, Janet, and I sat around Cole's couch with him. He was remarkably genial and friendly. Then someone came to the door and said, "Dinner is served." Everybody started to get up, so I just followed along. All of us walked down a little hallway, around a corner, and into the dining room;

when we got there, Cole Porter was already sitting at the head of the table.

I said to myself, *How the hell did he get there so quickly?* What I didn't realize was that Cole couldn't walk; both his legs had been broken in a horseback-riding accident. After the rest of us left him on the couch, two assistants had picked him up and hurried him through a back hallway and into the dining room before we could get there. I had always equated physical prowess with force of personality, but here was a guy who couldn't walk yet still dominated a room with his presence. Cole forced me to reconsider some of my basic assumptions. He was a remarkable man.

We all sat down and began the meal. I was sitting next to Janet, and I didn't know which fork to use, whether to use the big spoon or the little spoon for soup, that sort of thing. My lack of sophistication bothered Janet, always the perfectionist. She began poking me and whispering to me, making sure I didn't embarrass her with my inadequate manners. Her nagging pissed me off so much that I deliberately used the wrong knives and forks, which was childish but effective.

As we were sitting there, Ethel Merman picked up one of the wineglasses and gently squeezed it at the top. The wineglass was so delicate, and her touch so assured, that she could change its shape from round to oval without breaking it. I picked up my glass to inspect it, and Ethel said to me, "Go on. Try it."

I squeezed, and this beautiful, delicate wineglass shattered in my hand. Ethel, who was dear and kind, said, "Don't worry, kid, it could happen to any of us," and then she took her own glass and shattered it just to make me feel better. I looked over at Cole, and he was laughing, but Janet was furious.

One time after the wineglass incident, I went to La Grenouille, a famous French restaurant in New York, with my friend Gene Shacove and the Surrealist artist Salvador Dalí, who was staying at the same hotel I was, the Sherry-Netherland. I told them what had happened at Cole Porter's house. Gene tried it with his glass and shattered it. Dalí wasn't sure what we were doing, but he stood up in the restaurant, turned his glass upside down, and poured the wine onto his dinner; if we were somehow pushing the boundaries, Dalí wasn't going to let us do it alone.

There was so much about polite society that I just didn't know. One time Janet and I were invited to go to the racetrack to see the quarterhorses run. I had never been to a racetrack, so I wasn't sure what to wear. Janet said, "Just wear whatever you want." I decided to wear jeans, but when I got there the other men were all looking snazzy in their sweaters and trousers, two-toned shoes, and felt hats. I wish I could tell you it didn't matter to me, but the truth is that it made me feel inadequate. Those childhood wounds ran deep.

Janet's obvious discomfort with my manners and my New York accent didn't do much for my insecurity. She wanted to change me into Laurence Olivier, whose charm and polish were legendary. That was never going to happen. I was always going to stand out in a crowd, for better or for worse. And as time went on I got a stronger and stronger feeling that Janet thought it was for worse.

Janet and I had been nuts about each other when we first started going out. We loved the sex, and we loved the companionship; but it wasn't long before the differences between us that had seemed so exciting at first started to create friction. In many ways, I was the naive one in the relationship. I had never been married before, but for Janet I was husband number three — and she had been only twenty-three years old! She had already lived a lot in that time, and she had developed very firm ideas about how everything should be. Unfortunately, it wasn't long before she started trying to change me to conform to those ideas.

From my point of view Janet was bossing me around, just as my mother had bossed my father around. I could see signs in myself that I was becoming subservient, which only made my flashbacks to childhood more intense. Janet and I would go to a party together, and if I lit my cigarette without offering to light the cigarette of the person I was talking to, Janet would poke me with her elbow. She would always wait for me to introduce her to my friends, but I rarely did, because I never knew who she knew and who she didn't. This upset her every time.

She also had difficulty dealing with the attention that came with fame, whereas I enjoyed it. One time a studio hired a car to take us to a movie premiere at the Egyptian Theater in LA. When I got out of the car at the theater, screams erupted from the fans standing in the street. I reached into the car to help Janet out, and then we walked up to the entrance to the theater. On either side ropes kept the fans and the photographers from getting too close. The cameras were flashing, so I stopped to allow the photographers to take their shots. All the while, Janet was pulling on my arm to get me to go on in. Then she gave me a shove, and when I still didn't move, she pinched me in the back.

I turned around and looked at her. With her teeth clenched she said, "Don't stop and leave me out here like this. Get in there." I looked her in the eye. She was furious.

When we got home that night, I decided to ask her about the incident. She said, "Don't ever do that again. How dare you embarrass me in front of all those people? You made me look like a fool. How dare you treat me like that?"

When I look back on all the challenges we faced, what amazes me is not that Hollywood marriages fail at such an overwhelming rate; it's that any survive at all.

My grandparents in Hungary, c. 1920. Below: My first photo shoot, 1925.

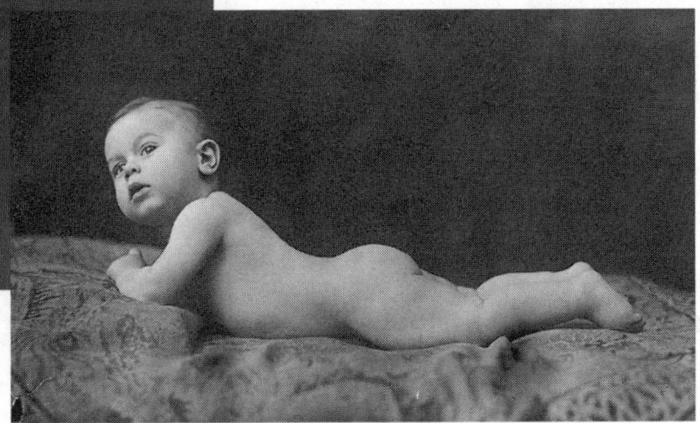

Me at 1 1/2, with my mother, Helen.

From left to right: My brother Julius, my father, Emanuel, and me.

Left and below: My parents with me and my brother Robert.

Although I never finished high school, I wore a cap and gown for an early head shot, 1946.

Bernard Schwartz and an unidentified costar in the play The Prince Who Learned Everything Out of Books, *1947.*

Left and opposite: Publicity shots for Universal, 1948.

Rehearsing a scene from Lysistrata *with Peggy Castle, 1950.*

An interview with Joe Franklin, 1952.

Above right: As an amateur photographer, 1953. Above left: On the set of No Room for the Groom, *1952.*

With Joan Crawford, 1950. Below: A publicity photo with Piper Laurie, 1951.

Technical adviser and magician George Boston shows me his tricks on the set of Houdini, *1953.*

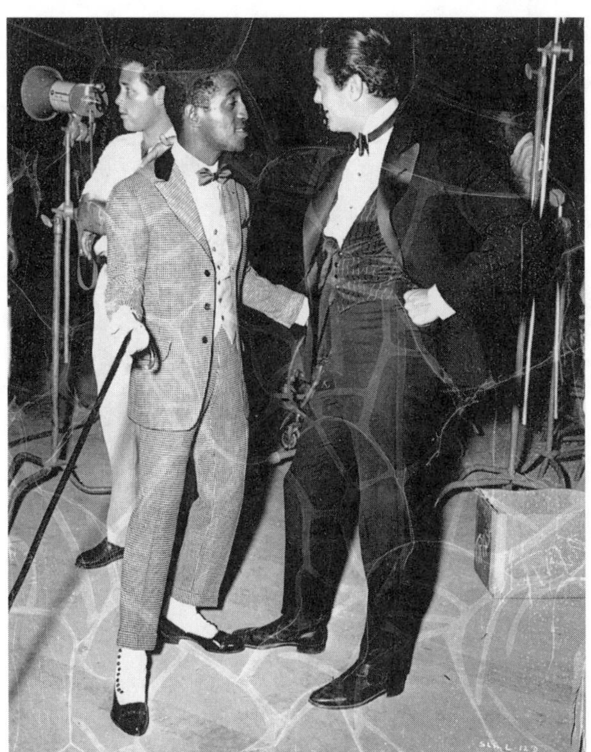

With Sammy Davis, Jr., 1955.

With Frank Sinatra, 1956.

From left to right: James Garner, unidentified actor, Craig Stevens, Paul Newman, Sammy Davis, Jr., Milton Berle, Peter Lawford, me, John Forsythe, Gene Kelly, and Cliff Robertson, at a "Share Party" fundraiser, 1956.

Taking direction from Billy Wilder on the set of Some Like It Hot, *1958.*

From left to right: Harold Mirisch, Barbara Rush, me, Lotti Mirisch, Warren Cowan, and Janet Leigh, at Barbara and Warren's wedding, 1959.

With Erroll Flynn, 1959.
Right: With Laurence Olivier in Spartacus, *1960.*

Above and opposite: With Kelly during the filming of Some Like It Hot, *1958.*

With Kelly in 1957, sporting the beard I grew for The Vikings.

Jamie at home, 1967.

With my third daughter, Alexandra, 1964.

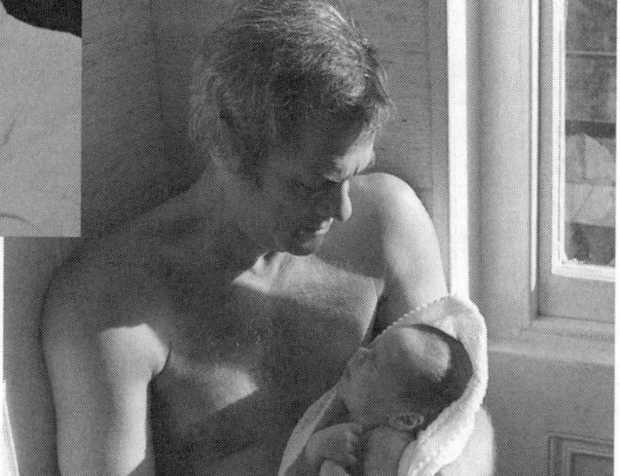

With my fifth child, and first son, Nicholas, in 1971.

Left and below: Nicholas and Penny, 1971 and 1974.

My fourth daughter, Allegra (left), and her sister, Alexandra, 1970.

With Penny and Kelly in Los Angeles, 1972.

My second son, Benjamin, 1974.

Jamming with Gerry Mulligan, November 25, 1959.

On the set of Operation Petticoat with, among others, Cary Grant (seated at left), 1959.

With Milton Berle, 1960.

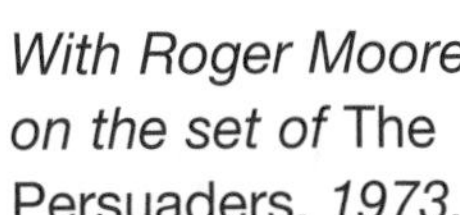

With Roger Moore on the set of The Persuaders, *1973.*

A scene from The Bad News Bears Go to Japan, *1978.*

With Walter Matthau and Jack Lemmon, 1986.

Below: At a showing of my work in Hawaii, 1986.

Above: With Jillie, 1998.
Left: With John C. Whitehead at the George Washington Awards dinner, December 10, 1991.

Malibu Beach, 1953.

10
Getting the Girls to Scream

I had a lot of good moments in my next movie, *Six Bridges to Cross,* a film about the Brinks armored car robbery in Boston. I played the ringleader who dies at the end of the movie. We went to Boston to film the exterior shots and shot the interiors at the Universal studio in LA. Sal Mineo played me as a kid.

Sal, who was born in the Bronx, was a gifted actor who had started out at Warner Bros. playing with James Dean in *Rebel Without a Cause.* Sal and I ended up being good friends. He was a good guy, and you could see he loved working in movies; like me, he felt privileged to get those jobs. But sadly, as he got older he soured because he was slight and boyish, so he always got the part of "the kid," but he wanted bigger roles. The movie that made him a star was *Exodus,* a picture made by a big studio, United Artists, with a handsome budget. They weren't trying to save money by hurrying the production, so Sal was able to develop his performance. In my Universal pictures, by contrast, the studio didn't want character as much as it wanted action, romance, or adventure. Sal suffered a tragic end when he was stabbed to death in West Hollywood by a mugger who didn't even know who Sal was.

All this time my mother had never stopped harping at me to get my brother Robert into the movies. When I mentioned to her that an actor was going to play me as a boy in *Six Bridges to Cross,* she said, "You should get Robert to play that part. He'd be a natural. He's your brother." I don't know what she was thinking. My brother was a schizophrenic, and you never knew what he would do next. But my mother was nothing if not persistent, so I mentioned it to the studio; they were kind enough to arrange to take pictures of him, but understandably they wouldn't take the chance.

My mother blamed me, and piled on the guilt. She said, "You're a big star at the studio. You should be able to get him the part."

"It's not up to me," I said. Not that she heard me.

Sammy Davis Jr. sang a song in *Six Bridges*

to Cross. In fact, he was driving to the studio to do some dubbing for the movie when he crashed his car and lost his eye. I don't know why, but Sammy was nuts about me. It may have had something to do with him being a little younger and less experienced than I was. He took an interest in everything I was doing — the movies I was making, my friends, the girls I liked, you name it. I came to like Sammy very much. He was a gifted performer who could do just about anything on stage, or in front of a camera. When I first met Sammy, he was a sweet and rather delicate person, but then he fell in with Frank Sinatra, and running with Frank's crowd got Sammy into some deep trouble.

Sammy was close to Jeff Chandler, a Jew from the Bronx who was also a close friend of mine. He was the guy who had done that cameo with me in the bar scene of Frank's film a few years earlier. Jeff injured his back while he was filming an action picture in the Philippines, and he was hospitalized until he could have surgery to relieve his pain. Tragically, he died on the operating table. By that time Sammy was spending a lot of time gallivanting around with Frank, and he didn't find a way to visit Jeff in the hospital. I was a pallbearer at Jeff's memorial service, and I noticed that Sammy didn't even arrive at the synagogue until after the ceremony had started.

When we all got up to leave at the end of the service, I went over to Sammy and said, "Jeff was looking for you."

"Well, I was around," Sammy said.

"No, you weren't," I said. "You were chasing Sinatra."

Sammy said, "I don't want to talk about it."

Things between Sammy and me were never quite the same after that, which was a shame, but I wouldn't have felt right just letting it slide.

The premiere of *Six Bridges to Cross* was held in Boston. When it was announced that I was coming for the premiere by train from New York, there was a mob scene at the Boston train station. So one stop before my train was to arrive in Boston I was met by a car and driven to the event. The ride took about an hour and a half, and my arrival was timed so I would arrive just in time for the festivities.

When we were ten minutes away, we pulled into a gas station, and I went into the men's room to change into a fresh suit. I also put on a trick shirt, with sleeves that were held on by only a few thin white threads. The idea was that one of the girls at the scene would pull on my sleeve and we'd have a photographer there to take a picture of fans tearing my clothes off.

We stopped two blocks away from the theater. Lined up in the street were hundreds of teenage girls, every single one of them waiting for *me.* When I got out of the car, there was a roar, and as I was hustled through the crowd girls started tugging at me. To the embarrassment of two ardent fans, the trick shirt worked to perfection!

I loved the fan response I was getting. I was having fun with it. Even though I wasn't doing the kind of movies I wanted to do, I was thrilled to see that I was becoming so popular.

In 1954 I starred in the only musical I have ever made, *So This Is Paris,* a film about three sailors on leave. Richard Quine directed it, and I danced in the film with Gene Nelson and Paul Gilbert, the other two sailors. Nelson, who staged all the dance numbers, helped me learn the steps. He said, "Put your hand on my shoulder. When you feel my weight shift, you shift." He was really the first person who ever taught me how to dance.

In the movie, Gloria DeHaven played a woman who ran an orphanage that we adopted. I had never forgotten that electric moment when I had locked eyes with Gloria as a teenager in the Navy, when she had entertained the troops at the Hollywood Canteen in LA. And here I was, years later, making a movie with her — and she was my leading lady! I told her about seeing her at the Hollywood Canteen, and she thought it was very sweet.

Gloria was a beautiful, gracious woman, and I wanted her badly. When we were doing the picture, she let me know it was okay for me to come after her, so between shots we started a relationship. This was one of only two times I actually fell in love with my leading lady (although I enjoyed many a romance that didn't involve love). I really felt deeply about Gloria. I liked everything about her, including her inherent grace, her beauty, and her ability to carry on our relationship without feeling guilt — or making me feel guilty. She never once put any pressure on me to get a divorce and marry her. It would have driven me to distraction if she had, but she was much too classy for that.

Gloria and I were fortunate enough to be able to spend almost an entire weekend together at the Beverly Hills Hotel. In those days we'd work half days on Saturdays, so this time, as soon as we finished, we both drove to the hotel, went up to our room, and spent the better part of a fabulous few days together. We continued to see each other for a while until everyday life intervened. I still run across Gloria every now and then. I love her to this day.

My next movie, *The Purple Mask,* was a cheap knockoff of *The Scarlet Pimpernel* — and my last swashbuckler. Angela Lansbury played my love interest. During the filming, Angela constantly smiled at me and made nice, but many years later she commented, "Things got so bad for me in the fifties that I had to make a movie with Tony Curtis." When I heard this I thought to myself, Things could never get bad enough for me to make another movie with you. This gives you an idea of how my career was viewed by some Hollywood insiders. Nor could I completely disagree with them. I was filling seats in the theaters, but the films themselves weren't classics. Not even close. They were a reflection of Universal's emphasis on profitable, low-budget movies, pure and simple.

No one outside show business understands how complicated it really is. Everyone thinks actors are rich and famous and lead charmed lives. But to get to the top, you can never be satisfied. I had wanted to be in pictures, and now that I had achieved that goal, I wanted to be in *quality* pictures, and that would mean making some changes.

The Purple Mask would be one of the last few movies I made at Universal. In 1955, I did two more films for the studio: *The Rawhide Years,* the only western in which I ever starred, and *The Square Jungle,* the Universal version of John Garfield's and James Cagney's boxing films.

Arthur Kennedy, an excellent actor who earned five Academy Award nominations, was my costar in *The Rawhide Years.* I also really liked my leading lady, Colleen Miller, a beautiful girl who had a brief film career. The director was Rudolph Maté, who had been a great cameraman for Harry Cohn at Columbia. He had photographed Rita Hayworth in the Oscar-winner *Cover Girl,* so they made him head photographer-cinematographer. Then he started directing movies, and this was the second movie I made with him.

During the first movie I made with Rudy, I had noticed that he would shake his head at the end of a scene. He'd say, "Cut. Print," but his head would be shaking, and I would be upset because I thought he didn't like what I had done. After a while I noticed his head shook like that all the time, and it had nothing to do with the acting. It was just a tic. Once I got past the feeling that I could never please him, I discovered that Rudy was a very lovable man.

The Square Jungle was fun to do too. I was a prizefighter, and Ernest Borgnine played my manager. Makeup fixed my nose so I looked like a boxer, and I did the boxing scenes myself, which made me feel good.

In 1955 Janet joined the cast of *My Sister Eileen,* along with Jack Lemmon and Betty Garrett. She had always wanted to be in a musical, and now that she was in one, she trained every day so her dancing and singing would be up to snuff. Her choreographer was Bob Fosse, who had a reputation as quite the lady's man, even though he was married to actress Joan McCracken.

While Janet was making her movie, I went off every other weekend to spend time with Frank. Janet was okay with that, since she wasn't around home herself. Then one weekend I came home and found a letter from Fosse to Janet. "I can't wait to see you," it said. "When you're coming, please let me know."

I couldn't be absolutely sure, but it certainly looked like Fosse had written a love note to my wife. I was wrecked. Even though Janet and I were distant, I became obsessed with the thought of Janet and Fosse in bed together; I imagined it over and over again, getting more upset each time. The letter brought back the feelings of jealousy I'd had when I pulled up at the studio to pick Janet up and saw Howard Hughes lurking in the shadows.

To make matters worse, Janet was working with Fosse day in and day out, so I got no relief from my jealousy. I decided not to confront her about the note, fearing that Janet would tell me she wanted a divorce. But that didn't mean I was going to be cuckolded and sit idly by. Sure, I had had affairs myself, but for one thing they always made me feel very guilty, and for another I made damn sure that Janet would never find out about them. I always hoped that if she ever got involved with anyone, I'd never know. Knowing changed everything, or at least that's what I told myself.

I decided then that I was going to get more out of life. I was thirty years old, in my prime, and I was at a stage in my life and my career when beautiful girls with fabulous figures were constantly throwing themselves at me. In the past I had turned down a lot more advances than I'd accepted, but I decided that from that point on I would partake more fully of the bounty being offered me.

By this time Hugh Hefner had become a

good friend of mine. To get away from Janet and Fosse, I flew to Chicago to visit with Hef. That weekend I met some very friendly Playboy bunnies, and I had not even the slightest pangs of guilt about having sex with them. After a week of debauchery in Chicago, I knew I was going to be all right.

If marital troubles had been my only problem, things wouldn't have been so bad, but I was getting lots of grief from my mother as well. I had bought a group of twelve garden apartments and I had given my parents one of the units to live in, with the understanding that my mother would be responsible for renting out the other units. Even though she had a real estate agent to help her, she was a real pain in the neck about it. She was constantly calling me with complaints about tenants and conflicts that were largely of her own making. Since she was my mother, I couldn't exactly avoid her calls.

In addition to my marriage and my mother, I had my career to worry about. I was working very hard making movies and doing publicity. My pictures were making a bundle, so the studio kept putting me in movies, but the movies I was in were B pictures, and it was time to step up to A pictures. But the way my contract was worded I didn't have the right to refuse any of the pictures Universal handed me; when a contract player like me refused a picture, his or her salary got reduced by a fee called a suspension — and I needed the full amount. I had my parents and Robert to support, not to mention my own household. The stress I was under became unbearable, and I sank into a terrible depression.

Bob Raines, who was now running the casting department at Universal, was a nice guy, a little bit older than I, and he could see I was having trouble. He suggested that I go see a psychiatrist, and when he told me the insurance would pay for it, I went along.

I would lie on a couch in the middle of the day, and Dr. Frym would analyze me. I don't know if it helped me, but I certainly liked the attention. He'd say, "Tell me how you're feeling," and I would rattle on about myself. I rather liked it. At first I'd randomly hit on something useful to explore, but soon I discovered that all I had to do was talk about my family in order to hit something worth digging into.

By the end of 1955, Universal had cranked up its publicity machine to make Tony Curtis a household name all over America. Having gotten me in all the fan magazines, the studio now tried to get me on as many TV shows as it could. TV was becoming very popular, so I would fly to New York and go on talk shows. I never talked very much on those shows. The host would say, "Ladies and gentlemen, please welcome Tony Curtis." I'd come on, they'd applaud, and the host would say, "Hi, Tony. So, your new film is *The Square Jungle.* How did you like making it?"

"I liked it a lot. I got to do my own boxing scenes."

"Who else is in it?"

I'd rattle off the names of my costars.

"And what's it about?"

"Well, it's about a grocery clerk whose father is a drunk and whose girlfriend doesn't think he's going to amount to anything. So he becomes a boxer, finds out he's a natural, and becomes the challenger in a big title fight. Like I said, it's a boxing movie."

"That's great. Tony Curtis, ladies and gentlemen." And off I went. There was nothing subtle about television interviews in those days. You get on, you plug the movie, and you get off.

I was a guest on *What's My Line?,* hosted by John Daly, and I appeared on one of TV's biggest hits, *The Ed Sullivan Show.* When I appeared on his show, Ed said, "I want you to meet the new bright star at Universal:

Tony Curtis." He knew the response he was going to get, and he got it: the girls in the audience all began screaming. I didn't want the applause and the yelling to ever stop. Now that I was making movies in Hollywood I didn't want to be known as a mere actor. I wanted to feel like a *star.*

In rehearsal for Trapeze, 1955.

11
"THE CAT'S IN THE BAG, AND THE BAG'S IN THE RIVER"

My agent, Lew Wasserman, had an uncanny instinct for making the right move at the right time. Lew's job was to provide my career with direction; my job was to put on some makeup and a costume and act. Early on Lew told me that the way to become successful was to take whatever parts came my way and not to give the studio a hard time. That's what I did. And it worked.

In fact, any advice he gave me always worked out the way he said it would. One time I signed to do a picture called *Lady L* for MGM. Orry-Kelly, the clothes designer, showed me some sketches he'd made of me in costume, and I was really excited about the part. But when the time came for me to shoot the movie, MGM wasn't ready to proceed, and they wouldn't pay me.

I went to Lew and told him how MGM was screwing me over. He said, "Go to MGM, ask where the stage for *Lady L* is, walk over there, and look for someone to tell you what to do." I did that, and of course there was nothing to do, but I stuck around for half a day. Lew encouraged me to keep going back. I did that for seven or eight days. My contract was guaranteed, and with me showing up ready to work day in and day out, Lew was able to say that I was holding up my end of the contract. He made them pay me, even though they weren't going to make the movie. They wound up dropping the project, although the studio revived it a year later with Paul Newman.

I did very well just by having Lew's advice in my ear — and following it. With him guiding me, I couldn't go wrong. It was like talking to an older brother.

Lew got along well with just about everyone in Hollywood. He loved Alfred Hitchcock, and Hitch loved Lew. I remember being at a party one evening and watching the two of them sitting in a corner talking. Lew was sitting there in his horn-rimmed glasses with his long legs crossed, while Hitch was perched on his seat — all five feet seven inches of him in that famous pear shape. To look at them, these two men couldn't have been more different, but they were bonded by the power of their remarkable intellects.

Lew loved to hear me talk about my life.

He was fascinated by stories about my childhood, because he came from such a different background. Lew came from money and was well educated, articulate, and comfortable with power. He could handle things. He was also very kind. Whenever I reached out to Lew, he always responded. It always meant a tremendous amount to me when someone really enjoyed my company. Lew obviously did.

One day Lew called and asked me to meet him at his office. When I got there, he said, "I'm not sure whether we can swing it, but United Artists is making a movie with Burt Lancaster called *Trapeze.* Harold Hecht is producing it. They're going to shoot in Paris, and they want you to play the younger guy, the 'flyer,' who gets flung around by the bigger guy."

"I love it already," I said.

"I knew you would," Lew said. "I'm trying to arrange it with Universal."

When Lew spoke to Ed Muhl, who was running Universal, at first Ed refused to let me go. "We're doing great with Tony now, and I don't think we want to loan him out anymore," Muhl said.

Lew, who ran one of the most powerful talent agencies in Hollywood, wasn't going to take no for an answer. He told Muhl, "Listen, you need to put Tony in that picture. Look how important he's going to be for you when he finishes making it. You have to consider that." But Muhl still wasn't convinced. So Lew had Burt Lancaster talk with Ed Muhl. Burt was a very energetic and imposing fellow, and with a few suggestions from Lew, Burt found a way to get Ed to say okay.

The director of *Trapeze* was Carol Reed, the Englishman who'd directed *The Third Man.* The producers were Harold Hecht, Burt Lancaster, and Jim Hill. Harold had discovered Burt on Broadway and brought him to Hollywood, and the two became partners in an independent production company. But after six or seven years Burt and Harold no longer got along. Burt felt Harold was imposing himself too much and he wanted to replace him, but they had a contract, so Burt hired Jim Hill to serve as a buffer between himself and Harold.

Of the three leads, Burt was an established star, Gina Lollobrigida was a certifiable Italian dish, and I was the up-and-coming kid. (Gina had come to Hollywood only a couple of years earlier and had starred in a movie called *Beat the Devil. Trapeze* was to be her second American-made picture.) So Burt got top billing, and I got second billing everywhere but in Italy, where Gina Lollobrigida wanted it. I didn't mind; I was happy just being in the picture. The only time I got upset was when Gina wanted me to cut my hair. She talked to Burt and Harold about it, so they came to me and asked me if I would mind going to the barber. I grudgingly went along. Gina was some dish, but after that I lost my appetite for her. Every time I saw her on the set I couldn't help but think about how much I missed my hair. If it sounds petty, I can't argue with that. I'm just reporting events as I experienced them.

I had expected Janet to join me in Paris, but she had signed to do a picture called *Safari,* which was going to be filmed in Africa. What's more, she had to go to England right away to do wardrobe and other pre-filming preparation. It had been too long since Janet and I had spent any good time together, and I found myself missing her, so I flew to London for three days before Janet left for Africa. My arrival in London made all the newspapers, which always made me feel good. And Rex Harrison and Marlene Dietrich hosted a dinner party for me. Rex, later the star of *My Fair Lady* and *Dr. Dolittle,* had a crazier married life than I did. Marlene, the star of *The Blue Angel,* had a heartbreakingly beautiful singing voice. When she sang "Falling in Love Again," men wept.

After dinner Janet and I went to a party with a lot of English celebrities, and Marlene was there too, leaning on a mantel with a drink in her hand. We started talking, Janet wandered off somewhere, and Marlene said, "How do you like London?"

I said, "I like it fine, but I'm going back to Paris in a couple of days."

She said, "I'm in Paris a lot, and I stay at the George Cinq. Why don't you call me when you're there?" I didn't know what to say. Janet was just in the other room, and Marlene was about fifty-five. I must have paused a little too long, because she said, "Don't be concerned."

I said, "Why would I be concerned?"

She said, "I'll treat you well."

Marlene Dietrich was a huge star, and I loved the way she talked and sang, but she was too old for me. I didn't have many firm rules, but not dating my mother (much less marrying her) was inviolable. Okay, Freud might argue that every man dates his mother in some form, but this was getting much too close.

I pleaded with Janet not to go and do the film in Africa. With Bob Fosse's note still lingering in my mind, I was afraid that we were drifting so far apart that our marriage was becoming irreparable. It was far from a perfect union, but for some reason I didn't want to let it go.

"Why are you doing this picture in Africa?" I asked her. The reason was simple: she wanted to work. It was a modest opportunity, but she liked acting. I was hoping she'd take this chance to choose me over her own work, but she refused. Here I was in this important movie, which gave her an opportunity to join me in a beautiful, romantic city, but she was running off to Africa. But there was no moving her. I understood Janet's choice only too well, but it was still painful when we went our separate ways and got to work.

During the evenings in Paris I was very lonely. Sometimes I'd go out to dinner with the movie crew, and the emptiness I felt was unbearable. There were also evenings when I sought out the company of beautiful French girls. They didn't mean anything to me, but for the short time we were together they managed to keep my mind off my loneliness.

Burt Lancaster and I stayed at the George Cinq, and Burt had the suite directly above mine. I would step onto my balcony, climb a lattice up to his balcony, and knock on his window. Burt would open his window and let me in. We'd talk and get loaded, and I'd stagger downstairs to my room. One night, after I returned to my room from dinner, Burt leaned over his balcony and called down to me: "Come on up here, Tony."

I climbed up, and there he was with two French girls. When my head came over the balcony railing, one of the girls screamed — not because she was scared, but because it was me!

Despite these diversions, I really missed Janet during my stay in Paris. She was in Africa, and there were only certain times during the day when I could call her because she had to travel from wherever they were shooting to where there was a phone. Janet's costar in *Safari* was Victor Mature. Janet later told me about a scene when she was in the Congo River, and she had to swim across to the other side. The script read: *A crocodile swims by.*

When they were discussing the scene, Mature said, "Where will I be?"

The director said, "You'll be in the water."

Mature said, "No, I won't."

The director said, "You don't have to worry. The crocodiles will swim around you."

Mature said, "No, they won't."

The director said, "I'm telling you, don't worry. I'll have a propman out there with a gun, and when you step into the water, he'll fire it, and the crocodiles will scurry away."

Mature said, "What if they're hard of hearing?"

Before we began filming *Trapeze,* I spent two months in Paris training with a fine company of acrobats attached to the Cirque d'Hiver. I had learned how to tumble before, but their routines were a lot more elaborate than anything I'd ever done. I also got some training from Burt, who had worked as a circus acrobat when he was a young boy, and from Fay Alexander, my stunt double. I was the flyer, and Burt was the catcher. I learned to swing on the trapeze and time my release so that my momentum would carry me to the point where Burt was on his trapeze, his arms extended to catch me. I also learned to throw my feet out when I swung to help my momentum carry my body across the space it had to travel.

The professional acrobats also showed me how to land on the net, thirty feet below. It was called a safety net, but you could still get hurt on it if you weren't careful. I'd hang from the trapeze, and Burt would yell, "Now!" Then I'd let go of the trapeze and lie flat, fall straight down onto the net and bounce. Fay taught me not to change the direction of my body as I was falling, not to look over my shoulder, not to do anything — just let go and wait.

There was only one serious injury during the making of *Trapeze.* We had some circus lions on the set, and everybody was nervous about them — with good reason, as it turned out. The girl who stunt-doubled for Gina Lollobrigida was in the pit with the lions when they started fighting with each other. She stood stock-still and waited for them to calm down. She wasn't attacked, but a little later on, when one of the custodians went into their den to feed them, one of the cats attacked him, bit him, and dragged him around. He didn't die. He was ripped up pretty badly, but he recovered. By the end of *Trapeze* I was a skilled flyer.

Alone in a strange land, I did what I could to keep myself busy when I wasn't making the movie. I'd always had a deep love of art, so while I was in Paris I looked up all the places where Modigliani had lived. Modigliani was loaded with talent, but he drank a lot, did lots of drugs, and came to a sad end. I went to his studio and stood at the spot where his mistress had jumped out of a four-story window the day after he died. I wasn't depressed enough to follow her example, but I was lonely enough to relate to how she'd felt.

Dean Martin happened to be in town while I was there, so I went to see him, and we palled around a little. He was in town to make *The Young Lions* with Marlon Brando and Monty Cliff. Dean was staying in the hotel right next to the George Cinq. Another day I spent some time with Billy Wilder and his wife, Audrey. They were in Paris making *Love in the Afternoon* with Gary Cooper and Audrey Hepburn.

I hated being separated from Janet at this difficult time in our marriage, but she hadn't been willing to give up her work to spend time with me, and I wasn't willing to make that sacrifice for her, either. I knew that doing this movie was definitely the right thing for my career. When I appeared on screen wearing white tights, my body hard and fit from having trained so much on the trapeze, my professional stock took a big jump up. After *Trapeze,* I could do no wrong. The big joke in town was that young ladies weren't the only ones I was attracting; gay men were supposedly lining up to see me in the picture. I remember a newspaperman who said to me, "I just came back from a prison up north, and you're their favorite actor. The inmates have got you all over their cell walls."

I got about a hundred and fifty thousand

dollars for making that picture, which was a ton of money in those days. I made more from that one picture than I would make in a year at Universal. So you can see why Universal didn't want to let me make the film. They didn't want me to get a taste of the money and the stardom that lay outside the walls of Universal. But now the genie was out of the lamp.

United Artists was thrilled with the way *Trapeze* turned out. The high quality of the movie only made me want to leave Universal more desperately. As grateful as I was to Universal for giving me my start, after I made *Trapeze* I just couldn't stand the thought of going back to my low-budget contract roles. Once again, Lew Wasserman came through for me. He said to Ed Muhl, the president of Universal, "If you let Tony do outside pictures, that's only going to enhance his value to Universal. Why don't we make it a brand-new seven-year deal, starting now, but you'll let him make every other picture for an outside studio?" Universal agreed. Both sides benefited, and Lew once again demonstrated that he was the smartest man in the business.

After *Trapeze* I did a movie for Universal called *Mr. Cory,* directed by Blake Edwards. We went to Lake Tahoe for the location shoot. Charles Bickford, a big, burly actor who played in a lot of westerns, was cast as my sidekick. In the movie, I play a busboy in a summer resort who becomes a successful high-stakes poker player. I make so much money playing poker that I open my own casino. Then I get in trouble with one of the other owners, who shoots me, but I survive and end up in the arms of one of the movie's two leading ladies.

Kathryn Grant, a sweet girl who always wore her hair in bangs, was in the picture. She was twenty-two years old, and I was attracted to her, but I didn't pursue her, because she was engaged to Bing Crosby. Martha Hyer was also in the film, and she was also very desirable, but Al Hart, the president of City National Bank in LA, was looking after her. She liked me, but she was scared that Al might show up and catch us fooling around, which would mean bye-bye to her house in Palm Springs.

After the success of *Trapeze,* Harold Hecht spoke to Lew and told him that he wanted to make another picture with me. I told Lew that that worked for me. Harold said, "We have a screenplay called *Sweet Smell of Success.* You'll play a tough guy. It'll be good for your career because —"

"I love it," I said. Harold didn't have to say

another word. I was never going to pass up a chance at a serious role.

The film was about a sleazy gossip columnist named J.J. Hunsecker, who was based on real-life gossip columnist Walter Winchell. In our initial conversation the movie's producers — Harold Hecht and Burt Lancaster — said they were going to get Orson Welles to play Hunsecker, and I would play Sidney Falco, a hustler willing to do Hunsecker's dirty work for a chance to get ahead. In the end the studio decided they didn't want Orson because his movies weren't doing much box office, so Burt ended up playing Hunsecker. After we began shooting I realized that Burt was a great choice for the role. He had a quiet strength that was perfect for conveying the brutal qualities of the character he played.

The director was Alexander Mackendrick, who had made *Tight Little Island,* an excellent European film. Burt and Harold were thrilled to get him, but what they didn't know was that Sandy, as everyone called him, was a perfectionist of the first order. A typical ten-day shooting schedule would take us a month or more. And once Sandy began directing the movie, he brooked no interference from anyone. He was going to film it exactly the way he wanted to, and he wasn't going to take any guff from anyone, including Harold and Burt.

The set was a replica of Manhattan's 21 Club. In one scene, Burt is having lunch at the club when I come into the club looking for him. Burt's line is, "Don't sit down, Sidney. You failed me."

I say, "Wait, give me a chance. Let me tell you what happened." Then I slide into the booth next to him, and we begin to talk. There's wonderful dialogue in the scene, but we had a problem with the blocking. Burt was sitting and eating on the outside of the booth's bench seat. So Sandy says, "Why don't we have Burt slide over and let Tony sit on the outside? That would make the shot more intimate."

But Burt didn't want to slide over. He wanted me to walk over to the other side of the table and sit down because he felt that his character wouldn't let anyone box him in like that. The character Hunsecker would have always made sure that he sat so he could get away quickly; he was a newspaperman who had made a lot of enemies.

Burt and Sandy started arguing about it. Sandy raised his voice to Burt, and then Burt went apeshit. He got up and pushed the table over, sending all the plates and glasses and food crashing to the floor. Then he raised his fist to hit Sandy. Sandy put his hands up to defend himself, but he didn't back down. He was a strong man, and he wasn't going to take any nonsense from anyone, even Burt. Burt took a deep breath, everyone calmed down, and we did it Sandy's way.

The truth was that Sandy had been driving Burt and Harold crazy right from the start of filming. Sandy wanted every detail to be just so, and too often Burt and Harold didn't think Sandy's perfectionism was necessary. If we were drinking cocktails, Sandy wanted the drinks to be a certain color. If we were having dinner in the movie, he wanted what we were eating to be the kind of food that the characters would choose. He insisted that all these things were necessary, but no one else saw the need, which only made Sandy surly and ill-tempered. He wanted his pictures the way he wanted them. Everyone agreed that details were important, but he was slowing the production down so much that it was costing Harold and Burt a lot of money.

Sandy was also big on delving deeply into the script and the characters. It wasn't enough to have a ruthless newspaper columnist pitted against a desperate press agent who would do anything to advance himself. Sandy wanted the tension between the two men to build in a way that satisfied his sense that it was happening naturally. Clifford Odets, the acclaimed playwright, had written the script, and Sandy was having Clifford rewrite it as we were filming. When we shot the film on location in Manhattan, Clifford would be sitting in the back of the unheated props van, typing pages in the freezing cold at two or three in the morning.

One night I went into the prop truck to see what Clifford was up to, and he said, "Come here, kid. I want to show you something." I looked over his shoulder as he typed, "The cat's in the bag, and the bag's in the river." In the scene he was working on, my character plants a bag of marijuana on Hunsecker's sister's boyfriend. Hunsecker then asks me whether I have done my dirty deed, and Clifford's rewrite of my answer was the "cat's in the bag" line.

A lot of the movie's characters had lines like that. Kello, the cop, had a line where he said, "Come here, Sidney. I want to chastise you." Police captains don't talk like that. "Get the hell over here, Sidney" would have been a lot more realistic. But I couldn't change Clifford's lines, and they were always undeniably poetic.

We all knew that *Sweet Smell of Success* would be a unique, interesting movie. What we didn't know was that it would get lots of review coverage, and that Walter Winchell and other gossip columnists would be furious about it. The film was good, but Sandy took so long to make the picture that Burt and Harold never forgave him. Sandy didn't work in Hollywood again for another six years.

As for me, people were surprised to see me playing such a serious part. The movie wasn't for teens, my core audience, and when the word got out that I was playing a despicable press agent, a bad guy, I got bum-rapped by Louella Parsons and Hedda Hopper. So I was very disappointed, not with the picture — I knew what a good film it was and what a good performance I had given in it — but with the reaction to it. The media just refused to acknowledge me as a serious actor.

After *Sweet Smell of Success,* I went back to Universal and did *The Midnight Story,* a contrived, completely forgettable movie about a cop who becomes obsessed with solving the murder of a priest. The more things changed, the more they stayed the same.

Around this time I was still spending a lot of time with Frank Sinatra. Frank didn't serve in the military during World War II, and his critics accused him of being a draft dodger, so he was constantly veering from being defensive to being pugnacious. On the one hand, he avoided getting into fights, especially about his patriotism, or lack of it, but on a lot of occasions — especially when he was drinking — he provoked them. Someone would stare at Frank, who after all was a huge star, and his response would be *What are you looking at me like that for?* The next thing you knew, Frank's friend and bodyguard Jilly Rizzo, who was a strong little motherfucker, would be busting heads.

At the time, Frank was King Kong in Hollywood, and I admired him for that. A lot of people hated him because so many people kissed his ass. Frank didn't give a shit. He had plenty of power, plenty of money, and plenty of muscle. He always had a couple of tough-looking guys around who looked after him, traveling wherever he went.

One night Frank and I were having dinner at a restaurant in Palm Springs, and some guy looked at Frank and yelled out something nasty. Frank got up out of his chair and started toward the guy. I could see from the guy's face that he wasn't afraid of Frank at all, but then Frank's two musclemen got up and took matters in hand, literally. One of them grabbed the guy by the throat, and the other pulled back his sports jacket and let the guy see he was packing a piece in a shoulder holster. They didn't even have to hit the guy. He got the message instantly. Those guys weren't fooling around.

Frank wasn't afraid of throwing his weight around, but he was also capable of great kindness. Paul Horn had taught me to play the flute for *Sweet Smell of Success,* so sometimes I'd come over to Frank's house and practice playing my flute for him. Frank was impressed that I was learning this new skill for my part in the movie, and he noticed that I was playing a cheap flute I'd picked up. So without telling me, he went out one day and bought me a magnificent flute, a priceless gift that I cherish to this day.

Frank used to call me up and ask me if I wanted to go to Vegas with him that weekend. He'd come by my house in his Karmann Ghia, and off we'd go. It was Frank who put the Sands Hotel on the map. When Frank started showing up at the Sands to perform, the Sands became *the* place to be seen. He sang there without a contract. When he was finished with his gig there, Frank would return home carrying a duffel bag full of cash.

I don't know how they did it — there were

no mobile phones in those days — but whenever Frank and I drove up to the Sands, a greeting party was always standing outside waiting. They'd take our luggage up to our rooms while Frank and I went right to the tables to play blackjack or craps. Then Dean Martin would show up, and Frank and Dean would sit in the lounge and drink Jack Daniel's on the rocks. I wasn't much of a drinker, and certainly not in their league. One night they insisted I drink with them, and by the time I had downed two Jack Daniel's, I was practically unconscious. I had a vague memory of Frank and Dean taking me by the arms and marching me outside, and the next thing I knew I was in the swimming pool, fully dressed!

I climbed out of the pool, dripped my way upstairs to my room, changed clothes, freshened up, and went back down to the casino. I was still a little dizzy, but at least I was keeping my eyes open. When Frank saw me, he said, "Where have you been?"

"Somebody threw me in the pool," I said. "I had to go upstairs and change."

Frank said, "Who in the world would do that?" I told him I thought he might have had something to do with it, but he denied it, and I couldn't be sure I had remembered it right.

Those were fun times, very carefree. My career was rolling right along, and when I was with Frank and Dean and the guys, I could forget about the sorry state of my marriage. They were all ten years older than I, and more experienced. Frank and the boys didn't even start functioning until late in the afternoon, so to fit in with their schedule, I would sleep late too.

Sometimes Frank asked me to be his beard. He'd meet a showgirl at one of the other casinos and arrange to have me come over at the end of her show and escort her back to the Sands. I would wait for her until after the show, and when I met her, I'd say, "Why don't we bring a few of your girlfriends as well?" Then we'd all crowd into a cab and drive to the Sands.

One time when Frank saw me coming with this bevy of beautiful girls, he said to Dean, "That's my boy. Look at that. I send him to get one girl, and he comes back with four."

Frank liked to have fun in Vegas, but his belligerence surfaced there just like it did in LA. I remember one night at the Sands when he got very drunk. He said something nasty to Carl Cohen, who was in charge of gambling at the casino, and Carl belted him so hard that Frank flew into the pit between the tables, and onto the floor. He was out cold. To his credit, Frank never held it against the guy. Or maybe he was just too drunk to remember it.

Frank was part owner of a casino called the Cal-Neva Lodge. It had lots of bungalows on Lake Tahoe, and as its name indicated, it sat on the California-Nevada border. The truth is that Frank bought his piece for Sam Giancana, who ran the Chicago mob. The state of Nevada had barred Giancana from even entering a casino, so Giancana found a way to "own" the casino through Frank.

While I was up there, Frank came over and said, "I want to introduce you to somebody, but don't bring anybody with you; come alone." I walked into this opulent suite at the hotel, and sitting there on a couch was a man wearing glasses. He got up, and although he was diminutive I could sense by the way he carried himself that he was important. Frank introduced me to the man, who was Sam Giancana.

Sam said, "I love the movies you make. Keep it up."

"A pleasure to meet you, sir," I said. Later, FBI wiretaps caught Giancana at the Cal-Neva, and as a result Frank was forced to sell his interest in both the Cal-Neva and the Sands. Giancana never forgave Frank for the loss of the Cal-Neva. Frank was lucky Giancana didn't have him killed. Disappointing friends like Sam Giancana could be a very dangerous business.

In 1958 I did a wonderful movie called *The Vikings* with Janet, Kirk Douglas, and Ernest Borgnine. We shot our boat scenes on the fjords in Norway, we did our interior shots in Germany, and we filmed our castle scenes in Belgium. We also shot some scenes in France on the Loire River. Kirk Douglas's company produced the movie under the auspices of United Artists. Kirk had made a lot of excellent movies, and he was tough, both as an artist and as a businessman. You couldn't get a nickel out of him, and you also had to be careful not to upset him or he would cut your lines out of the script. And since he was making the picture, he always made sure he was the most important actor in the movie.

Eventually Kirk and I got to be excellent friends, although it took a little doing. We first met at a party, where I was talking with him and Burt Lancaster. I made some kind of little joke, and in response Kirk made a move like he was going to knee me in the balls. I just looked calmly at Kirk and kept on talking. I think Kirk respected that he couldn't intimidate me. Once we started working together, we got along very well, which wasn't always easy with Kirk.

Three months before *The Vikings* started filming, Kirk gathered all the male actors together and said, "I'll give every one of you a two-hundred-dollar bonus to grow a beard." We all took him up on it, and three months later, I was in the company of "Vikings" who all looked like I did. Kirk was the only one who was clean-shaven.

Kirk was a perfectionist on the set of the picture. He wanted every shot a certain way, and the cameraman, an Englishman, had to do exactly what he was told. Kirk also took over the production company, which became a problem when he decided to pay no attention to the production manager, whose job it was to monitor how long it was taking to shoot the movie.

It took three months all told to shoot *The Vikings.* My two-year-old daughter, Kelly, was in it, along with Kirk's son Peter, who was three. During filming I received an unexpected — and unwanted — visit on the set from my brother Bobby, who was thirteen. He stood around the set, performed his usual array of eye-catching tics, and engaged me in endless, inane conversations.

He'd say to me, "Are you my brother?"

I'd say, "Yes, I am."

He'd say, "Are you really my brother?"

I'd say, "Yes, Bobby, I'm really your brother."

He'd reply, "How do I know you're really my brother?"

You get the idea. Bobby was only on the set for about a week, but I have to admit I hated every second of it.

Off the set, Janet and I weren't fighting, but things weren't good between us, either. I should have been happy that Janet was working alongside of me, but I wasn't. My feelings had changed drastically after I got home from making *Trapeze.* I had started feeling that my marriage had become a trap. When I look back on it, I wonder why I had such a strong urge to be free. I think I just wanted to live my life the way Frank was living his, and Frank was nothing if not free. To complicate matters, when Janet and I returned home to California, she informed me she was pregnant again, which was good news, but it made me feel even more trapped in my marriage.

I found that Kirk was a good person to talk to about my difficulties. Kirk was demanding professionally, but he was a very kind man. If someone around Kirk was having problems, Kirk would always do what he could to help that person out. I was looking for a brother figure, someone to fill the hole that Julie's death had left in my life, and Kirk became that for me. He was a person who could always make me feel better about myself.

Ironically, Kirk suffered from moods as black as mine, although he seemed to shake his off faster than I did. One day Kirk and I were sitting under the set of a wooden ship in the Hardanger Fjord while it was raining, which happened frequently there. We'd been shooting nicely when it started to pour, so we just took a break, stayed in costume, and waited for the deluge to end. Half an hour later, it was still raining. Kirk looked at me and said, "You want to buy a movie company cheap?"

My next film was *Kings Go Forth,* a United Artists production with Frank Sinatra and Natalie Wood. Frank very much wanted me in the picture, and anything he asked for, he got, so there I was in the film. Despite the fact that we were friends, I wasn't sure how well we'd mesh as actors because of his reputation for being difficult. If Frank didn't want to work, he just didn't show up. If he wanted to bust the director's chops, he did. Even the toughest production manager was afraid of Frank; people worried that if they pissed Frank off, he might have them bumped off the next day. Everybody tiptoed around him. Despite all that, I have to say that Frank was always nice to me. We were pals. Frank called me "Boinie," and I called him "Francis Albert."

Frank had a unique way of working. He liked to do a scene in one take. He liked it so much that he wouldn't give the director another one. I knew how Frank worked before we started shooting *Kings Go Forth,* so I made a decision: *I will give them the very best I have in the first take.* That helped, but there was only so much I could do on my own. There still would be times when Frank would blurt out his lines, and if they didn't come out right, too bad. He'd say to the director, "Look, you have other film you're going to shoot, so just cut to Tony, or cut to the dog." Having Frank around complicated a moviemaking process that was already complicated by its very nature. If things got too difficult for him, all of a sudden fun-loving Frank would disappear, to be replaced by the New Jersey kid with a mean streak.

In the movie, set near the end of World War II, Frank loves Natalie Wood, and at first it looks like she loves him, but then she sees my character playing the trumpet in a club in Paris, and I captivate her from afar. I start taking her out, and Frank stops pursuing her because he sees she no longer loves him. Then she gets pregnant, and we find out her child is black, and that changes everything. She tries to kill herself. Frank and I are soldiers, fighting together in France. I'm shot, and he cradles me in his arms as I die. He comes back to France many years later, and Natalie's character is teaching school.

Natalie was a wonderful actress. She had been training since childhood, and she brought real artistry and insight to bear on even the most ordinary part. I was attracted by her intellect, but I didn't feel any romantic attraction for her. Frank didn't become involved with Natalie, either. I knew this because Frank didn't take any days off during shooting.

United Artists wanted to have the premiere of *Kings Go Forth* in Hollywood, but Frank said, "I'm not coming back there. I'm in Monte Carlo." So, presto, the premiere gets moved to Monte Carlo. The next thing I know, I'm on a Constellation prop plane flying sixteen hours from New York to Monte Carlo. I hated those prop planes because the vibration drove me crazy.

The highlight of my trip was meeting Princess Grace and Prince Rainier of Monaco. I had known Grace Kelly from a couple of parties we both went to in LA. At one party, she and I had been talking shop about the movies, then we went somewhere quiet and we started kissing. In person, Grace was a lot earthier than her ethereal screen persona, and she spoke with a Philadelphia accent that belied her delicate features. After necking with her, I wanted her badly, but I never got that far. When I saw her again at the premiere in Monte Carlo, all I could think of was how lucky I had been to have had her alone for even a couple of minutes.

With Sidney Poitier, 1958. © BETTMANN/CORBIS

12
The Defiant One

After making *Kings Go Forth,* I let Lew Wasserman know that I wanted another dramatic role and, as always, he came through for me. My next movie was *The Defiant Ones,* another United Artists project. The movie was about a white man and a black man who break out of prison in the South, but they're still chained together as they try to stay ahead of the law. When I read the script, I thought it was a little too intense in some parts, and it needed a stronger sense of location, but I liked the fact that the two lead actors were chained together until almost the end of the movie. My part was well written, I would make a nice chunk of dough, and Lew arranged it so I had approval of who the black actor would be.

My first choice to play the other lead would have been Harry Belafonte, because of our friendship and because I felt he would have been good in it, but his name was not on the list the studio gave me. Sidney Poitier was on the list, and I was very impressed with him when he was introduced to me. He was just starting out as an actor, but he was my choice for the part. I insisted that he and I share top billing, because I felt that if my name was on top of the title and his name ran below it, that would contradict the entire premise of the movie: that these two convicts from different races had to accept each other as equals.

For a while it looked like the director, Stanley Kramer, wasn't going to be able to raise enough money to make the film. He told me he was short about a million dollars. Fortunately, I knew a guy who invested in movies, a fellow Hungarian Jew whom I liked a lot, so I figured I'd give him a try. Al Hart was a sweet man, but I wasn't sure if he would be able to help us because this was 1958, years before the start of the civil rights movement; the topic of race guaranteed that this film would be controversial. But not only did my friend Al come on board, he helped us get the money we needed from a number of different investors.

Director Stanley Kramer was the rebel in town, who wanted to make socially conscious movies. He also wanted to send a message to supporters of the late senator Joe

McCarthy that he wouldn't be intimidated by the senator's anti-Communist rampage, so he hired Nedrick Young, who had been blacklisted, along with his partner, Harold Jacob Smith, to write the script for *The Defiant Ones.* Ned and Harold also played bit parts: they were the two guys in the bus taking Sidney Poitier and me to prison at the beginning of the picture.

Since I played a convict in the movie, I decided I needed to change the way my face looked. I had never done this before, but I knew that Larry Olivier and a couple of other actors I admired had done it, so I put on a fake nose. Costuming helped too, of course; I wore a shirt open at the neck, jeans, heavy boots — clothes that were perfect for the character I was playing.

We shot the movie in the Kern River Valley in California. In one scene Sidney and I, chained together, had to cross a fast-moving river. Sidney didn't swim, so his stand-in did the swimming. Stanley Kramer wanted my stuntman, Davy Sharpe, to swim for me, but I said, "Stanley, you don't need Davy. I can do that."

Stanley was skeptical. "Tony, it's too dangerous," he said.

Davy said, "No, Stanley, let him do it. I know he can."

I was delighted that Davy came to my defense. I did the scene with no mishaps, and I was always grateful to Davy for that.

The Defiant Ones was a groundbreaking movie for its time. It also made me much more aware of racism in America. Sidney and I would sit and talk about the inequities that he had suffered from his whole life. As a Jew who'd dealt with plenty of anti-Semitism, I had some understanding of his situation, so we got along really well.

Sidney Poitier was to the movies what Jackie Robinson had been to baseball, but at the time no one talked about it. Sidney and I wanted to speak out against racism, but our views were printed only in obscure black magazines. Sidney's name would never even come up on national television talk shows, which really offended me. I wanted to kick up a fuss, but I realized the best thing I could do was to make the movie and let it speak for itself. So that's what we did, although the picture didn't play in the South at all.

One of the members of the cast was Carl Switzer, who had played Alfalfa in the *Our Gang* comedies, one of the first integrated movie series to feature blacks who weren't just playing servants to whites. The producers knew they could get away with it because the actors were kids. Carl didn't get much work after he played Alfalfa, so he was happy to be part of the cast. We used to play poker a lot between shots, and he'd pass the time by telling me stories about filming *Our Gang.* There was one scene in the show where a bear was supposed to come over and take a bite out of Carl. Carl said, "I ain't gonna do it." The director said, "Believe me, there's no way you'll get in any trouble. He'll open his mouth and yawn." Carl said, "I don't want to do it."

The guy who owned the bear said, "Carl, there's nothing to worry about. He's a very gentle animal." And in front of the cast and the crew, he went up to the animal. He said, "This is what I want you to do." He put his face up to the bear's mouth, and the bear bit his cheek off. Needless to say, the bear scene was edited out.

Tragically, Carl was shot to death not too long after we finished shooting *The Defiant Ones.* He got into an argument with a friend over borrowing a hunting dog, and when he barged into his friend's house in a drunken rage, the other man shot him to death. Carl was thirty-one years old. The bitter irony was that in *The Defiant Ones,* Carl played a hunter who got in an argument with a police sergeant over his hunting dog.

I was sure *The Defiant Ones* was going to be a huge hit, but it wasn't. At that time United Artists didn't have the promotion budget or distribution of some of its bigger competitors, so its movies never hit the way they should have. UA would spend two hundred thousand dollars on a film and make two million, but if almost any other studio had made the film, it would have been much bigger.

The Defiant Ones was important to me, because I was still building a case to be seen as a serious actor. Obviously I'd made the right choice with this movie, because Sidney and I were nominated for Oscars. But this year they weren't going to give an Oscar to a black man or a Jew. The winner for best actor that year was David Niven for *Separate Tables,* a movie about an Englishman with very little money who goes to a resort and meets a lady who becomes infatuated with him. I thought, *What the fuck is the Academy doing?* But hey, I was prejudiced.

I said as much to Lew Wasserman, who replied, "Don't worry about it, Tony. They're not ready for you yet. You need a few more pictures."

But I was angry, and disappointed in my profession. I felt *The Defiant Ones* was making an important statement about the times we lived in. I also felt my own time had come. I was making important pictures, and I felt I deserved some acclaim from my peers. But Lew was right. *The Defiant Ones* was ahead of its time, and I needed to wait my turn.

My next movie, directed by Blake Edwards, was *The Perfect Furlough,* the story of a soldier who wins a date with a femme fatale, played by Linda Cristal. I played the soldier. To keep me in check on my date, the army sends two chaperones along, one of whom was played by Janet. I climb out my window to go into what I think is Linda's room, but it turns out to be Janet's room. It was very amusing. Blake did a good job with it.

The next big event in my life was personal. In September 1958 I got a phone call from my brother Robert, who said, "Daddy has gone to sleep." I knew what that meant. Janet and I jumped in the car and raced over to my parents' house. We walked in and found my father lying on the bedroom floor, next to the bed. He was dead.

My mother said, "He came to me, and then he just fell off." I decided that must have been her roundabout way of saying he was having sex with her when he died. I thought, *That's nice for him. What a perfect way to go.*

My family and I sat shiva for my father, and a lot of family friends showed up to offer their condolences and to tell stories about the old man. After the funeral, I bought my mother a house to live in. Things were good for me financially, but my father's death triggered one of my major depressions. Despite my prosperity, my endless struggle to build on my success didn't seem worthwhile anymore. No matter what I did, I still felt like the same mixed-up kid I had been when I was growing up on the East Side of Manhattan.

Then things went from bad to worse. As long as Lew had been my agent, I felt that my career was in the best hands possible and that everything would be okay. But then MCA, Lew Wasserman's company, bought Universal Studios. Now Lew was going to be a studio exec, which meant he was no longer going to be an agent. I asked him how I was going to be affected.

"Don't worry about it," he said. "I can't represent you anymore, but now I can see to it that you're free to go and do your outside movies whenever you want."

So I gained a sympathetic new head of the studio that owned my contract, but I lost my agent, and the trade-off was not a good one. I had thought Lew and I would stay together forever. Losing him as my agent was devastating — and it would be another couple of years before I would feel the full impact of our parting.

A publicity shot with Jack Lemmon, 1959.

13
Some Like It Hot

I was walking down Beverly Drive one afternoon when a man stopped me in the street.

"You don't know me, do you?" he asked. I shook my head.

"I'm Harold Mearish. I produced *Beachhead.*" This was the film I had made in Hawaii several years earlier, with Frank Lovejoy and Mary Murphy. Harold was a Jew who had made a fortune selling chocolate bars in the movie theaters of Milwaukee. He had wanted to get out of the chocolate business and into the movie business, so he approached studios and got them to agree to make his films if he would finance them. Howard Koch had line-produced *Beachhead,* but Mearish had put up the money.

Harold said, "You know, in the first two months of release we made back all the money we spent on that film, and it was all because of you."

"Thanks a lot," I said. "I appreciate that."

After we met, Harold Mearish started inviting me over for dinner or a screening. I think he enjoyed my exuberance. One afternoon Harold called and said, "I want you to come over to my house. Billy Wilder is here, and he wants to talk to you."

Billy Wilder had gotten his start as a screenwriter in the German film industry. When Hitler came to power, Billy left Germany and came to Hollywood, speaking no English whatsoever. That didn't stop him from making some of the most memorable movies in the history of film, including *Double Indemnity, Sunset Boulevard, Lost Weekend, The Apartment, Sabrina, Love in the Afternoon, The Seven Year Itch,* and *Irma la Douce.* Much later he even worked on the script of Steven Spielberg's extraordinary *Schindler's List.*

I didn't know what Harold had in mind, but I was hoping Billy might have some work for me. After *Trapeze* I had half-expected that all sorts of important directors would think about using me, but it hadn't turned out that way. So I kept working on my craft and on polishing my rough edges, both as an actor and as a player in Hollywood's social game. I was getting better about which fork to use and how to make conversation at parties, but that didn't stop some people from looking down on me. I was nuts about Phyllis Kirk, a raving beauty who starred with Vincent Price in the movie *House of Wax,* but she wouldn't even spit on me. But I was still young and I was still learning, and today I was driving to meet Billy Wilder, who wanted to see me.

Starring in a Billy Wilder film would be a great coup, putting me in Hollywood's most rarified air. Billy was an Academy Award–winning director who was also a brilliant screenwriter. He had the skills to make movies that looked nothing like the typical run of the Hollywood mill. Most Hollywood movies were conceived primarily by producers, who might say, *Why don't we make a movie called* All American? *We can get this Italian kid who's rough, put him in a fancy school, cut his hair, and show how he can become an American too.* That was actually a movie I made at Universal; in real life I was Jewish instead of Italian, but Universal's producers didn't care about that.

There were a lot of things that most producers and directors didn't care about, but Billy was different. *Double Indemnity* is a prime example, as you can see from just the story alone. This guy who's an insurance salesman on the road comes to a house where a beautiful woman is living with her husband, an older man who's an oil executive. The guy and the wife get to know each other and plot the murder of the older husband. They almost get away with it, but the insurance agent kills the wife; he then confesses and is sent to the electric chair. *That's* Billy Wilder's idea of a movie. To put it simply, it's got depth.

Harold Mearish's house was on a nice quiet street in Beverly Hills behind the Beverly Hills Hotel. Harold had created a beautiful projection room in his home, where I'd seen a number of screenings. I parked my car, came inside, and Harold introduced me to Billy Wilder. Shaking Billy's hand I felt like a prizefighter who wanted to be a contender. I just needed to get a big part in a Billy Wilder movie to show everyone that I was the real thing.

Billy took me into a small room and shut the door so we could talk privately. I was so nervous to be in his presence that when we sat down I thought to myself, *Are we sitting all alone because he's embarrassed to be with me?*

That wasn't it at all, as it turned out. Billy was indeed offering me a part in a movie. He said, "I'm making a picture about two musicians who are working in a speakeasy during Prohibition, when the place gets raided.

They escape, but the man who owns the place loses his business because a rat blows the whistle on him. So the mobsters who run the speakeasy find the rat and kill him. But the two musicians witness the murder, so now the mobsters want to kill them too. To escape, they dress up as girls and join an all-girl band." That was the hook, the Billy Wilder touch that set this film apart. The title? It would become *Some Like It Hot.*

Billy said, "I want you to play one of the musicians, the one who gets involved with one of the girls in the band, and I'm going to get Frank Sinatra to play the other one. And Mitzi Gaynor is going to play the girl."

I thought, *Get whoever you want to play the other parts. It makes no difference to me.* I was thrilled just to be sitting in a quiet room with Billy Wilder, and absolutely stunned that he was offering me a big part in his next movie. There were dozens of talented actors who would kill for this part, but I was the one he wanted!

Of course I told Billy I'd do it. About a week later Harold invited me to a screening at his house, and Billy was there too. Billy called me over and said, "I'm not going to use Sinatra. He's going to be too much trouble."

"What kind of trouble?" I said.

Billy said, "He'll have to dress up as a woman every day, and I just can't see Frank doing that." I knew what he meant. Along with Frank's arrogance came oversized insecurities, and there was no way he was going to dress up like a woman for a movie role. Billy said, "I'm going to use Jack Lemmon instead."

I was delighted to have Jack as a costar. He was a good friend and a wonderful actor, and for some reason I never felt the slightest twitch of competitiveness from Jack. Perhaps it was because he was so comfortable in his own skin. I loved the work he did in *Some Like It Hot,* and much later he was totally amazing as Felix Ungar in *The Odd Couple.*

Mitzi Gaynor never got the part. When I ran across her a number of years later, I asked her, "Did you know you were going to play Sugar Kane Kowalczyk?"

"I heard," she said. "Do you know what happened?"

"When Marilyn became available, Billy said he was going to use her, difficult as she was," I said. Billy was certainly right about Marilyn being difficult, and he was even more right about casting her for the part. Can you imagine anyone else playing that role?

The script for *Some Like It Hot* was written

by I. A. L. Diamond, who had worked with Billy before. Izzy understood the New York idiom, and he had a great sense of humor. When you took his jokes, combined them with the great storyline, and then threw a girl like Marilyn into the mix, you got a perfect movie. At least you did if you were Billy Wilder.

Billy also showed great judgment in his choice of his supporting actors. He was a big fan of the movie *Manpower,* which had starred George Raft and Edward G. Robinson, so he wanted both of them to play gangsters in *Some Like It Hot.* Unfortunately, Robinson and Raft had gotten into a fistfight while making *Manpower,* and Robinson had sworn he would never work with Raft again. In an effort to get Robinson to take the part, Billy signed Robinson's son, Edward Jr., to play in the movie, but Robinson still turned Billy down. By the way, you can see Edward G. Robinson Jr. in the scene where he's flipping a coin in the air. When George Raft grabs the coin in midair, he says to Edward Jr.'s character, "Where'd you learn to do that cheap trick?" The reply? "I saw George Raft do it." That was a typical Billy Wilder touch.

To play the part of the yacht-owning millionaire who falls in love with Jack Lemmon in drag, Billy selected Joe E. Brown, a great character actor. Even though Joe had been in the movies since the 1930s, he treated me as an equal, which totally won me over.

To my surprise, I was very uncomfortable the first time I put on women's clothing for the movie. I was in the dressing room putting on a jacket that looked like it belonged to Eve Arden and a garter belt that looked like it belonged to Loretta Young. Not to mention the shoes with the three-inch heels. Jack Lemmon was in there too, just screaming with laughter, which didn't help. I refused to come out of the dressing room.

Billy Wilder came in and looked at me and said, "What's the matter, Tony?"

I said, "Billy, look at me." Even as a woman, I wanted to look good, and these clothes were not doing the trick.

Billy said, "Don't worry, Tony. We'll get some clothes made for you. Come on out." Gradually, he coaxed me from the dressing room. After all those years of putting up with guys coming on to me and hearing rumors about my own sexuality, dressing like a woman felt like a real challenge to my manhood. To calm myself, I recalled a lot of tough experiences I'd been through in life, and I told myself this couldn't be any tougher than those.

As I stepped outside the dressing room

clutching my purse, I was horrified to see a crowd; there were some fifty members of the crew standing there waiting to see what I looked like as Josephine. I felt deeply embarrassed, but actor that I was, I turned that into material for my performance: I blushed and put my hands over my face, coyly acting the part of the reluctant diva.

Jack, on the other hand, had no such reservations. When he emerged from the dressing room for the first time, he came out fully in character, shrieking, dancing, prancing, looking cute, and exaggerating his femininity. I watched him with envy. I couldn't imagine doing that.

Billy Wilder had hired a female impersonator to teach Jack and me to move like a woman, and I worked with a voice coach who trained me to speak in a softer, higher voice. *Some Like It Hot* was a real acting challenge for me, because, in effect, I played three characters: Joe, the sax player; Josephine, Joe's identity when he's in drag in the all-girl band; and Junior, an identity Joe assumes to help him woo Sugar. Junior is supposed to be a millionaire who owns a yacht. For my scenes as Junior, I was dressed in a blue yachting blazer, white trousers, open shirt, and a captain's hat. The big question in my mind was, what should Junior sound like? As Joe, I was harsh and tough, a guy who had been around and who had fucked every vocalist in any band he was in. Josephine, of course, was softer and more demure. When I played Junior, I could have used a variation on the same voice and mannerisms that I used for Joe, but I wanted to do something more interesting.

I thought about it and I decided that the voice I liked best for the part was Cary Grant's, but I chose to exaggerate it to the point of caricature. I played it saucy. I kicked up my voice a little bit higher, and I extended certain words and made them a little longaaah, but I didn't swallow the *g* like the British did. By putting more emphasis on the "gaaaa," it came out as a mix of London and New York, which told you right away, *This guy is not English. He is a New Yorker trying to sound English.*

In the first scene I shot as Junior, I was sitting in a deck chair on the beach when Sugar walked by. Billy said to me, "When she runs by you, trip her." I complied, and Marilyn took a great fall onto the sand. She turned around and looked at me with surprise. In my exaggerated Cary Grant voice, I said: "I hope I didn't hurt you. Are you all right? When people find out who I am, they sue for a bundle of money."

Billy yelled cut. I said, "Billy, was that all right?"

He said, "It was great."

"Did you hear the accent?" I said.

"What accent?"

I said, "I was doing a little bit of Cary Grant."

He said, "If I had wanted Cary Grant to play the part, I would have gotten Cary Grant." That was all Billy had to say about the accent, but he didn't tell me not to use it, so I kept it up. The accent helped me establish a character whom I had an absolutely wonderful time playing.

As I got more into the character of Josephine, I began to enjoy playing that part too. I imagined myself as Eve Arden or Grace Kelly, or sometimes even my mother. I learned that in order for a woman to walk like a woman, she didn't have to try to tighten her ass or maintain good posture. She just walked easily, which I tried to emulate.

I had a great time working with Jack Lemmon. He was very friendly and easygoing with everybody, and he never played the prima donna or did things to make himself look good at the expense of the other actors. Jack was smart and fun, and he was a very positive guy. He was fairly reticent on the set and wouldn't talk much about his personal life, but when I met him at one of Billy's parties, he was much more gregarious and open. I had the feeling that Jack was never satisfied with anything, even with his performances, which may explain why he drank a lot. Drinking allowed him to relax and quiet that critical inner voice.

On the set, Jack's performance was spot-on, and in this case that meant being very theatrical. He had a funny way of reaching into the words and exaggerating them for effect. He was always very animated, so his characters sparkled with life.

Marilyn was perfect in the movie that was our final product, but on the set she was a loose cannon. Part of the problem was her relationship with Lee and Paula Strasberg, who ran the Actors Studio. Marilyn wanted to be an intellectual, and they played to that desire by treating her as one of them, which made Marilyn very dependent on them. She had completely succumbed to the Actors Studio philosophy that it's better to mumble your words, what I called the Marlon Brando style of acting. The problem was that only Marlon could do that.

I came to hate the Actors Studio for what they did to Marilyn. Lee Strasberg was a great acting coach; in my opinion the problems came from Lee's wife. Paula's presence made things harder for Marilyn, because she felt torn between Paula and Billy. Marilyn played the ding-dong for Paula, and she played the diva with Billy, giving each of them what she thought they wanted, because that was how Marilyn was wired.

At the time that *Some Like It Hot* started shooting, Marilyn had caused so many problems around town that some studios were refusing to hire her. Twentieth Century Fox had put her on the shelf. Fox's executives figured that if she sobered up and got herself together in a couple of years, then maybe they'd be able to work with her. They weren't wrong in their assessment of Marilyn's problems, but Marilyn also had an incredible gift. She really was a first-rate comedienne. Billy may not have been sure about Marilyn when he signed her, but he quickly saw that she was exactly what he wanted.

Still, taking on Marilyn meant taking on Marilyn's problems. Lew Wasserman was still her agent at this point, so Billy worked with Lew to try to keep her under control. As a backup plan, Billy and I discussed a list of actresses who we thought could play the part if Marilyn didn't work out. Billy knew she was perfect for the role, but he made it clear to me that he was willing to replace her.

"This is *not* the story of Sugar Kane," he would say. "It's the story of two musicians who have to dress up like women, and one of them happens to fall in love with a beautiful girl singer."

From the beginning, Marilyn was difficult. She refused to wear the clothes the wardrobe department gave her. She demanded that she use only her own makeup. Her hair had to be the way she wanted it. She was so unreasonable in so many different ways that we weren't even sure she would last through the first week of shooting.

We began by filming the train sequence on the back lot at MGM. This was Marilyn's first shot, when she comes walking down the platform holding her ukulele and boards the train. It sounds simple, but Marilyn was very unsure of herself. Before we rolled film, she was walking down the platform rehearsing the shot, and Billy was directing her. About twenty feet behind him stood Paula Strasberg. As I watched, I could see Marilyn looking not at Billy but at Paula. Marilyn did this take after take. She might have been talking to Billy, but her eyes were always darting away toward his left, where Paula stood behind him. I thought, *How interesting is this? Paula's gonna direct the movie. She's going to take over, and Marilyn will work only if Paula says so, and she's gonna do only what Paula wants. God, if it turns out like that, we're going to be in a lot of trouble.*

Finally it was time to start shooting. Billy bellowed, "Action," and Marilyn started walking, and then she stopped before she hit the mark.

"All right, let's do it again," he said. I'd heard that Billy had a reputation for being harsh and unsympathetic on set. But here he was, with an actress who had given him so much trouble before a single frame of film got shot, and he was strictly business. No sign of emotion whatsoever. She went back and did it again.

"Cut," Billy said, but the problem this time wasn't Marilyn. "I don't want the passerby crossing in front of her until after she gets past this point; I want the scene to be only about Marilyn," Billy said. Strictly business; strictly practical. "All right, roll 'em."

After the fourth or fifth take, Marilyn came down the platform perfectly, and Billy said, "Cut." Marilyn looked over at Paula, and Billy turned around and looked at Paula too. He said to her, "How was it for you, Paula?"

Of course it was fine for Paula, but that wasn't the point. The point was that Paula hadn't pulled that scene out of Marilyn; Billy had, and everyone knew it. Billy asking

Paula her opinion only made it more obvious. In that moment, any influence Paula might have had on the movie simply vanished. The company didn't rally behind her; Billy had simultaneously taken Marilyn in hand and cut Paula out of the loop. You had to admire the way he worked.

Billy was that rare combination of an artist with a strong practical streak. There was one scene on a yacht when Marilyn was supposed to come into the stateroom and look for a bottle of bourbon. Paula's direction would have been, "You're coming into the room and looking for the thing that's going to calm you down. Where could it be?" Billy would say, "The bourbon's in the top drawer in the chest. Take three seconds looking for it, then find it." Marilyn followed Billy's direction, and she did it very well.

But the struggles with Marilyn weren't over. Every now and then she would simply not show up for work for a couple of days, which is one of the worst things you can do in the movie world because it wastes everyone's time and it wastes money. It also made everyone nervous: was Marilyn going to show up today, or wasn't she?

Even after the first third of the filming was completed, the studio was considering shutting us down for a week, recasting Marilyn's part, reconfiguring the story to work in the footage we'd already shot, and then going back to work. Most people on a movie set were expendable, including the stars. A classic example was when Jean Harlow collapsed on the set in the middle of filming *Saratoga.* She was taken to the hospital, but she died of kidney failure at the age of twenty-six, and the studio finished the movie by shooting over the back of a stand-in.

The producers could have easily replaced Marilyn, but everyone could see that she, in spite of herself, was conveying that funny, special quality she had that would sneak into a scene and make it great. Even in the rushes you could see that Marilyn lit up the screen.

After a week on the back lot, we began filming the beach scenes in San Diego at the Hotel del Coronado. Billy wanted to shoot at an actual hotel because he wanted Marilyn to live on site, thinking that would make it harder for her to refuse to show up for work. Unfortunately, things got worse between Billy and Marilyn after we got to San Diego. She'd come to work late; she wouldn't know her lines. She put a huge strain on the entire company.

I went to Billy and said, "I'm having trouble sleeping because of all this shit with Marilyn." He said he was too, and he had something that could help. He went into his hotel room and came back with a little bottle. He gave me the bottle and said, "These are French suppositories. Slip one in your *tuchis* and you'll sleep all night."

That night I inserted one of the suppositories and slept. The next morning Billy asked me, "Did you take the suppository?" I said yes. "How did it work?" he asked.

"My ass fell asleep instantly," I said.

The problem with Marilyn was that the vulnerable quality that made her portrayal of Sugar so affecting on screen was also her biggest drawback. When she wasn't being selfish or rude, she could be quite charming, and she didn't lack for friends. Marilyn's dressing room was adjacent to mine, and it was interesting to see who came to see her. Paula Strasberg came by a lot, of course, as did a friend of mine named Sam Bagley, an extra on the film. Sam was also good friends with Clark Gable. Sam was a character; he'd always carry a cigar and a big wad of bills, with a hundred-dollar bill on top and a stack of singles in the middle.

Visitors in the dressing room were one thing, but Marilyn didn't like people visiting the set when we were filming. She would become enraged if a newspaperman, a member of the Mearish family, or even an assistant director walked in on us unannounced. From the time she got to the set to the moment she left, she'd go through a hundred and fifty different emotional changes. She just couldn't relax. It was more than work; the problem was that she wanted to control every single man she met. Depending on the man, it was either "I love him" or "I hate him." But she was incapable of *not* paying attention to a man. She felt she had to play to every one.

I felt affection for Marilyn all through the picture. I knew her well enough — and was enough like her — that I understood how she was feeling. Being comfortable was just not something she did very well, although she seemed to be having fun during our love scene on the yacht in *Some Like It Hot.* We did that scene over and over, and I loved every take of it. We were revisiting the feelings we had had for each other years earlier, those dinners, those drives around town in my Buick convertible with Dynaflow Drive, and our times together in Howard Duff's beach house. Once again we were incredibly young, and I knew that she was enjoying those memories as much as I was, although we never spoke of them.

During this time Marilyn was married to Arthur Miller, and every once in a while he would come to the set. He'd pull up in a limousine opposite the entrance to the stage, and he'd stand by the stage door and wait for Marilyn to finish work. You know what I've noticed? All the guys Marilyn went with looked like Abe Lincoln, every one of them: Arthur Miller, Joe DiMaggio, Yves Montand, the whole lot. I think the look fascinated her. It wasn't the Hollywood look, and it certainly wasn't my aesthetic. They were all a little off-kilter in their looks, but they all were great talkers. Marilyn loved articulate men.

After about the third week of shooting, I heard rumors that Marilyn was pregnant. It was impossible to tell just from looking at her, but once the gossip mill started up, the producers began to get alarmed. How many months along was she? We finished the movie without mishap, but later on, after the movie wrapped and we went back for retakes, we heard that she'd had an abortion.

Marilyn continued to butt heads with Billy, and by the end of shooting he was furious with her. He had suffered from so much stress that his back had gone out. One night we were having dinner at my house, and Billy was so tense that he couldn't get out of his chair. We helped him lie down in our bedroom, and Janet called a doctor to come and give Billy a muscle relaxant.

Sometimes Marilyn caused stress with her efforts to make a scene better. In one scene in *Some Like It Hot,* Marilyn and I are drinking champagne on the yacht, and then we start to become romantic. Marilyn has just come from singing at a nightclub, and she's wearing a see-through dress. Orry-Kelly, the film's dress designer, figured out how Marilyn could wear it in the nightclub by adding a little extra cloth to cover her nipples. Marilyn decided the scene on the yacht would work better without the cloth, but MGM got panicky about it. What if we shot the scene without the cloth, and then the censor bureau said they wouldn't allow it? But Marilyn insisted that she wouldn't do it any other way. As she became more and more important to a picture, she exerted more and more control. She got her way, and I guess Billy got creative with the lighting during the shot, because the censor board didn't say anything.

Marilyn and I had a lot of scenes together, and as we spent time together she began to turn to me more and more for support. If Marilyn felt she was having trouble, she looked to me to become her co-complainer. Her trouble became my trouble. If she felt there was too much noise on the set, she'd look at me, and I'd say, "Yeah, too much noise on the set." Or we'd be doing a scene, and right in the middle she would look at me and say, "How's my makeup?"

I'd say, "It looks good." That wasn't a line in the script, needless to say. Then she'd keep right on going.

There were times when I walked onto the set and Marilyn would be sitting in one of the director's chairs with her name on it. She'd catch my eye, and so much would happen between us in those few moments we looked at each other that I felt like I had had a whole love affair with her before I even sat down.

She enjoyed it when I would visit her in her dressing room. I'd knock on her door and say, "Hello, Marilyn. It's me." She'd invite me in, and I'd say, "I hope you don't mind my coming in. I just want to sit here quietly before Billy calls us."

She'd say, "Please, sit down." I'd sit there relaxing while she read her script. That was all. We'd sit together ten or fifteen minutes, until Billy called for the cast, and we'd come out. I really liked those moments we had together. They meant a lot to me, and I could see she enjoyed them too. They seemed to make her a bit calmer. Every time I looked at her she would be smiling at me.

Before we shot the romantic scene on the yacht where Marilyn was going to cure me of my impotence, she was in her dressing room, and she asked to see me. She had opened a bottle of champagne, and she wanted us to get a little loose before we shot the scene. I had one glass, but I wouldn't drink any more, knowing my limits when it came to booze. She had another glass and murmured, "If it could only be like what we had before." I knew what she meant; it was the first time either of us had openly acknowledged what we had once meant to each other. I gave her a long kiss, and she seemed to relax a little bit. I was glad for that, because this was going to be a difficult scene.

By the time we shot the scene, Marilyn was into it. When we kissed, I was on the receiving end of her tongue, and of her grinding. I had a hard-on (but don't tell anybody) all through that scene, and she knew it, which made her even more aggressive. She knew I wasn't acting when I expressed my desire for her. She could feel it — in more ways than one — and when Billy yelled "Cut," she pushed herself off me and gave me a big, satisfied smile.

In the end it turned out that we all had misunderstood Marilyn. We knew that she was a powerful woman and a consummate actress, but we didn't realize that her way of finding out who she was came from acting. In her early career, her films were flimsy, poorly written affairs, so of course she had trouble getting a handle on the material. But in *Some Like It Hot* the material was beautifully written, and she absolutely shone.

After the scene in which Marilyn and I were kissing, some of the crew and I stood around to watch the rushes, and afterward they wanted to know what it was like to kiss her. I figured a question that stupid deserved a stupid answer, so I flippantly responded by saying, "Kissing Marilyn is like kissing Hitler." I was right — it *was* a stupid answer. What I should have said was, "What do you think kissing her is like, birdbrain?" Or I could have had the good sense to just say nothing. But my thoughtless comment became public knowledge, and the story still makes the rounds. So let me use this book to set the record straight once and for all: I *hated* Hitler. This is the kid who threw condom-bombs on the pro-Nazi parades, remember? I loved Marilyn Monroe. And she was a terrific kisser.

After *Some Like It Hot* wrapped, I saw Marilyn again at Peter Lawford's house at the beach. A lot of her friends were there. We talked for a minute, but somehow working with her on *Some Like It Hot* had brought a sense of completion to my feelings for her. The more we talked, the more I realized another love affair had bitten the dust. It seemed like working with me had changed things for her too, or maybe it just represented the natural end of something we'd shared. When I saw her at Peter's party, she was really out of it. She looked like death warmed over, which saddened me, but I knew there was nothing I could do about it.

When I was invited to attend the Moscow International Film Festival, the government liaison for the event asked me to bring a copy of *Some Like It Hot* with me so they could show it at the festival. The studio arranged for all the clearances, so I embarked on the long flights from California to London to Moscow. At the festival, a giant screen had been set up at one end of a huge gymnasium, and on one unforgettable night the bleachers were packed with people watching *Some Like It Hot* without benefit of subtitles. Fortunately for some, a translator stood by the screen with a microphone, translating the dialogue as the movie went along. At the end of the movie, when Joe E. Brown learns that Jack is a man and says, "Nobody's perfect," the gymnasium exploded with laughter. You know a joke is good when it translates into another language without losing any of its punch.

I had never thought it was that amusing for guys to dress up like women. I had seen pictures of Eddie Cantor dressed as a ballerina, and I didn't find that very funny. But when *Some Like It Hot* was finished, I was overwhelmed by how good it was. The dialogue, the photography, Marilyn's character, Jack's character, and the way my role turned out: I was very pleased with all of it. At times during the making of the film I had felt discouraged by the thought that Jack and Marilyn had the most interesting parts, and that I was just playing the straight man for the two of them. It felt good to see my own work holding its own with all the wonderful acting in that movie.

In the end, Jack Lemmon got an Oscar nomination for his acting in *Some Like It Hot,* which was richly deserved, but my heart ached that I didn't get nominated too. I loved the overwhelming reaction my role generated from my fans; don't get me wrong, that was very important to me. But all of us who work in the movie business long for the special recognition from our peers that comes with an Academy Award. Nothing. Nothing?

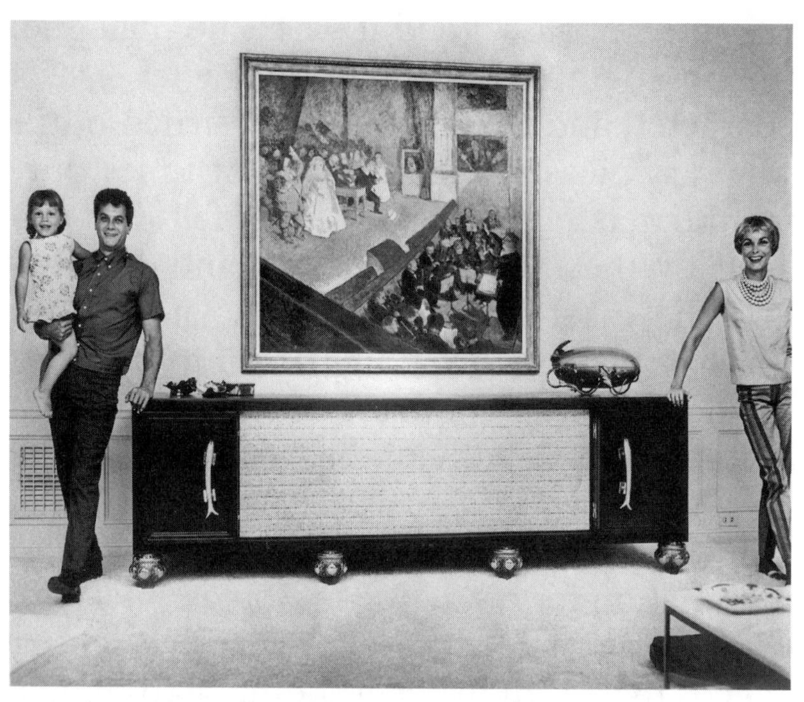

Kelly, me, and Janet, 1958.

14
The End of a Marriage

After I completed *Some Like It Hot,* Universal asked me what I wanted to do next. By this point in my career I had some leverage, so I said, "I want to make a submarine picture with Cary Grant." After all, Cary Grant's role as a submarine captain in *Destination Tokyo* had inspired me while I was in the submarine service. Cary agreed, with the proviso that after seven years he would own the movie. The studio bought in too, and so it was that *Operation Petticoat* came into being.

The movie, directed by Blake Edwards, was the story of a submarine that had been sunk in the Philippines at the beginning of World War II. It was raised from the bottom and ordered to make its way to Australia to be refitted for combat. On one Philippine island the sub picks up a bunch of nurses. On another island the sub is painted pink, in the absence of either enough red or enough white paint to cover the entire hull. Cary plays the sub commander, and I play his supply officer, a con man who will go to any lengths to keep the ship running. The nurses create a lot of trouble for the crew, of course. In one scene, Cary is at the conning tower getting ready to fire the sub's only torpedo at a Japanese ship while Joan O'Brien, playing one of the nurses, is talking to him about the value of taking vitamins. She bumps into him just as he says, "Fire one," and the torpedo runs across Tokyo Bay and blows up a truck on the shore.

Cary's character eventually ends up with Joan, and I end up with Dina Merrill. This was the third movie Blake Edwards and I made together, and by this time we were great friends. He and his wife spent many an evening with Janet and me. Blake and I were about the same age, and we were both very caught up in our manhood; one drunken night we went so far as to see whose dick was too big to fit through the hole of a 45 rpm record. As best I can remember, neither of us won that contest, but another time Blake and I asked a girl we had both dated which one of us was better in bed. She replied, "I'll never tell," which was smart of her, and good for our friendship.

A year after Blake made *Operation Petti-*

coat, he started casting for the movie *Breakfast at Tiffany's.* After I read the script, I felt I was perfect for the lead. I called Blake, and he invited me over to his office at the studio. I told him how much I wanted the part, and he danced around the issue for a while. Finally he told me, "I'll do what I can," but whatever he did turned out not to count for much. After that meeting I never heard from Blake again. George Peppard, a wonderful guy, got the part. But, sadly, the silence from Blake hurt me a lot.

There were other important parts I didn't get. Audrey Hepburn made a picture called *Two for the Road* that I would have loved to be in, but Albert Finney got the lead I was hoping for. I was pretty sure Audrey liked me, but later I heard that when my name did come up, Audrey's husband, Mel Ferrer — who made those decisions for her — didn't want me in the picture. That's how Hollywood works; it's all about relationships. They can make you, and they can break you. If you're around long enough, they'll do both.

My next movie was *Who Was That Lady?* with Dean Martin and Janet. Its plot was so ridiculous that even Bob Hope turned it down. In it, Dean plays a television producer, and I play a college professor whose wife catches him kissing one of his students.

I call my friend Dean to help me keep my wife, played by Janet. Janet and I were terrific in the film, but by this time our marriage didn't have much life left in it. We'd been faking it for years now. We had two beautiful little daughters, Kelly and Jamie, but the relationship between Janet and me was miserable. We fought all the time. We had lots of reasons for disagreements, but having Janet's father handling her business affairs was a constant thorn in my side.

Truth be told, Janet and I still lived under the same roof, but that was about the extent of it. In the evening, she went out with her friends, and I went out with mine. I'd go to parties with my buddies, or go visit Hef in Los Angeles. Sometimes I'd fool around with one of Hef's bunnies, but by now I no longer had feelings of guilt about my extramarital escapades. Quite the opposite; I knew these short-lived pairings actually made it easier to stay in my marriage. I could pay attention to someone other than my wife, who clearly didn't love me anymore.

When Lew Wasserman was still at MCA, he represented both Janet and me, and he also represented Alfred Hitchcock, a favorite client of Lew's. Lew got Janet her role in *Psycho,* where Anthony Perkins stabs her to death in the shower. It was a small part, but it became the part for which she'll always be remembered. It was a horrific scene, but what made it presentable was the stylized way Hitchcock shot it and edited it. I was very happy for Janet, because I was sure that all the attention she was getting for *Psycho* was going to result in her getting a lot of other movies.

After *Psycho* came out, all the press wanted to talk about was the murder scene. Janet had never enjoyed media attention, and when the pressure of this new celebrity began to get to her, she started to drink a lot. And when Janet had a few drinks in her, she became a different person: belligerent, accusatory, and downright nasty. I didn't want to provoke her rages, so I started staying away more and more. Eventually I decided I needed another life, but I had no idea where I was going to find one.

My next film was called *The Rat Race,* in which I costarred with Debbie Reynolds. It's the story of a musician and a dance-hall hostess who share an apartment. What I remember most about that movie was the sparks that flew between Debbie and me, and I don't mean the angry kind that I was seeing at home. Up to that point few of my leading ladies had been able to deny me.

Debbie was one of the exceptions. We snuggled together quite nicely during the kissing scenes, and I spent a lot of time hanging out with her in her dressing room. In order for the sparks to turn into a full bonfire, however, Debbie and I needed a lot more time than we had on the set. Debbie had been in show business since she was a kid, and as a result she had a hard shell that was tough to crack.

My next film after that was *Spartacus,* which was made by Universal, believe it or not. The only reason the studio went for it was that Kirk Douglas, who starred in the film, also produced the picture and offered it to Universal as a package. The studio never would have paid Kirk what he was asking in those days, but the package deal gave Universal a chance to get him cheap. In the movie, Kirk plays Spartacus, who leads a slave revolt. Laurence Olivier plays the Roman general out to stop him. I play a slave purchased by the general, and after the general tries to seduce me, I run away and join Spartacus.

The screenwriter for the film was Dalton Trumbo, one of the writers who'd been blacklisted during the 1950s for supposedly being a Communist sympathizer. Trumbo had been writing under a pseudonym for the past ten years, but Kirk wanted him to get full credit for writing *Spartacus,* and as the producer, he made sure it happened. Trumbo was named in the credits as the writer, a brave move on Kirk's part, and a historic decision that broke the power of the blacklist.

When I first read the *Spartacus* script, I didn't think it was anything special; it read like an adventure movie in the mold of *Ben-Hur.* But I was under contract to Universal, and I owed them a picture. Universal told me that I would only have to be on the picture for twelve days, but the exec who told me this didn't know director Stanley Kubrick — or Kirk — very well. I didn't wrap up this movie for four and a half months!

Anthony Mann was the original director of *Spartacus.* When Mann began filming, Kirk didn't like what he saw in the rushes. He wanted sharper performances from his all-star cast. I hadn't started shooting my scenes yet, but I was told that Kirk and Anthony were bickering a lot. Not long after, Kirk fired him and hired Stanley Kubrick to replace him. Kirk had done a World War I movie with Kubrick called *Paths of Glory,* so they knew they could work together. That was an understatement. In fact, they understood each other so well that when I listened to them working out how they wanted to shoot a scene, I had no idea what they were talking about. They talked in shorthand and literally finished each other's sentences.

Stanley Kubrick told me that ever since he'd been a little kid he had loved taking pictures with his black-and-white Brownie camera. As a director he had an artist's genius for putting his own imprint on a film, regardless of its content. He was like Elvis in that way. Stanley was also a perfectionist. He would shoot scenes, and then after shooting later scenes he'd go back and reshoot the earlier ones so that everything fit together flawlessly. The studio didn't like that because it drove up costs, but Stanley didn't care.

One evening Kirk and I were doing a shot in which we were sitting and talking before a big battle. Behind us were a bunch of men being crucified. Kubrick had orchestrated a complex system for how he wanted those actors to moan and groan in between the lines of the conversation Kirk and I were having. Each crucified actor had a certain sound he was supposed to make on cue: the first guy was supposed to say "oooh," and the second guy was supposed to say "ugh," and the third guy was supposed to say "aaaah," and so on.

Their cue was a flag that Stanley waved at them.

So Stanley said, "Roll 'em," and Kirk and I started doing our scene. Stanley started waving his flag, and the guys on the crosses started moaning and groaning.

I said, "Why is life like a pomegranate?" *Ooooh!*

"Well," *Ugh!* "a pomegranate, like life, can be eaten." *Aaaah!*

Marshall Green, the assistant director, was in charge of making sure the moaning and groaning was happening properly. At one point Stanley looked up and noticed that one actor farther up the hill wasn't moving, or saying anything, and he pointed the guy out to Marshall. Stanley said, "Marshall, didn't we assign him anything?"

"Yeah, I assigned everybody a sound," Marshall said.

"Then how come this guy isn't doing anything?"

"Well, maybe he's not paying attention," Marshall said. "You want to do it again?"

"Before we shoot any more, why don't you go up there and find out what's wrong with him?"

So Marshall walked up the hill, finally stopped, and looked up at the guy on his cross. From where I was sitting, I could faintly hear Marshall's voice as he yelled up at the guy: "What's going on?" The guy didn't say anything, so Marshall said, "Look, if you've got to pee in your pants, pee in your pants. Don't worry. It's only wardrobe." Then Marshall stopped. He stood still and looked up at the guy for a few seconds, and then he turned around and slowly walked back down the hill to where Kubrick was waiting for him.

Kubrick looked at Marshall, and Marshall said, "It's a fucking dummy — a mannequin." Kirk and I laughed so hard that we almost peed in our pants.

Stanley Kubrick was constantly in conflict with Russ Metty, Universal's top cameraman. Kubrick was a newcomer, and Metty was a veteran of some twenty-five years. For one scene that we shot in a tent, Stanley said he thought the lighting was too dark, but Russ thought there was plenty of lighting. Standing next to Russ's chair was a light on a wheeled pole, so without getting up, Russ kicked the light toward the actors. The light rolled into the shot, and Russ yelled, "Now I'm ready." Stanley had his hands full with Russ, but somehow he kept the film moving forward.

One of the highlights of making *Spartacus* was acting with Larry Olivier. This was the first time we had acted together in a movie. I loved Larry. He was a total character. He would sit and watch everything like a hawk. When things got crazy, as they often did, I would glance over at Larry, and the look on his face seemed to say, *I know what I'm doing. I know you do, too. Don't take the rest of it seriously.* The film's editors cut the one scene we did together, the famous hot-tub scene where he tries to seduce me with his "oysters and snails" line, but the scene was restored when the movie was reissued in 1991.

One unusually powerful scene in the movie takes place near the end, when Spartacus and I are forced to fight to the death. Spartacus defeats me, and I say to him, "I love you, Spartacus, as I loved my own father." He says, "I love you like the son I'll never see," and plunges his sword into my heart. The next morning the Romans crucify him, but before he dies, his wife comes and shows him his baby son, and she vows that their infant will grow up as a free man.

I had no idea that *Spartacus* would have such power. I had thought this was going to be just one more sand-and-tits movie with a Roman twist, but I didn't take into account the level of talent involved in every aspect of the picture. (Even Russ Metty fought through his drunken stupor to do an amazing job!) When the picture came out, I got as many raves as anyone, even though I had a small part.

Having friends like Frank Sinatra meant I got a chance to meet some extraordinary people, and I don't just mean Sam Giancana. One day Frank introduced me to his friend Jack Kennedy. Jack was a big fan of Hollywood movies, and of the beautiful women who starred in them. I saw Jack with Marilyn one time, but I couldn't tell for sure whether they had any sort of relationship, although everyone now says they did. I also met Jack's younger brother Bobby and played touch football with him. Bobby was quiet and soft-spoken, and I liked him a lot.

Through Jack and Bobby I met their father, Joe. I later found out that Joe had always loved Janet because she had a great chest. Joe told me he loved watching my movies because I got all the girls, and because I reminded him of the kids he grew up with in Boston. I couldn't get over it: this Irish Catholic guy was reminded of his childhood by a Hungarian Jewish kid!

Maybe another reason Joe liked me was because I could introduce him to Hollywood starlets. The two of us attended a movie premiere party where I just happened to know a lot of people, so I went from girl to girl introducing him. "I want you to meet my friend Joe," I'd say, and then I'd lean in and whisper, "He's John Kennedy's father." The girls' eyes widened, which was fun for Joe, and fun for me.

After Jack Kennedy won the 1960 presidential election, Peter Lawford asked Janet to host a luncheon for Jackie Kennedy at our house. Although Jackie was the guest of honor, I hardly spoke to her; I must admit that I was intimidated by her elegance. She had extraordinary poise, and everything she wore seemed so perfect. I remember thinking, *What should I call her? First Lady? Mrs. Kennedy? Jackie?* I didn't want to expose my ignorance, so I kept my distance. Later I discovered that Jackie was such a class act that she would have found a way to make me comfortable.

In January of 1961, I was staying at the Sherry-Netherland in New York when Joe Kennedy invited me to come to his home in Palm Beach, Florida. Joe had his own DC-3. I didn't like flying, but I loved Big Joe a lot, so the two of us got on his plane and flew to Joe's huge Spanish-style house in Palm Beach. In the morning I'd swim and work out a little bit, while Joe read the papers and talked on the phone. Then we'd both watch the news on TV to find out what was going on in Washington.

One evening we were sitting in Joe's den when the phone rang, but it wasn't the house phone I'd used earlier; this was a special phone, and Joe picked it up at once. He talked for a little while, and then said to me, "The president sends you his best wishes." They talked a moment longer, and then Joe said to me, "He wants to read me his inauguration speech. No one has heard it as yet."

"Great," I said. "I'll go for a walk."

He said, "No, stay." Then he said, "I'm ready, son, whenever you are." He was silent for a while, as Jack recited his speech over the phone. Then Joe motioned for me to come over to the phone, lifted it away from his ear, and said, "I want you to hear this." He said, "Say that again, son." I put my ear to the phone, and I heard Jack Kennedy say, "Ask not what your country can do for you; ask what you can do for your country." The words were absolutely electric; they gave me goose bumps, and I told the president-elect so.

The night of the inauguration, Janet and I went to a party where Jack Kennedy was also in attendance. As we slowly made our way through the huge crowd, I heard someone say, "Tony, Tony." I turned, and about fifteen feet away was President Kennedy, who said, "My dad ran an advance screening copy of *The Great Impostor* last night, and the scene of you pulling Edmond O'Brien's tooth was the funniest thing we ever saw. I wanted to tell you that."

I said, "Thank you, Mr. President, I really appreciate that." I knew I wasn't likely to ever get a compliment to top that.

My next film, directed by Delbert Mann, was an interesting movie about Ira Hayes, the Native American Marine who helped raise the American flag on Iwo Jima. It was called *The Outsider,* and it shows what happened to Ira Hayes after he became famous. While he was in the Marines, his best friend introduced Ira to alcohol, and after Ira got back from the war, his life fell apart. People tell me I should have won an Oscar for my portrayal of Ira, but even though a lot of people went to see the picture, there wasn't enough buzz about it to move the Academy's voters. But I loved playing this role; I felt a special empathy for anyone in pain, especially the pain of being shunted aside or treated poorly.

If my movie career was going great guns, my personal life was a shambles. Janet was drinking heavily, and her love affair with the bottle was poisoning her life and our marriage. I wasn't sure exactly what she was going through. Perhaps she was having a midlife crisis; after all, she had married me when she was very young. These days her career was going well, and her roles were getting better and better, but the bigger she became, the more discontented she was. She knew that no matter how successful she was, she could never compete with actors like Elizabeth Taylor, and it drove her insane. I certainly related to that. I could never compete with Marlon Brando, and sometimes that drove me crazy too.

One afternoon in August of 1961, Janet's mother, Helen, called me. She and Janet's father, Fred, had divorced acrimoniously, but at this moment she was worried about him because she'd been trying to reach him all afternoon at his office without success. I didn't see what the big deal was, but she asked if one of us could go look in on Fred. Janet wasn't around — she was somewhere in the south of France, attending a film festival with Jeannie Martin, Dean's wife, and the Kennedys — so I told Helen I'd drive over and check on him. Privately I thought Fred might be with his mistress, who just happened to be his ex-wife's sister, but needless to say, I didn't mention my suspicions. I hung up with Janet's mother, hesitated for a moment before calling the police, and drove over to Fred's office.

I got there before the police did. I saw a light on in the office, and the door was unlocked. There was Fred, slumped over his typewriter, dead. I couldn't tell how he'd died; there was no blood, no pills, and no gun. But in the typewriter was a note that read, "I hope you're satisfied, you bitch." I pulled the sheet of paper out of the typewriter and stuck it in my pocket. I lifted Fred off the typewriter and leaned him back in his chair. Then I called Helen and told her that her fears had been confirmed.

Five minutes later the police showed up. They called an ambulance and took Fred away. Maybe I shouldn't have removed that letter, but I didn't want Janet's mother to see it. The police later concluded that Fred had died of natural causes, which was just as well.

My next movie was *Taras Bulba* with Yul Brynner. The movie was going to be filmed in Argentina, and because I hated to fly, I booked passage on the S.S. *America,* which took three days to go from Miami to Argentina. Janet, the two girls, and I took the train from LA to Miami. Getting Janet to make the train trip was a major coup, because she didn't like to do anything unless it happened quickly.

Once we got to Miami, Janet and I started drinking in our hotel room, and she got very angry with me in front of the girls, screaming at me and complaining that my neuroses had forced her into this boat trip instead of going by airplane. Kelly and Jamie looked on as Janet raged at me and threw things. I didn't say a word. I didn't realize how strongly she felt about having to take our boat trip until we arrived in Florida, when it was too late to change our plans. But as Janet stood there showering me with abuse in front of my children, something shifted inside me; I realized I couldn't take her outbursts anymore.

The next morning, the four of us went down to the pier and boarded the boat to Argentina. Our time on board allowed me to have a lot of fun with Kelly and Jamie, who were five and three. We swam together every day in the pool. I loved this opportunity to be with the girls without any outside distractions, and I couldn't help wishing I had spent more time with them instead of letting my work schedule keep me far from home. After we arrived in Argentina, Janet and the girls stayed for five or six days and flew home. After they left, I resolved that it was time for me to move out and move on. My marriage was over.

With Christine Kaufmann on our wedding day, 1963.

15
My Teenage Bride

Janet left Argentina because she had a movie to make, but the reason for her leaving as quickly as she did may have been jealousy of my beautiful young costar, Christine Kaufmann, who played my love interest in *Taras Bulba,* a Ukrainian version of *Romeo and Juliet.* I was playing Andrei, Yul Brynner's son, a Cossack who falls in love with a Polish princess. The Cossacks and Poles are enemies, and to make our love affair even more complicated, I kill her brother in a sword fight. What no one knew at the time was that I didn't have to act in my love scenes with Christine, because I really did fall in love with her.

To make the situation even more ticklish, Christine was only seventeen years old. That gave me pause, but there was a freshness about her, an exuberant joy in living that made me go all funny inside. To me, she represented all those girls I would have liked to have dated when I was a poor kid living in New York. I had never gone out with a girl like that, and now I was playing love scenes opposite one.

If Janet and I had been getting along, I might not have been so emotionally vulnerable, but that was not the case. Needless to say, the fact that my marriage was not in good shape meant that Janet and I rarely had sex, which didn't help either. Christine made life fun again, and I wanted to be with her in the worst way. My dream came true when Christine and I launched into a torrid affair for the first three weeks of shooting. Then her mother arrived on the set, at which point she and I agreed to bury our feelings and stop seeing each other.

That wasn't the only off-screen drama that was taking place during production. Yul Brynner disliked me because he'd wanted top billing, but United Artists had given it to me. Brynner was very pretentious and overbearing, not unlike the characters he played in his film roles. It got back to me that Yul was telling people I wasn't a good enough actor to play the part of his son. Yul's wife also made clear her distaste for me. On location she would bring a big pitcher of orange juice to the cameraman and the boom operator, and she was very obvious about not offering me any. I just shook my head.

Yul smoked all day long, and he had a lackey whose job was to light his cigarettes. When Yul was talking, he'd pull out his long cigarette holder, insert a cigarette, and then nod, which was the signal for his man to walk over and light him up. It was just another way for Yul to publicly demonstrate his power. He used this ritual to assert himself when he talked with the director, J. Lee Thompson. He'd say, "I don't think the scene will work this way, Lee. Why don't you have the horses come in from the other side instead?" Then he'd pull out a cigarette and wait for it to be lit.

After a while, I couldn't take Yul's behavior anymore, so I went out, bought an eyedropper, filled it with water, and brought it to the set. I stood behind Yul and waited for his servant to walk over to light his cigarette. After the cigarette was lit and Yul took a puff or two, he'd set it down in an ashtray. I'd tiptoe over, squeeze a couple of drops of water onto the end of the cigarette, and put it out. When Yul went to take another puff, the cigarette would be dead. After three days of this, Yul was about ready to kill his servant. I didn't want to be responsible for Yul firing the guy, so I finally let Yul in on what I was doing. I have to give him credit: he laughed.

Another actor who didn't like me was a bit player named Mickey Finn, a guy who weighed in at an impressive two hundred and eighty pounds. One day Mickey was sitting on his horse teaching a couple of other actors how to fence, and he said, "It's like throwing confetti." When I heard that load of horseshit, I realized Mickey had no idea what he was talking about, and I just had to correct him.

"You can't do it that way," I said. "You have to get close." I got on my horse, rode up right alongside a mounted soldier, and struck him twice with my sword before he finally parried. I said, "That's what you've got to do." When one of the riders followed my example, I said, "You've got it." Mickey became furious that I was showing him up, but there wasn't a lot he could do about it because my suggestion worked. I'd had a lot of experience fencing in movies.

One night at a cocktail party Mickey decided to vent his frustration by picking a fight with me. He came at me like a gorilla. I just stood there, thinking, *If you want to kill me, give it your best shot, Mickey, but if you so much as touch me, you're out of a job.* I was the star of the picture, which meant I could have easily seen to it that Mickey was fired. I prepared to defend myself using some self-defense moves that my stuntman friends had taught me. Perry Lopez, who was playing my brother in the film, alertly jumped in between Mickey and me, preventing what could have been a very ugly scene.

J. Lee Thompson, our director, had directed a huge hit the year before: *The Guns of Navarone.* He was a forceful director who knew how to control a set. When we had to shoot some military scenes, he contacted the head of the Argentine army and said, "We need two or three battalions out here for a week, and we'll pay you thirty thousand dollars." The next thing I knew, we were dressing two thousand Argentine soldiers as Poles. We'd shoot a Polish army scene, then the shot assistant would say, "All right, let's get these Poles turned into Cossacks." An hour later, thousands of soldiers who had been Poles would come riding onto the set as Cossacks.

After we were through filming in Argentina, the entire cast and crew flew back to Hollywood to finish the picture on United Artists' back lot. Christine's mother came along, and I went home to Janet. Christine and her mother were both staying at LA's Chateau Marmont, but I knew they were staying in separate rooms. I desperately wanted to be with Christine, but I knew the situation was fraught with danger.

I came up with a plan that involved driving up to the Chateau Marmont at five thirty in the morning. Christine would let me into her room, and we'd have our fun until about eight thirty. Then I would leave and go directly to the set, making sure her mother didn't see me on the way out. When Christine and I met on the set that morning, we'd greet each other as if for the first time that day. The sneaking around made our trysts even more romantic.

I may have been fooling Christine's mother, but Janet could tell something was up. She came by the UA lot one day when we were shooting and said something odd to me: "I want to see this Christine girl."

"What are you asking me for?" I said. "Go on the set and see her."

"Will you introduce us?" she asked.

"If I'm around, I'll introduce you, sure," I said. Janet was letting me know she suspected something was going on, but she didn't come right out and accuse me. I couldn't bear living with Janet anymore, so I often stayed overnight with Nicky Blair, a friend of mine who owned a restaurant in LA, or with Hugh Hefner. Whenever I needed to get away, Hef would let me stay in one of his rooms.

One night Janet and I were at home, having one of our terrible fights. Janet was drinking scotch and crying while she was trying to fix her makeup in front of a little mirror. There was a bottle of pills on her dressing table next to the mirror, and while I was standing there she opened the bottle, shook a handful of red pills into her palm, and threw them down her throat. In a panic, I slapped her hard on the back, causing her to cough up most of the pills.

That was the last straw. Soon after, I told Janet I was moving out. At first she took it calmly. "So move out if you want to," she said.

I packed a few clothes, and after I walked out the front door to my car, carrying a small valise, Janet came and stood in the doorway, holding Kelly by the hand and Jamie in her arms. She didn't say much, but she was crying, and when I saw the two girls, my heart was torn apart.

I should have found a better way to end things with Janet, but I had run out of energy. So instead, I just left. I found a hotel close by, and I stayed there while I finished the movie. Janet and I had parted, and not on good terms. Sad to say, Kelly and Jamie have always held it against me. It's understandable. Janet had full custody of the girls, which was typical in those days, and I'm sure she filled their heads with all sorts of negative stories about me.

Meanwhile, the movie magazines were buzzing with rumors about Christine and me. One day I got a message on the set saying that Hedda Hopper was calling. I got on the phone, and Hedda said to me, "Listen, Tony, God help you if you lie to me, but are you going with a teenager?"

I said, "No, Hedda, that's not true at all."

All that did was postpone the inevitable. The story of Tony Curtis leaving his wife and two kids for the teenage daughter of a German air force officer made every newspaper in America. The media frenzy made Janet even more bitter, if that was possible. She was being humiliated in public, and she never forgave me for it. I managed to get visitation rights to see our daughters, but Janet often found ways to keep me from seeing them.

After the movie wrapped, Christine went back to Germany, and that cooled down the rumors about us, but we talked on the phone long distance every night.

After Janet and I separated, I made a movie called *40 Pounds of Trouble.* The picture was about a five-year-old waif my character had taken in who tries to get me together with Suzanne Pleshette, the actress who would later become famous for her role on *The Bob Newhart Show.* Suzanne was a Brooklyn native who'd gotten her start as a stage actress on Broadway. She had wowed the critics when she replaced Anne Bancroft in the stage production of *The Miracle Worker,* and now here she was in Hollywood, making movies. Like Christine, Suzanne was young and smart and beautiful, and I often wonder whether I might have fallen for her if I hadn't already fallen for Christine.

We were the first company allowed to shoot a film in Disneyland, which had opened in Anaheim in 1955. We also filmed at the Cal-Neva Lodge near Reno, the place that Frank Sinatra owned as part of his under-the-table arrangement with mob boss Sam Giancana. Frank's relationship with Sam Giancana was the reason that Jack Kennedy had been forced to cut Frank off as a friend after he got elected president. J. Edgar Hoover knew all about Frank's mob friends, so he told Kennedy to keep Frank at arm's length, which Kennedy did. That was very hurtful to Frank, who had been an important campaigner for Kennedy, and Frank never forgave Jack for turning his back on him.

Frank took his anger out on Peter Lawford, because Peter was married to Jack Kennedy's sister Patricia. Frank had never been that crazy about Peter anyway. Peter was British, which he thought gave him special status, and he seemed to look down on the rest of us — especially me, whom he saw as some sort of New York gangster wannabe. Peter could also be rude. Sometimes Frank would be talking and Peter would interrupt him right in the middle of a sentence, and Frank would say, "What the fuck are you doing interrupting me? Shut the fuck up." Once Jack Kennedy severed his ties to Frank, Frank turned right around and cut Peter Lawford out of his life completely. It was as if Peter no longer existed.

After *40 Pounds of Trouble* wrapped, I got a call from director Richard Quine, asking me to do him a favor. Dick was making the movie *Paris — When It Sizzles,* starring William Holden and Audrey Hepburn, but Bill Holden had been drinking too much and had been forced to check into a rehab clinic partway through filming. Dick asked me if I would take a small part that they would write in for me, to reduce the amount of time that Bill had to be on screen. I agreed. I was happy to be working, but I was sad about Bill, because I admired him so much. It had been a stroke of genius for Billy Wilder to cast him in *Sunset Boulevard.* "No one else thought Bill could do it," Billy had told me, "but in that movie he proved himself." Billy had wanted a great performance of a guy going downhill, and he'd gotten it. Now Holden was going downhill in real life.

Paris — When It Sizzles didn't have much of a story, which turned out to be helpful when they had to write me in at the last minute. I did a good job, but having me in the movie didn't turn it around. After my part in the picture was finished, I flew to London, where I bought a Jaguar coupe and drove to Munich to see Christine, who was making a movie there. I checked into the Bayerischer Hof, a beautiful hotel where the cast was staying. I couldn't wait to see her.

Christine was shooting nights, and Munich was chilly. I would go to her film location, park my car, and keep it running so the heater stayed on. Whenever Christine got a break, she would come and sit with me in the car. After a couple days of this, other cast members who were friends of Christine's started joining us. On any given night we could have half a dozen people warming up in that car.

At the end of my fourth or fifth night of

visiting Christine at the set, I drove back to the hotel and left the car with the doorman. Before I went inside, he said, "Can I show you something, Herr Curtis?" He walked me around to the back of the car and pointed: someone had jammed rags into both exhaust pipes. I was lucky I hadn't died of carbon monoxide poisoning. I could see the headline: *Tony Curtis gassed by Germans.* I was sure somebody in the company had done it, perhaps because I was a Jew seeing a beautiful German actress.

Janet filed for divorce while I was away in Europe. I was making significantly more money than she was, so I gave her the house in Palm Springs and our house in LA. Things were bad enough between us; I didn't want any more trouble over money. Also, I had two little girls to support, and I wanted to be sure they didn't want for anything.

Janet remarried with remarkable speed, and in my ongoing desire to not make things worse between us, I agreed during the divorce settlement to pay one-third of all Janet's expenses, which included whatever her new husband, Bob Brandt, spent. So here I was, paying a third of the cost of Bob's toothpaste, Bob's shaving cream, and Bob's neckties. Could Janet have been seeing Bob behind my back? I never asked, and I didn't want to know, especially if it was true. It was hard enough seeing her new husband move into the house I had bought with *my* hard-earned money, to live with *my* daughters, even though Bob was a nice guy.

Almost overnight, I went from being the happiest man in Hollywood to being miserable. I was in love with Christine, but now I felt my other problems were overshadowing the joy in our relationship. I had enjoyed being one of the most popular actors in town, but now I was roundly despised for having dumped Janet, who was very well liked. It was a terrible time for me. Anyone who tells you there's no such thing as bad publicity has never lived life in the public eye when things take a turn for the worse. I suffered a lot as I kept asking myself, *How did I get in a mess like this?*

After the divorce, strict limits were placed on the amount of time that I was allowed to spend with Kelly and Jamie. If I wanted to take them to the beach, I had to ask permission. Sometimes I'd go over to the house and bring them little presents, but Janet or Bob or someone else would always be in the room, keeping one eye on the clock, and asking me to leave the moment the legally prescribed time had elapsed. The girls have blamed me for not spending as much time with them as they would have liked, but after a while the battle to see them just became too difficult.

To make things worse, Harold Hecht cheated me out of a big chunk of money from *Taras Bulba.* I was supposed to get a percentage of the profits, but after Harold's creative bookkeeping, I got nothing. Not a penny. The studio would send Harold money, and after he paid expenses on location, he would fly to Buenos Aires and deposit the rest of the money in private bank accounts. According to Harold, the money owed me was spent on production. He was the one keeping the books, so he could say he spent whatever he wanted on expenses, lowball the net figure, and pocket the difference. How was anyone at the studio going to know what the real expenses were?

Getting my share of that picture would have changed everything for me, because now I was completely broke. I was paying for Janet and the kids, in addition to supporting my mother, father, and brother, not to mention my aunt and uncle back in Hungary. Then I got a flicker of hope: I was offered five hundred thousand dollars to make a film called *Lady L* for MGM, but the project fell through. And boy, did I need that money. I had painted myself into a corner, and I needed to find a way out.

Through it all I did what Lew Wasserman had told me to do: I kept making movies. In 1963 I had made a film called *Captain Newman, M.D.,* about an Army psychiatrist played by Gregory Peck. My character was a neurotic orderly whose antics forced Captain Newman to pay attention to his patients. It was a great part. Angie Dickinson played a nurse assigned to the ward, and Bobby Darin played a shell-shocked airman. He gave one of the worst performances I ever saw, and to my astonishment he was nominated for an Academy Award for that picture. To this day I can't understand how that happened. Go figure that one out!

In 1963 I had also worked a little in a movie called *The List of Adrian Messenger.* A lot of big-name actors, including Burt Lancaster, Frank Sinatra, and Robert Mitchum, were signed along with me to play people suspected of being traitors during World War II. The idea was that the audience, having been presented with a number of possible culprits, all famous and all in heavy makeup to "disguise" them, had to try to guess whodunit. It was a clever gimmick. I played two bit parts: an Italian with an accordion, and an organ grinder with a monkey.

John Huston was the director, and he was a big worry to me. I knew he was incredibly talented, and because I'd never worked with him before, I just assumed he must have something against me. I figured he was probably saying to himself, *That Curtis is a New York bum.* I was so insecure sometimes. It turned out that I couldn't have been more wrong about Huston. When I met him, I could tell right away that he liked me. He was appreciative and kind, and he put me completely at ease. Being in his movie meant a lot to me, given Huston's extraordinary accomplishments.

On February 8, 1963, Christine and I were married in Las Vegas. Kirk Douglas was my best man. Kirk had made *Town Without Pity* with Christine, and he understood why I was so nuts about her. I was touched by how considerate and supportive Kirk was. Kirk's extraordinary wife, Anne, was maid of honor. Anne loved the fact that I was marrying a European girl because Anne herself had been a reporter for a French magazine, which was how she met Kirk.

I was thirty-seven when we married, and Christine, at eighteen, was too old for me. She was such a special person. No other woman in my life — certainly none of those

Hollywood girls, including Janet — had ever been so sweet and generous with me. I was madly in love with Christine. It was a wonderful, almost magical, experience.

Christine's mother was adamantly opposed to the wedding. She didn't like the idea of her daughter going with a Jew. She told me Christine was going to be a great star, that one day she would light up the sky in Germany, and I should stay away from her. But one day Christine's mother came to me and said she needed money; if I gave her ten thousand dollars, she told me, she would end her opposition to the marriage. I gave her the money and I said, "Stay out of my way." She did.

I was nervous about meeting Christine's father, because he'd been a German air force pilot during World War II, but he was nicer to me than her French mother was.

My wedding attracted a lot of press, and none of it was good. Most stories took the angle that Tony Curtis was abandoning his family to marry a teenager. It hurt, but there was nothing we could do about it. If a magazine wanted to interview you for a story and you turned them down, they were even nastier than they would be otherwise, so I just met with reporters and did the best I could. The studio decided that the best way to make the furor over our marriage go away was to put Christine and me in a movie together, so we signed on to act in a film called *Wild and Wonderful,* in which a poodle creates all sorts of marital problems for us.

Christine's mother was her agent, and at first she felt this film wasn't good enough for her daughter. I talked to Christine and shared my Hollywood philosophy: Make as many movies as you can. If a movie's a hit, great. If it isn't, so what? You get paid either way, and, more important, you never know whether a movie will be good or bad until after you've made it. After Lew Wasserman advised her to do the movie, Christine finally agreed.

Wild and Wonderful turned out to be a very amusing movie. Christine was terrific in it. There were moments in it when sparks flew between us, and we enjoyed the experience. In the movie, I was trying to romance her, but I was bedeviled by her dog, a French poodle that was constantly peeing on my leg. In the movie the dog hated me because he saw me as a rival for Christine's affections. This was uncomfortably close to real life, where, instead of a dog, it was her mother who wanted me to shove off. The dog stole the show, emerging as the real star of the picture. I liked that dog so much that when the movie was over, Christine and I got a dog just like him.

Wild and Wonderful turned out to be Christine's last movie for some time. I didn't know it at first, but I found out that Christine wanted to focus on being a wife and mother, and was willing to put her career on hold. When her mother found this out, she went crazy. But it was a good thing for my new marriage. And after she gave birth to two beautiful children, Alexandra and Allegra, Christine was more convinced than ever that she had made the right decision.

Once I married Christine, my life settled down. I had to start over financially, but I was making good money, and for the first time in a long while, I was happy.

With Susan Hampshire in Those Daring Young Men in Their Jaunty Jalopies, 1969.

16
Top of the World

Goodbye Charlie, the next movie I did for Twentieth Century Fox, starred Walter Matthau, Debbie Reynolds, and me. Like *Some Like It Hot,* it had a plot that revolved around ambiguous sexuality. Walter, a jealous husband, shoots a no-good philanderer who's messing around with his wife. The philanderer dies but returns to Earth in the body of a woman, played by Debbie. I play the philanderer's best friend, and after he "dies" I meet Debbie and fall in love with her — which means I'm really falling in love with my best friend. If you think this sounds like a perfect movie for a gay audience, you wouldn't be wrong. Happily, the picture was a big hit all across the board.

The director was Vincente Minnelli, who, even though he had been married to Judy Garland, was rumored to be gay. Big fucking deal. Who gave a shit? All I knew was that he was a refined, reserved man, and a great film director, with a broad knowledge of movies and filmmaking. What I remember most about the movie was the bickering between Vincente Minnelli and Ellen McRae, a Broadway actress just starting out in the movies, who later married and became Ellen Burstyn. The two of them were so regularly at each other's throats that I would come to work thinking, *Here we go again.* I felt like I was back home with my parents. I would always side with Vincente in his battles with Ellen, or with anyone else on the set. I liked him. Every once in a while someone would try to demean him by calling him a "faggot" (not to his face), and I'd make a point of not letting that pass.

Donna Michelle, the 1964 Playboy Playmate of the Year, was also in the film, and the other girls in the film responded to her presence in ways that were less than hospitable. In fact, they were downright cruel. They always seemed to find some way to step on her lines or do something to distract her at a crucial moment. Debbie Reynolds was their ringleader. For once I was lucky just to be the leading man. Pat Boone was my only competitor in the film, and Pat was just what he seemed like: a really nice, friendly guy.

One day I was on the phone with Joseph Heller, whose classic novel, *Catch-22,* had been a recent bestseller, and he said to me, "Hey, Tony. I'm going to write a movie treatment for *Sex and the Single Girl.* How would you like to star in that?" With my friend Dick Quine directing and Jack Warner of Warner Bros. hot to do it, I quickly said yes.

When I was a kid, I used to go see Errol Flynn and Olivia de Havilland in *The Adventures of Robin Hood* and all those other great movies Warner Bros. made in those days. Little did I know that one day I would be in a Warner Bros. picture myself. This was another one of those moments when I had to pinch myself. I had always told myself that my life would turn out like this, that it was supposed to happen this way, but I couldn't help but be surprised and delighted that it had. If you remember, Jack Warner and I had met and made a good connection on that very first plane trip I took to Hollywood. In those early years I would sometimes see him at parties, but we rarely connected. One time, though, when he was visiting Universal, he saw me in the commissary and called me over to his table.

Jack said, "Hi, Tony. Good to see you. Say, have you ever met your boss?"

"No, I haven't," I replied.

Jack turned to the man sitting next to him. "This is Bill Goetz," he said, "and he's your boss." Goetz and I smiled at each other and shook hands. Not only had I never met Goetz, I'd never even heard of him.

Sex and the Single Girl was based on a book written by Helen Gurley Brown, but the movie had nothing to do with the book. Joe Heller took the title and then wrote a story about a female publisher of a smutty magazine who happened to be a virgin. That character was played by Natalie Wood. In what I thought was an odd bit of casting, the studio hired Henry Fonda to play a Jewish clothing factory owner. Fonda was as far from being Jewish as a man could be, but I didn't say anything. His wife was played by Lauren Bacall, who was Jewish, although nobody knew that at the time.

I had known Natalie for ages. Janet and I often saw Natalie and her husband, Robert Wagner (known as R.J.), at all those Hollywood parties we went to. They remained happily married until she fell in love with her agent, Richard Gregson, and ran off with him. R.J.'s heart was broken. I saw him at a party one night not long after that, and it was obvious he hadn't eaten or slept properly. I felt so bad for him. I put my arm around R.J.'s shoulder and said, "Listen, things are going to get better. There are a lot of good-looking girls in this town. Don't worry about it." He kind of smiled. During that time he often stayed with friends, including me, rather than staying at home alone. That was one way we all took care of each other.

Natalie, meanwhile, had gone off to England with her agent lover, but she returned to make *Sex and the Single Girl.* She and I were costars, and it was sheer pleasure to be working with a friend who also happened to be an outstanding actress and a wonderful comedienne. I never had to worry about the leading lady giving me what I needed in our scenes together. When two actors are in sync, one throws the line, and the other one carries it. Forget the director; forget the way the script is written. Forget all of that. The relationship between the actors is what's most important to a movie's chemistry.

Around this time I realized it was time for me to find a new agent. The trouble was that when Lew Wasserman had stopped agenting to run Universal, he had left behind impossibly large shoes to fill. One day when I was visiting Christine in Germany, we went to see a movie, and a man sat down next to me. I looked over and was amazed to see that it was an agent from MCA.

"What are you doing here?" I asked, my surprise making me less than tactful.

"I called Christine's house and her parents said you were at the theater, so I came down here to find you. I'm here to see if you'd like to be my client."

I didn't answer, and although I took his business card, I never called him. I knew that particular agent's reputation, and he wasn't for me. A number of Lew's MCA colleagues — Arthur Parks, Jay Kanter, Jerry Gershwin — were available, but I decided to go outside the agency to pick the best-known Hollywood literary agent at the time, Irving Lazar. Irving, who went by the nickname "Swifty," took only four-star clients. He represented mostly writers; in fact, I was the only actor he handled. There was nobody like Lew, but Swifty was intelligent and wise, and I felt like I was in good hands.

After I did *Sex and the Single Girl* for Warner Bros., Jack Warner wanted me to be in another picture called *The Great Race.* He said he wouldn't make the picture unless I was in it. Blake Edwards was the director, and he wanted Robert Wagner to play my role, but Jack Warner had overruled him. Blake then suggested George Peppard or Burt Lancaster, but Jack kept saying no; he wanted me, and he wouldn't make the movie without me. It upset me that Blake didn't want me for the film. I figured it was some weird holdover from our tests of manhood during the making of *Operation Petticoat.* Or perhaps the assertive way I had sought Blake out and asked him for the part in *Breakfast at Tiffany's* had left him feeling uncomfortable. There was no way of knowing for sure without asking him, and I had no intention of doing that. The important thing was this: as long as Jack Warner wanted me in the picture, Blake was the one who was going to have to make the adjustments.

Irving Lazar went to see Jack to make my deal, knowing that Jack Lemmon and Blake Edwards had signed to do the film for a hundred thousand dollars each. Irving told Jack Warner, "Tony won't work for that. You have to do better." And Jack did, by twenty-five thousand. Then Irving said, "You can't give Tony a raise and not do the same for Blake and Jack Lemmon," and Jack Warner said, "You're right." So everybody got a nice raise, thanks to Irving.

If someone had done that for me, I'd have gone over to his house with roses, saying, "Thank you for what you've done for me." But I never heard a word from either Jack Lemmon or Blake. Times like this left me feeling alone, and perplexed. Was I way off base in my expectations, or was there some difference between Gentiles and Jews at work here that I didn't understand? Was this how blacks felt in a white world? There seemed to be a sense of entitlement that came naturally to Hollywood's ruling elite, but it never came naturally to me. No matter how well I did, I always felt like an outsider.

As it turned out, Irving Lazar not only got me a boost in salary, he also got me a piece of the film. After the movie came out, I got a small check every month. So far I've gotten more than two hundred thousand dollars in royalties from Warner Bros. for *The Great Race.* And I made sure to let Irving know how much I appreciated his efforts on my behalf!

Natalie Wood played the leading lady in the movie. She really didn't want to do it, but Natalie owed Warner Bros. a picture, and when her agent couldn't get her out of it, she really had no choice. By this time she had been nominated for three Oscars — for *Rebel Without a Cause, Splendor in the Grass,* and *Love with the Proper Stranger* — and had starred in two acclaimed musicals, *West Side Story* and *Gypsy.* Natalie was not part of Swifty's deal with Warner Bros., so I was surprised when her agent came to me and asked if I would give Natalie a percentage of what I was getting.

"I don't know why I would do that," I replied.

He said, "Because Natalie's in the movie."

I declined, thinking perhaps he could have come up with a more persuasive rationale. Truth is, I had never heard of asking an actor to give part of his or her salary to another actor. Natalie was a friend and an asset to the movie, but if she was having trouble getting properly paid for her work, that certainly had nothing to do with my financial picture.

In the movie Jack Lemmon played the bad guy, and I played the good guy, but we were more like Laurel and Hardy — and Blake Edwards loved Laurel and Hardy. It was the first time Jack and I had worked together since *Some Like It Hot,* and we picked up as though it had been yesterday. Jack and I understood each other's gifts so well that we were like one person. If I was in a scene with Jack, he knew I had his back, and I knew he had mine. Neither of us ever did anything to take the focus off each other on the screen, and we complemented each other beautifully.

Production of *The Great Race* was marred by constant tension between Jack Warner and Blake Edwards. (Are you beginning to get the idea that filmmaking can be a contentious business?) Early on, Jack even fired Blake, and the studio publicly announced that Jack was taking Blake off the project, but Natalie and I defended Blake. I didn't claim to understand the man, but I did appreciate his ability to get the best out of actors. We never heard a harsh word from him; he knew how to get us to give him what he wanted without ever demeaning us or acting abusive. All the actors and some of the crew felt the same way, so we approached Jack and told him we wouldn't work unless he reinstated Blake. Jack capitulated to our demands and reinstated Blake on the film, although I suspect Jack was going to do that anyway. After letting Blake twist in the wind a bit, Jack put him back on the picture. I think he was just trying to let Blake know that Jack Warner was still in charge.

Once we started filming *The Great Race,* something happened between Natalie and me that often happened with my female costars. Natalie warmed up toward me, and we began to feel a strong attraction for each other. In one scene she was lying on my lap on a couch, and at the end of the scene, Blake yelled, "Cut!" Then Natalie sat up, moved up close to me, and affectionately toyed with a lock of my hair, so I kissed her on the lips. With that, she put her hand behind my head and pulled me down close to her. We just nuzzled each other for a few moments, indifferent to the people around us, and I felt a deep, delicate warmth move through me. Up until then I had been trying very hard not to get goose bumps from Natalie Wood. So much for that.

Now I felt a strong desire to be with Natalie, just to be near her. Every time the camera would stop, I would go over to her and start talking nonstop. I'd ask her what she thought of the scene, what kinds of movies she wanted to make — just chitchat, anything to hear her voice. I felt exhilarated whenever she was around, just the way you feel when you're falling hard for somebody new.

At one point we were working on Stage 9, the big stage at Warner Bros. that included a giant lagoon for filming water scenes. Natalie and I were acting in a water sequence where we were both on an iceberg floating in the middle of the water. After the third day of shooting on the iceberg, we wrapped around five for a dinner break, and the assistant told us we'd start shooting again around seven that night.

My trailer was right next to Natalie's. It was going to be a long break, so there was no point staying in costume. I changed and went over to visit Natalie. I didn't know why. I didn't have an invitation. It just felt right.

I knocked on the door. Her hairdresser came to the door and said over her shoulder, "It's Tony." I heard Natalie mumble something, and the woman said to me, "Come on in." I stepped through the trailer door, and the hairdresser said, "I'll see you later," and Natalie said, "Great." The woman left.

After I sat down on the couch, Natalie walked across to the trailer door and locked it. She came back to where I was sitting, sat down next to me, and kissed me deeply. It was a kiss that spoke of longing, a kiss that perfectly expressed the feeling that had been exquisitely building between us for weeks as we worked together.

We both came up for air, and then she leaned forward and kissed me again. That was when I realized that she was naked under her robe. I tore off my jacket and shirt. I don't remember how I got my pants off, but I must have, because the next thing I knew we were making crazy love on the sofa of that trailer. For me it was a highlight not just of working on that picture but of my entire life. We didn't say anything, before, during, or after. Nor did we need to. It was perfect just the way it was. No explanations.

After we finished shooting on the Warner Bros. lot, we all went to Salzburg, Austria, to shoot on location there. Natalie had someone she was interested in join her in Salzburg, so although she and I worked beautifully together for the rest of the shoot, neither of us ever spoke of our moment in her trailer. We still took every opportunity to talk and spend time together between shots, and it was always sweet and gentle, but what was between us remained unspoken.

As things played out, the pace of our shooting schedule in Salzburg kept us from finding a time when we could be together again, and in truth that was fine with me. I was happily married to Christine, and our first child, Alexandra, had already been born. Once we were done shooting the picture, I went back to my life, and Natalie went back to hers, and we both knew that was best for both of us.

In the fall of 1965, George Pal, my director in *Houdini,* introduced me to several executives at Hanna-Barbera — the company that had created the cartoon *The Flintstones* — to explore the possibility of using my voice on the show. Was I interested in helping to create a new cartoon character named Stony Curtis? I said, "Let's do it." I loved the idea, plus *The Flintstones* was one of the most popular shows on television. Later, people asked me why I did it. I did it because I was invited to, and because it looked like it would be fun! And it was.

My next film, which I did for Paramount, was called *Boeing Boeing.* It was about a newspaperman who has three stewardesses living with him. Because of their busy schedules, the stewardesses don't know about each other. Jerry Lewis plays my roommate, and Thelma Ritter plays the housekeeper who screws up the scheduling and causes all hell to break loose when the girls find out about each other.

The film did very well, and I was very pleased with it. The only problem I had was that Jerry, being Jerry, was tirelessly moving from one crazy gag to the next. I remembered how this used to infuriate Dean Martin, and it was starting to get on my nerves too. We'd be standing around waiting for the lights to be readjusted for a scene, and Jerry would take his cigarette and drop the ashes on the shoulder of my suit. I had put together a really beautiful wardrobe in this picture, and I didn't want this schmuck setting me on fire. I'd brush the ashes off, and I'd seethe, but I wouldn't say anything.

When I was in a scene with Jerry, he'd take things and put them in my pocket as a joke. He was completely unrepentant when his gags ended up disrupting an entire scene. It was his way of showing off on the set, and he thought it was funny. The director, John Rich, wasn't much good at reining Jerry in, but you could hardly blame him for that. After all, this was Jerry Lewis we were talking about, so everyone, including John Rich, let Jerry be Jerry.

Working with Jerry was like working in a jungle: you never knew what was coming at you next. It was the total opposite of working with Jack Lemmon, for instance, who was so gracious and steady and generous. When I was making *Operation Petticoat* with Cary Grant, I would have nailed my shoes to the floor to make sure I was standing still when Cary was delivering his lines. I would have done anything to keep from distracting the camera. But Jerry couldn't help himself. He thought he was the greatest comedian who had ever worked in movies, and he made sure everyone knew it.

After I made *Boeing Boeing,* I was spending some time in New York with a friend of mine, Richard Feigen, a prominent art dealer. My childhood interest in art had only grown stronger over the years, although my movie career didn't allow much time to explore my desire to paint. One day Richard said to me, "Let's go see Joseph Cornell."

Cornell, a reclusive artist, had confided to Feigen that he would like to have been a movie star, and I had told Feigen I wanted to be an artist, so Richard figured the two of us had to meet. He took me out to Queens, where Cornell lived with his brother and mother, off Utopia Parkway.

Cornell's brother, Robert, had cerebral palsy. He was confined to a wheelchair and had difficulty speaking, but like Frank Sinatra he loved electric trains. After I met Robert, I would send him an engine or a boxcar here and there for his collection. Joseph Cornell made the most incredible wooden boxes for his brother. He'd take one of his mother's empty powder boxes and glue slivers of mirror to the outside in beautiful patterns. On the bottom of one box he stuck a couple of dozen pins, and on top of those pins he placed thimbles. He cut one hole in the side of the box and another in the top so light could get in. When you held the box up to your eye, you saw a thimble forest. The effect was surreal.

Meeting Cornell and seeing his boxes reminded me of some of the artistic impulses I'd had as a kid. I used to ask my dad for his empty cigar boxes and use them to store all kinds of crazy stuff — skate keys, chewing gum wrappers, stamps, marbles — whatever

I could think of. Whenever we moved, I made sure to take those boxes with me. Joseph Cornell's fascination with his mother's powder boxes reminded me of my father's cigar boxes, and I decided to start using them again.

Cornell was a loner, and in my heart of hearts so was I, so we got along very well. Like me, he also had a fascination with female beauty. Cornell had an extensive collection of still shots of movie actresses, some of which he placed inside his boxes. He was delighted to meet Christine, and he asked to shoot a whole series of photos of her. I suspected the photos might also provide him some sexual excitement, but I didn't question him about it. If that made him happy, so be it.

Things took a lucky bounce for me in 1966. The Keck family had discovered oil in the Los Angeles area, and their oil field lay right behind MGM's studio lot. The Keck family estate was a twelve-thousand-square-foot mansion, complete with eighteen rooms, an Olympic-size indoor swimming pool, a projection room, an elevator, and a massive wine cellar. There was even a secret room hidden behind a carved wooden panel in the den. The estate sat on four acres of land overlooking the Los Angeles Country Club. Originally, Joe Schenck, a cofounder of Twentieth Century Fox, had bought the house from the Kecks. When I was going out with Marilyn Monroe, this was the house where she stayed with Joe Schenck on weekends. It was for sale again, and the asking price was three hundred thousand dollars.

My attorney, Marvin Meyer, came to me with the news that the Keck house was available, and then he said, "I just found out that the government wants to encourage wealthy people to spend their money, so they'll let you buy property with prepaid interest." The prepaid interest was five percent. He said, "You can live in the house for five years for just the cost of the prepaid interest, and after five years you can either buy it or give it back to the seller." I paid the fifteen thousand dollars in interest, and Christine and I moved in. I thought I had died and gone to heaven. When my friends in LA saw it, they asked me, "When did you become a multimillionaire?"

I said modestly, "I just caught some lucky breaks." Christine loved the house as much as I did, and for the next few years we lived like royalty.

With Judy Garland, 1969.

17
Downward Spiral

I'm not sorry I married Christine, although that doesn't mean that in retrospect I think it was a good idea. The problem was that I married her for the wrong reason: her youth. I had never been seventeen in the ordinary way, and by the time I was twenty-two I was already immersed in a career. When I met Christine, it looked like I was being given a second chance to experience all those things I had missed out on. We went to the malt shop; we went to movies together and snuggled in the balcony; we went to the beach; we even went to rock concerts together.

Being married to me was good for Christine, too, because as Mrs. Tony Curtis she was granted access to anyplace she wanted to go. She'd go to an exclusive club, and they'd let her in as one of the beautiful people. We were having so much fun; I just wish it had lasted a little longer.

■ ■ ■ ■

In 1966 I appeared in a picture called *Not with My Wife, You Don't!* Made by Warner Bros., it starred George C. Scott, Italian film star Virna Lisi, and me. It was the story of two pals. I'm married to Virna, and while I'm stuck in the Army, George C. Scott begins wooing her. I thought the movie was badly cast, but that was out of my control. To my way of thinking, the roles should have been switched. I should have played the gigolo, but George was a very powerful actor, and they wanted him in that role. It worked out okay, but the picture wasn't as good as it could have been. Virna was a very good actress, though, and a beautiful woman, very aristocratic. I liked her a lot.

Over the years I had a powerful tendency to fall for my leading ladies, and usually I found some way to make my feelings known. If a woman seemed receptive, I might make an advance, and if I got a good response to that, I would keep pressing my case. There's no question about the fact that I was driven to conquer every woman I met. I liked to think of myself as quite a ladies' man, and I felt compelled to prove it.

Oddly enough, perhaps, sometimes I respected the women who didn't fall for me more than the ones who did. Virna Lisi was one of the former; she kept me at arm's length. She was married, I don't know how happily, but that didn't matter. She wasn't going to fall in love with me, or run away with me for a weekend. Not only did I admire her for that, but in this case it made it a lot easier to get the picture made. I didn't have to stay up until four in the morning waiting up for her. At the end of a day of shooting, I would go home, and she would do the same.

I didn't stray in my next picture either, but this time it wasn't so easy. The film was originally called *Arrivederci, Baby,* but after it was finished Paramount decided the title was too vague and too Italian, so they renamed it *Drop Dead Darling.* I took the job because of the excellent script by Ken Hughes. I played a cad who searched through fashion magazines looking for wealthy women to marry for their money. I had not one but four love interests in the movie: Zsa Zsa Gabor, Nancy Kwan, Anna Quayle, and an Italian actress named Rosanna Schiaffino. Although I wanted to chase them all, I limited myself to the romantic activity called for by the script.

Nancy Kwan was a sensitive beauty, with a wonderful, saucy smile, and we became great friends. I was attracted to her, but she was in a very involved relationship off the set, so nothing happened between us. Anna Quayle and I didn't really get along, so nothing happened there either. Then there was Zsa Zsa. When it came to some things, Zsa Zsa wasn't too sure what was going on, but when it came to men she knew exactly what she was doing. She knew exactly which guy she was going to bed, and how, and when. She was quite a bit older than I was, though, so I was lucky.

Rosanna Schiaffino had an impressive support system of family members, all of whom were dedicated to making her a star. Her husband was her manager, and her uncle ran the business. I had a great time with Rosanna. She had a wonderful sense of humor, and we laughed through the whole movie. Her sister came onto the set one day, and she seemed a little ill at ease, so I brought her some coffee, and we started to talk. I said, "I'm so happy to be here working with your sister. She's a wonderful girl."

Rosanna's sister said, "Do you like her?"

"Yes," I said.

"If you're sensitive enough, perhaps you two could become lovers."

"Do you think so?"

"Not a chance," she said. "If you have any

ideas about that, don't."

I laughed and said, "You know, it's not completely up to me."

"I know," she said. "It's up to my sister. And she has to be careful, so please be kind."

"What do you mean, 'kind'?"

"Don't go near her," she said.

The dialogue between Rosanna's sister and me was at least as good as the dialogue in the movie. She and I bantered all through the making of the movie. I'd be standing there with my arm around Rosanna's waist, like you do with a friend, and her sister would walk by us, and when she got out of Rosanna's line of sight, she'd make a face at me, as though to say, *Take your hands off my sister.*

At one point, Rosanna's sister said, "Go ahead and do it." I wasn't sure if she was serious.

She said, "Shall I help you?"

"How?" I asked.

"I'll tell you what makes Rosanna crazy: the back of her neck and her tummy."

"How am I going to get close enough to touch her in those places?"

"Get her alone in her dressing room, of course."

In the movie, Rosanna is the last of my conquests, and we end up in Naples, Italy.

The camera pans to a neighborhood where the laundry hangs outside the windows, and as the shot comes closer to a house, the audience can see that I'm inside it with Rosanna, and we have six children. I look out directly at the camera, and I say, "What are you looking at?" before I close the window.

The problem with the picture was that it was disjointed. The individual scenes were funny, but the production company couldn't figure out a way to link them all together. It was around this time that I began to feel the full impact of parting ways with Lew Wasserman. I missed Lew terribly. He had treated me so wonderfully. I really enjoyed his company, and when I feel that way about a person, I can be free and easy and have fun with them. And Lew had been busy doing great things for my career to boot. Did I want to make a submarine picture and have Cary Grant play in the movie? Lew arranged it. Did Burt Lancaster want me in *Trapeze*? Lew arranged it.

But once Lew left agenting to run Universal, I was on my own, figuratively and literally. Yes, I had hired Swifty Lazar to replace him, and Swifty certainly had his strong points, but he didn't have the clout Lew had, or Lew's experience in the world of film. In fact, Swifty turned out to be a terrible choice.

If you combined Swifty's shortcomings with the fact that a lot of influential Hollywood people were pissed off at me for divorcing Janet and marrying Christine, you'll understand why, in 1966, I started accepting movie roles I never would have taken otherwise. That's before you factor in the hefty alimony and child support I was paying to Janet. When my accountant told me I needed to make some money, I took whatever movies I could find.

The first of these was a picture called *Chamber of Horrors,* made by a small, independent studio. It was about a killer who strangles his victims. I don't remember much about it except that the studio's check cleared. My next film, *Don't Make Waves,* wasn't much better. It was a film version of the book *Muscle Beach* in which I played a professor, and I had two beautiful costars, Claudia Cardinale and Sharon Tate. The plot was utterly ridiculous, but I agreed to appear in the film because I got a percentage of the gross. When Martin Ransohoff of MGM asked me to recommend a director, I suggested Alexander Mackendrick, with whom I'd worked on *Sweet Smell of Success,* and when MGM decided to use

Sandy, they also gave me a producer's credit for bringing him on board.

As a result, Sandy had his first chance to direct in six years. I liked him because he was so good with his actors. Like a lot of actors, I needed constant reassurance that I was good at my job, and Sandy was great at that. While we were working together he would call me up and say, "Tony, I'm so happy you're working on this picture. You are the finest American actor I know." Sandy always managed to give me the sense that perhaps I was a better actor than I realized. It didn't take much for me to get down on myself, and he always helped to counteract that tendency.

I was sure that with Sandy directing, this would be an interesting, different kind of film. Marty Ransohoff was enough of an avant-garde producer to appreciate Sandy's style. My only reservation about Sandy was his famous perfectionism, and sure enough, once again we ran into problems with the schedule and the budget. Ransohoff complained that Sandy wasn't working fast enough, and Ransohoff also didn't like the way the picture was coming out. Here too Sandy was focusing on details no one else had even considered — details about the decor inside a car, the titles of books I was carrying, you name it.

Claudia Cardinale was gorgeous, but her boyfriend at the time was rumored to be an important politico, so Ransohoff delicately told us, "Hands off." Sharon Tate was living with Roman Polanski — whom she married in 1968 — and I was a good friend of Roman's. We would meet at parties, after which I would go over to their house and make myself comfortable there. A few years after we made *Don't Make Waves,* Sharon was brutally murdered by Charlie Manson and his "family." Roman had gone to London to shoot a movie, and while he was away, Manson's band of killers invaded his house and murdered Sharon and the baby she was carrying. It was a terrible tragedy.

By 1967, it was clear to me that I might be on somebody's shit list, or maybe on more than one list. I simply wasn't getting any good offers to make movies in Hollywood. Swifty said to me, "Go do pictures in Europe. Clint Eastwood did it when he made those spaghetti westerns. Those pictures will give you great exposure all over Europe, and you'll come away from the work more bankable than ever." So I went ahead and made *The Chastity Belt* in Italy with Monica Vitti. The plot was simple: a husband locks his wife in a chastity belt before he goes off to the Crusades. I played the husband. I made a lot of keys and gave them away to my friends.

I loved filming in Italy. I enjoyed hearing Italian spoken all around me, and in Europe people treated me with a lot more respect than they did in Hollywood. Monica Vitti, though, made things very difficult. She was being romanced by the cameraman, so she felt that gave her some entitlements. For one thing, she insisted that she not be filmed in profile, because she was convinced her ass was too big. For another, she almost always showed up late. She did everything a leading lady shouldn't do. Next to this woman, working with Marilyn was wine and roses.

I went to the line producer and said, "Don't take her shit. She's putting the production at risk. Somebody from Warner Brothers is going to come along and close down the movie because of all the delays and added costs, and we'll never get it released. We've all got too much invested in this, too much time and energy. If she keeps this up, why don't you just ease her out of the picture?" They took my advice. The director, Pasquale Campanile, began to cut her scenes.

As part of the deal for making that picture, I insisted I be paid by certified check. When

I arrived in Italy, they said they couldn't do that, so I said, "I'm leaving." I went to the hotel and started packing my luggage. The producer, Francesco Mazzei, followed me to my hotel room and begged me not to leave.

"How am I going to get paid?" I said.

"We'll pay you in cash," he said, and they did. They gave me the money in a suitcase. I locked it, took it down to the concierge, and said, "Here. Hold on to this for me." When the picture ended, I took the suitcase through customs, showed the customs agents my papers indicating what I was owed, and said, "This is my salary." As soon as I got to LA, I asked my accountant how much I owed the IRS on that money, and I paid it. One thing I had learned way back when Bob Goldstein had insisted I set aside money for my SAG dues was that I never wanted to get behind on payments for anything.

I did have a great thrill in 1967 when I found my face on the cover of the Beatles album *Sgt. Pepper's Lonely Hearts Club Band.* When I was in England making *Drop Dead Darling,* I had become friends with Peter Blake, the artist who designed the album cover. He had seen some of my own sketches, he liked them, and he encouraged me to paint. His enthusiasm meant a lot to me. For the *Sgt. Pepper's Lonely Hearts Club Band* album cover, Peter wanted lots of famous faces, so he used images of W. C. Fields, Karl Marx, Albert Einstein, and a whole slew of people, including me. Marilyn Monroe was on there too. It was particularly uplifting for me partly because I was feeling so downhearted, so upset that I wasn't getting the movies I wanted to make. I remember that Beatles cover as an emotional oasis during a tough period in my professional life.

I had an opportunity to meet Paul McCartney when I was filming *The Chastity Belt* in Italy. He was in Venice, and the Beatles were giving a concert one night in the big plaza in front of the Doge's Palace, so I went to see them after work. I came a little late, and while I was underneath the bleacher seats walking toward the stage, I could hear Paul saying, "We're dedicating tonight's concert to Tony Curtis." Paul was incredibly nice to me. As I said, I badly needed strokes from my fellow entertainers. I was feeling very alone and underappreciated, so I was especially grateful when someone whose work I so respected let me know he appreciated mine.

Around this time I began to wonder how

well I really knew my wife Christine. She had been very young when she married me, and it didn't take her long to start feeling out of place among my circle of friends, who were all twenty years older than she was. She became restless and wanted to go out with her younger friends.

Sometimes that worked out fine. After I came home from making *The Chastity Belt* in Italy, for instance, we went out to the clubs in LA, where at one point we met the Rolling Stones. I became great friends with Ron Wood, who was not only a great guitarist but a terrific painter. I loved talking to him about painting and about technique. I remember one party we went to with the Stones when I got up and started to dance with a chair that had ball bearings for feet, so I could spin it around and make some crazy moves. It knocked everyone out.

On other nights, when I wanted to stay home, Christine would go out anyway. This is how she met Dean Martin's son Rick. It wasn't long before everyone in town knew they were seeing each other — everyone except me. When I found out, I confronted Christine, and we had an ugly scene. I had to really work hard to control myself, because while we were shouting at each other I felt the most horrible, violent impulses. Every married man fears that his wife will cuckold him. Even when I had nothing to worry about, the thought of my wife fucking another guy could make me really upset. So when I found out that it was actually happening, I almost went crazy. And it certainly didn't help when I realized that everyone else already knew about it. What a nightmare!

After this particularly ugly argument, Christine decided she was going to fly back to Germany. She took our daughter Alexandra and flew the first leg of her trip, the flight to New York, but when she got there, she had second thoughts and came back home. I took her back, but I wasn't very happy, and I was exasperated at having to pay for the canceled airfare to Germany.

Soon afterward, I was contacted by Richard Fleischer, a director with a track record in a wide range of movies. He was interested in having me play Albert DeSalvo in *The Boston Strangler.* But he said he didn't want me playing DeSalvo looking the way I did; he wanted me to look more sinister. He said, "What can we do to make you look like Albert DeSalvo?" I knew exactly what to do. Knowing what DeSalvo looked like, I got some putty and worked it onto the bridge of my nose, so it looked broken. I mussed up my hair and put dark makeup around my eyes. Then, holding a camera at arm's length from my body, I took photos of myself as though I was being booked in a police station: profile and front-facing.

I sent the photos to Richard Fleischer, and he took them to Richard Zanuck, the producer, son of the legendary Darryl Zanuck. What Richard hadn't told me was that Zanuck didn't want me for the part. He had told Richard, "If he plays the role, as soon as Albert DeSalvo comes on screen, everyone's going to know he's Tony Curtis."

Richard put the photos on Zanuck's desk, and he said, "There's your Albert DeSalvo."

"You're right," Zanuck said. "Who is that?"

Richard said, "It's Tony Curtis. Give him the part." And Zanuck did. It was the one film I made in 1968, and it was a quality picture.

After I got the part, I went out and bought brown contact lenses to hide my blue eyes. I put on about fifteen pounds, and I used ankle weights to change the way I walked. I wore a pea coat, a stocking cap, jeans, and big, heavy boots. Up to that point I had mostly played the romantic love interest, but I knew there was no reason I couldn't play a psychopath. My lack of self-confidence was focused mainly on what other people thought about me; I always had a pretty good sense of what I could do when it came to acting.

The costar of *The Boston Strangler* was Henry Fonda, who played the DA trying to track me down. I knew Henry from the days when I was married to Janet. He was part of that Gentile group I mentioned earlier, but he'd always been friendly. When I had owned a home in London, I had let Henry and his wife live in it while he was making a picture, and when I went to New York to rehearse a play, he'd let Janet and me stay in his apartment. So we were pretty close, or so I thought. But I was forced to revise my opinion when we started making *The Boston Strangler.*

Henry Fonda was very cold to me, or so it seemed to me. I was working my ass off to give a performance, and never once did he say, "That was a good scene," or "Nice job," or even "You could have done better." He hardly talked to me at all. Maybe he treated me that way because he was intent on staying in character. Some actors like to work that way, but that certainly wasn't my style. I tried hard not to be offended by Henry's remoteness, but at times it was a real struggle.

We shot some scenes of *The Boston Stran-*

gler in LA, and during that time Christine and I were having terrible fights. Some nights I stayed on location because I couldn't bear to go home and face her. Apparently there were some nights when Christine didn't feel like staying home alone, so the following day I would hear that she'd been seen out somewhere with Rick. Once after I finished shooting, I went to a club where I was told Christine hung out, and there she was with two or three of her friends. She was surprised when I walked in, but she didn't act like it was a big deal. Rick wasn't there, but something about the scene made me fear I'd do something I'd regret, so I just left without a word. I still had a picture to finish.

I suppose my problems with Christine helped me in one sense, because I was able to take my rage and express it through the character of Albert DeSalvo. I felt Christine had violated my trust, which made me want to explode. Sure, I hadn't always been faithful to her, but I'd always been discreet. And I'd always figured that after I'd had a little fun I'd go home to the woman I loved most of all. In any event, while my rage may have helped my portrayal of Albert DeSalvo, it didn't make me much fun to work with. There were times when, after we finished shooting, someone would come up to me and say, "How's Christine?" I'd growl, "I don't fucking want to talk about it." The question was probably asked innocently, but I was incapable of hearing it that way.

I was so distraught that I started seeing my psychiatrist again. He was really good with me. One day he said, "Tell me about the parts of your life that you think are similar to Albert DeSalvo's."

I said, "I don't feel comfortable at home anymore, and every now and then I want to go out in my car and just drive around. When I do that, I'm not looking for women; I'm not looking for anything. I just need to be alone, which is a first for me. I've *never* wanted to be alone. I may have felt like a loner, but I always needed company."

He stayed with it. "Let's go deeper than that. What is it about being alone that is so terrifying to you?"

I'd tell him it took me back to my early childhood, and away we'd go.

For a couple weeks after I finished filming *The Boston Strangler,* I tried to carry on as though nothing was wrong. By this time Christine and I had had two daughters, Alexandra and Allegra, whom I loved deeply. There were also times when Kelly and Jamie Lee, my daughters from my marriage to

Janet, would come over and play, and that calmed me. But I was unable to control a deep sense that I had lost everything that mattered to me, that I had started two families but I was going to be left with nothing and no one. I knew my life would no longer be the same. I felt devastated.

Eventually Christine moved out of our big mansion, leaving me to suffer alone in that empty palace. Without my knowing it, Christine went to Juarez, Mexico, and got a divorce, which was foolish of her, at least financially. Had she sought a divorce in the United States she might have been eligible for half of my assets plus child support, but she didn't pursue it. I'm not sure why she made this decision, although perhaps her very public infidelity may have had something to do with her reluctance to fight for her share of my net worth. I just don't know. To this day Christine claims that she still loves me. I don't believe her. I'd like to, but I don't.

On the set of Casanova & Co., 1977, with Britt Ekland, Marisa Berenson, Jenny Arasse, and Sylva Koscina.

18
"What Time Is the Enema?"

While I was filming *The Boston Strangler,* I met the woman who would become my third wife. Her name was Leslie "Penny" Allen, and she was a friend of my friend Bob Friedman, a stockbroker in New York City. He'd been a fan of mine ever since my early years, and whenever Bob would see me, he'd shout at the top of his lungs, "TO-NY CUR-TIS! TO-NY CUR-TIS!" He'd arrange to meet me in public places just so he could yell when I arrived. Bob was a lovable gentleman and a great connoisseur of young women. I don't know how he managed it, but it seemed that whenever an incredibly beautiful new girl was hired by one of the top modeling agencies, someone would call Bob, who got himself assigned to show her around town.

Bob knew how despondent I was after the breakup of my marriage to Christine, and he said to me, "Don't worry about a thing,

Tony. I'll fix you up." That was how I met Penny Allen, who was twenty-three and working for the Ford Modeling Agency. I was absolutely bowled over by her beauty. I told her I was filming in Boston and asked her if she'd like to visit me there. Penny's mother lived in Boston, so she agreed to come and see me there, which would also give her a chance to visit her mother. Almost immediately, Penny and I became lovers.

I was a real mess because of my breakup with Christine, but I kept that hidden from Penny. A big part of me felt beat-up and numb, but another part of me was yearning to find a new relationship, any new relationship, and that was the part that won out. I focused all my charms on Penny and won her over. I felt she was special — so beautiful and so young — that I didn't want her ever to leave my side. Like Janet and Christine, Penny was the shiksa goddess of my dreams. Heaven knows, when I was a kid I couldn't have imagined even *talking* to a girl who looked like Penny Allen.

After I was done filming in Boston, Penny flew out to California to be with me. I was still living in the Keck estate, with its twelve thousand square feet of space and two safes in the basement, one for wine and one for gold. I started taking Penny on a grand tour of the house, and while we were walking together, I asked her to marry me.

She said, "If you have an elevator, I will marry you."

I took her by the hand and walked her across the dining room to a back hallway, where I pressed the button in the wall that summoned my elevator. The elevator came, and we got on it and rode up to the second floor, and by the time we got there she said yes. After a whirlwind romance, Penny and I were wed on April 20, 1968.

After our marriage, I flew off to Rome to film *Those Daring Young Men in Their Jaunty Jalopies,* a new take on *The Great Race.* Two great English comedians, Terry-Thomas and Dudley Moore, were in it. I was the star, and my love interest was Susan Hampshire, who was married to a French film producer. The thing I liked best about Susan was that she kept falling in love with everybody around her, even me. We became lovers, but just while we were working on the movie. I couldn't help myself — marriage or no marriage. It didn't mean anything, but for some reason I needed to do it. I guess at this point I wasn't sure of anything or anybody — least of all myself.

In my next movie, *Suppose They Gave a War and Nobody Came?,* once again I fell hard for my leading lady. Only this time I really thought I'd found true love, and *that* didn't happen often. In this movie I was playing opposite Suzanne Pleshette, who had been my costar in *40 Pounds of Trouble.* We had avoided an entanglement that first go-round, but this time there was no escaping it.

At the end of the first day of shooting, I said to her, "Will you be making breakfast?"

"What?" she said.

"Will you be making breakfast? You don't have to make the bed, but just a little breakfast when we get up would be nice."

She smiled and said, "You're so funny."

I said, "You'll notice I didn't mention the laundry."

She laughed, and from then on I teased her in that flirting way throughout the making of the picture. Somewhere in the middle of the film, she said to me, "Will we have separate checking accounts?"

"Of course we will," I said. "You get yourself whatever you want, I just don't want to know." Soon it became apparent that there were real feelings behind all the jesting. I liked Suzanne enormously, although I tried to hide my feelings from everyone but her. I was protecting her, and I was protecting my marriage. Eventually Suzanne and I started meeting in secret, just to talk. We knew that if we were seen together too often we'd start tongues wagging. The intrigue made our feelings for each other even more exciting, although we were careful to keep things platonic.

It made me happy to be around Suzanne. I loved to see a woman's behavior toward me change from politeness to real interest, from "How do you do?" to "Hello there!" It made me feel alive. I still get a jolt of vitality when a woman finds me attractive. I'm a little embarrassed to admit this, because I don't want people to think badly of me, but it's part of my makeup, and I can't pretend otherwise. Some people need alcohol. Some people need drugs. I need the attention of beautiful women.

One night Suzanne invited me to come by and see her place, and I did. She had planned a little dinner, and by the time I arrived she was wearing comfortable clothes, and so was I. Believe it or not, we didn't consummate the affair. I didn't want to, because I wasn't going to leave Penny, and I didn't want to do anything that might hurt Suzanne. I'd never felt this way before, and I explained that to her.

She took a moment to consider this, and then she said, "Is it true? Did you really have affairs with all those leading ladies?" I told her I had. She said, "Would you do me a favor? I'd like to be included in that group. Could you just tell everyone you had an affair with me?"

I said, "All right, dear. You're in." We chatted some more, and I went home.

That was Suzanne Pleshette.

I find it fascinating how people become attracted to each other. What causes those little sparks? Whenever I started flirting with a girl, I'd keep close touch with how it made me feel. Sparks flying was what mattered most. If I didn't feel sparks, then it was no go. If I did, then look out!

Suzanne and I remained good friends. Many years later, she called me and let me know she was getting married to Tom Poston, a good comedian and a wonderful guy who had starred in Bob Newhart's 1980s sitcom *Newhart.* I went to their wedding reception, and I was genuinely happy for her. She and Poston were perfect together. They both died recently, less than a year apart, which saddened me greatly, although I'm sure they're happy to be together, wherever they are.

The last movie I made for a while was for Columbia Pictures, and it was called *You*

Can't Win 'Em All. I went to Turkey to shoot it, and when I got there I discovered that the director, Peter Collinson, was a rabid anti-Semite. A friend of mine who happened to be Jewish came to see me on the set, and Collinson asked, "How come you Jews always stick together?" I told him to go fuck himself. Needless to say, this was not the best way to start off a working relationship. To make matters worse, the picture was terrible. Collinson understood the technical aspects of filmmaking, but he didn't have the necessary leadership skills to make a movie, so my costar, Charles Bronson, and I took over. Charley was a thoughtful, intelligent man, and he and I got along very well.

Turkey was an interesting country. A local Columbia Pictures employee recommended that I go to a Turkish bath in Istanbul, but when I went into the place and got undressed, I discovered a lot of guys standing around with erections. As calmly as I could, I delicately turned around, put my trousers back on, and got the hell out of there.

I was also directed to a massage parlor with rooms decorated in the Turkish style. The masseuses wore flouncy Turkish harem clothes with bloomers. One of the women must have seen my films, because she took me under her wing. She picked out a group of gorgeous girls for me to spend time with, and I found myself involved in some very exotic sexual play.

After this very pleasant break I went back to work. We were shooting a street scene, and I noticed that one of the bystanders watching us was a girl from the massage parlor. During a break in shooting, I went over and talked to her, and she invited me to go out with her. I thought I was going to a party, but instead I wound up at her parents' home. She came from a well-to-do family. She introduced me to her folks, and we had a lovely time; I never once let on where we had met.

When movie offers stopped coming in, Irving Lazar said to me, "I don't want you to stay out of sight for too long, so do some talk shows."

I said, "Will they want me?"

"They're all going to want you," he said. "So don't be shy about it."

Dan Rowan and Dick Martin had invited me to appear on *Laugh-In* five times over the past several years. I had always wanted to do sketches and stand-up comedy, and this was my opportunity. I was delighted with the results, and I was happy that they liked me too. Then Mike Douglas called, and I went out to Philadelphia to do his talk show.

Irving Lazar continued to do what he could to get me parts, but the offers had dried up. An agent I knew, Freddie Fields, who had a lot of action in Las Vegas, asked me to go there and work as an emcee for a couple of weeks. He had hired a bunch of variety acts, and my job would be to would introduce them; as part of the gig I would also perform some magic tricks. The audience loved it. When we got to the end of the run, the hotel people begged me to stay on longer, but I had had enough.

When I saw I wasn't being offered movie roles, I decided to become a producer. I tried to produce a film called *The Night They Raided Minsky's,* which was going to be about a burlesque house and the strippers who worked there. Each stripper thought she was going to end up being a star like Gypsy Rose Lee. I was going to play the lead. I thought the movie would be very funny, but we didn't end up with a suitable script, so I wound up not producing it. Norman Lear took the project on, and did a great job with it.

I didn't work in a single movie between 1971 and 1974. My star had fallen so far that I couldn't even get work on an American TV show. I did get a role on an English

TV show called *The Persuaders,* with English star Roger Moore. Roger had played Simon Templar on the TV show *The Saint* for six seasons, and later he would star in a string of James Bond movies. *The Persuaders* was about two millionaire playboys who roamed Europe fighting bad guys. It was similar to James Bond, but perhaps a little more realistic.

Before I flew to London to start shooting *The Persuaders,* I carelessly threw a little marijuana in one of my bags. By this time pot had become very hip in Hollywood, and everyone and his brother was smoking it. Marijuana was cheap, and it wasn't addictive. The worst feature of smoking pot was that you tended to eat a lot of munchies. That, and the possibility that it might accidentally find its way into your luggage. To make matters worse, for some reason I must have thought I might need protection across the pond, so I packed a .38 pistol in another bag.

When I got to England, customs inspectors went through my suitcases, and they found the marijuana and the gun. They confiscated them and allowed me to go on to my hotel, but a few hours later I received a summons to come to court the next morning at ten. When I arrived the next day, the British police kept me in a jail cell until my case was called. Everyone treated me very nicely, but I was beginning to get worried. When it was time for my case, the police officers led me up a spiral staircase, and at the top I found myself in the middle of a courtroom.

The judge, a woman, asked me to explain myself.

I said, "Well, ma'am, I don't drink alcohol, because of what it does to me. But marijuana seems to calm me down. And I honestly don't know why I brought the pistol. I just threw it in my bag without thinking. I had no intention of using it."

She let me off easy, with a fifty-pound fine, but the incident made all the papers in England and America. One headline read, TONY CURTIS BROKE AND BUSTED. I felt humiliated, but there was nothing I could do about it except give myself a pep talk. I said to myself, *Go ahead, world, do your worst. I've had it up, and I've had it down. Whatever happens, it won't be as bad as my childhood.*

Penny and I decided to buy a house in London on Chester Square while I was making *The Persuaders.* Lew Grade, who was financing the show, intervened with the bank to make it possible for us to buy the house. I later found out that Penny had tried to make a secret deal with Lew and the bank so that if she and I ever got divorced, she would get the house. I was furious, and my sense of trust was badly shaken.

Penny and I were walking down the streets of London one evening when a car pulled up beside us. A window rolled down, and there was Paul McCartney. Paul later told me he had idolized me because I had been the first movie star to wear my hair long, a real rebel. He said my look had inspired him to dress however he wanted to.

Paul yelled out the window, "We're going to a party. Want to come along?"

"Great," I said. We got into Paul's car, and he took us to a place that looked like some kind of futuristic auditorium, gleaming white and antiseptic. When we got there, we sat and listened to a speaker who went on about spaceships and the future. If this was what parties were like in the future, then send me back to the past! Well, maybe not. The Beatles were the future, and I certainly liked them. We always had a good time together.

Meanwhile, Penny was also making friends in London. One night she took me to a party at the home of a famous British musician — I can't remember his name — and she chased after this guy the whole time we were there. That really ate me up. My idyllic third marriage was starting to spring some leaks.

The interior shots for *The Persuaders* were shot in London, and the exteriors were shot in the south of France, so we could take advantage of the extraordinary beauty of the place. There's a river near Nice that runs right out into the sea. The estuary at that spot is half a mile wide, and producers liked to shoot adventure stories there because it looks like the sea but is much, much calmer.

When we traveled for location shoots, Penny usually stayed behind in London. Despite my own dalliances, I was devoted to her, and I thought it would be easier for her to stay home because my shooting schedule was always so hectic — two nights in one place, one night in another, three nights in another. Also, it made more sense for Penny to stay home now that she and I were spending a lot more time with my daughters from my marriage with Christine, Alexandra and Allegra.

I had unexpectedly won a reversal of the custody decision from my divorce with Christine, because I'd discovered that the kids really needed their father in their lives. In 1971 the girls had come to France and I had had a chance to see them for the first time since the divorce. I wanted them to eat healthier foods. They had been eating so much candy that it was a wonder they weren't toothless!

I went to attorney Marvin Mitchelson, a good friend of mine, and sought his help in gaining custody of the kids. And that is exactly what happened: I was awarded custody. Penny and the girls got along well, which made me feel great.

While we were working on *The Persuaders,* Roger Moore and I became the best of friends. We had a wonderful time together, shooting twenty-four fifty-minute shows in the first year. We worked with a variety of talented European film directors who couldn't find movie work, so we had good directors and all the best European leading ladies. One of those was Joan Collins, a British actress best known for later playing Alexis Carrington on the American TV soap opera *Dynasty.*

Joan's bizarre behavior made her rather difficult to work with. In one scene, we were supposed to drive a little truck a couple of hundred yards to where the camera had been set up; then I'd stop the truck and we'd both get out. When the time came to do the shot, the assistant director waved a flag, which was my signal to start driving, but Joan said, "Don't go yet. Please. I'm not ready. Let me get into the mood."

I leaned out and shouted, "She's not ready." Joan started fixing her makeup in the side-view mirror. I waited and waited. Every now and then I'd look over at her. She kept fiddling with her face. Finally I lost my temper. I said, "Joan, will you stop acting like a cunt? Let's go get this shot, and then we can break for lunch."

She said, "What did you say? You called me a cunt."

I said, "I'm sorry, Joan, but can we please go?"

The assistant director waved the flag, and I drove to my mark. When I stopped, Joan leaned out the window of the truck and screamed, "He called me a cunt!" She leaped out of the truck and said, "I'm going home!"

Going home? I thought. *You're lucky to be working.* She stalked off to her trailer.

The producer, Bob Baker, said to me, "Tony, you've got to do something about Joan."

"What do you want me to do?" I said. "I apologized in the truck."

Bob sent a runner to go buy some flowers, then he brought them to me and said, "Take these to her."

I went to Joan's trailer and knocked, and she opened the door. I said, "Here, Joan, these are for you. I'm really sorry I said what I did. I got nervous when we were doing the shot. Please forgive me."

"Well, that's all right," she said. "I forgive you."

She closed the door, and I whispered under my breath, "You cunt."

After the episode wrapped, I called Lew Grade and said, "Any more episodes with Joan Collins, and you'd better get somebody else to do them, because I won't work with her again."

During the two years I spent in Europe I met some very interesting people, including the artist Balthus, who lived in Rossinière, Switzerland. Balthus was thrilled to meet me because he loved the movies and enjoyed meeting actors, and I was thrilled to meet him because I loved art and wanted to meet artists. I bought one of his paintings, which, sadly, I was later forced to sell when I was strapped for cash.

After we finished shooting the first season of *The Persuaders,* it was summertime, so Penny and I decided to take a family vacation on the island of Sardinia, in the middle of the Mediterranean. By this time she had given birth to Nicholas, so we invited Alexandra, Allegra, Kelly, and Jamie to join us. It was a rare opportunity for me to have all my children together in one place. I loved Sardinia; the water was gorgeous. The only off note was Penny's mood; she seemed distant and unhappy. By the end of the summer, I felt we might all do better going back to the States.

The Persuaders was a huge hit, a very successful TV show in England, France, and Germany. On the nights *The Persuaders* aired in England, the streets literally emptied because everyone wanted to be home or in a local pub so they could watch the latest episode. It was the biggest television show in England.

The show's success couldn't alleviate the stress I felt. I now had five kids — with one more on the way! Penny and I were soon to be blessed with the arrival of a second son, Benjamin. But how was I going to support my growing family when I couldn't get a movie role? Looking back, I see that I was always so busy concentrating on my work that I never took the time required to be a good family man. I guess I wasn't wired to be a good father. Whenever I fell deeply in love with a girl, I knew that the only way to keep her loving me was to marry her; but once she gave in and married me, children became involved, and somehow I was never prepared for that. I guess I had a hard time sharing the affections of the woman I loved.

To make a buck and stay in show business, I agreed in October of 1973 to star in a play called *Turtlenecks,* which was renamed *One Night Stand.* Written by Bruce Jay Friedman and produced by David Merrick, it was bad by either title. The play opened in Detroit, and I had a lousy time of it. The director was incompetent, and the other male lead, William Devane, was a miserable guy to work with. The director sat next to Bruce Jay Friedman on opening night, and they laughed uproariously at the dialogue, but I knew better. The show closed in Philadelphia without ever making it to New York.

After that I made a couple of TV movies, including *The Third Girl from the Left* and *The Count of Monte Cristo.* I would have liked to star in a TV series of some kind, but I made good dough from those TV movies, which took maybe ten to fifteen days to film. I was also able to tell myself I was still making movies, even if they were for television. Lots of people saw them, which meant they knew I was alive and working, and that helped make it okay.

In 1974 I finally got a film. I was hired by two Israeli producers, Menahem Golan and Yoram Globus, to star in *Lepke.* The film was about Louis "Lepke" Buchalter, the Jewish American gangster who was the only mob boss ever to be executed for his crimes. In March of that year, while we were still filming *Lepke,* I got a call from Memorial Hospital in Culver City, California. My mother was in the hospital, suffering from heart failure.

I flew to California, but before I even made it into her hospital room, I could hear her voice from the hallway. She was yelling, "Tony! Tony!" I stood outside her room, filled with rage as I remembered all the things she'd done to me during my childhood, all the cruelty I'd never confronted her with.

A nurse walked out of my mother's room into the hallway and saw me standing there with my hands in my pockets. She said, "Are you Tony?" I nodded. She said, "Well, what are you waiting for? Go on in and see her. She's been calling for you."

I shook my head and said, "You don't understand." That was all I could manage.

The nurse said, "You're her son."

I said, "You don't know what she put me through."

I tried to force myself to walk into that hospital room, I really did. But I'm ashamed to say I just couldn't do it. I walked out, and never went back.

My mother died about a week later. I didn't know how to feel about that. All my life I had resented the way she had treated me, but now that she was dead, I wondered if maybe I had been too hard on her. My guilt lasted until I opened her safe-deposit box and read her will. She had ten thousand dollars in cash, and her will stipulated that the entire sum go to my brother Robert, in the mental hospital. I had told her earlier that if she left anything to him, the state would just take it, but she left him that money anyway. She did it deliberately. She knew how to stick it to me, even in death.

After my mother died, I hoped that her death might finally free me of the bitterness I felt toward her. Our relationship had been so ugly for so long. I had felt no warmth or kindness from her since I was a very small child, when she used to sing to me in Hungarian. I remember her beautiful voice and how it made me feel when she sang to me. But those memories would give way to my recollection of years and years of terrible loneliness as I came to understand that I was never going to find in this woman the love that I needed so badly. The beauty of those early moments faded quickly, but the anger and bitterness lingered for a lifetime.

■ ■ ■ ■

I enjoyed making *Lepke,* and the movie did well, but I could see that my career was in serious trouble. For one thing, I wasn't properly connected to the film industry anymore. Nobody wanted to take a chance on me, whereas in my salad days if you put me in a movie, it was money in the bank. I really didn't know whom to talk to about this. Lew Wasserman was no longer by my side, and Irving Lazar was no help. I could have talked to someone at William Morris about it, but I wasn't sure William Morris would have done better for me anyway.

My stomach was in knots all the time. There I was, growing into middle age, and nobody cared. I would read in *Variety* about upcoming pictures that seemed like they might have parts for me, and a couple of times I even swallowed my pride and called producers to ask them, "You got a role for me?" But that never works. Being your own agent is like being your own lawyer: you have a fool for a client.

Fortunately I had a little money from several real estate ventures. On the advice of my attorney, I had bought two hundred and fifty acres of land in Perris Valley, California, that I leased out to vegetable farmers. I had tied up a big chunk of that land with a thousand dollars of prepaid interest. As I started paying off the principal, the land became more and more valuable. After a while I was able to sell ten acres for a hundred thousand dollars. Then, as the California land boom hit, I sold another piece, and another, until I was making more money from real estate than I was from the movies.

After *Lepke* in 1974, I didn't make another movie for almost two years. Then Elia Kazan asked me to play Rodriguez in the movie *The Last Tycoon.* Robert De Niro played studio boss Monroe Stahr in a cast filled with wonderful actors. When Elia called me, it brought tears to my eyes, because at that point I really thought my career was over. The character I played was a guy who couldn't have sex with his wife anymore. He had been a great actor, and all the fans loved him and wanted to see him, but when he got home with his wife, he just couldn't get it up.

In the film I take my problem to De Niro's character and say, "What am I going to do?" The purpose of the scene was to show how the head of a studio has to know everything about everybody. The part of my wife was played by Jeanne Moreau, the famously sensual French actress known for movies like

The 400 Blows and *Jules and Jim.* I was overjoyed to find myself with an outstanding part in a very powerful film. Elia, who was a fantastic director, even let me direct one of my scenes, which made me as happy as I could be.

Some people in Hollywood were angry at Elia because he had named names before the House Committee on Un-American Activities during the Red Scare of the early 1950s, but no one in the cast cared. That wasn't any of our business, and it had happened a long time ago. For me, I understood only too well how tough it could be to get hired when the tide had turned against you; the pressure was unbelievable.

One thing I remember about *The Last Tycoon* was how great I looked in it and how much some of the older actors like Ray Milland and Robert Mitchum hated me because of that. My character had a great wardrobe, and I had dark hair with sexy sideburns, and it just killed those two to see me like that. Ray Milland in particular was a total prick. He'd be talking with another actor, and I'd walk over to them, and he'd mutter, "Forget it," and walk away. His coldness was very unpleasant, but there was nothing I could do about it, so I shrugged it off.

Ray Milland was best known for playing a

falling-down drunk in the famous *Lost Weekend.* He was part of the WASP old guard, and I always felt he might be an anti-Semite. One time I overheard him and his group discussing the usurpers who were trying to get into Hollywood. He wasn't talking about me, but he mentioned a producer's wife who was Jewish. I knew he was one of the people who subscribed to the theory that I had married Janet Leigh as a career move. Milland was poison, so I just stayed away from him as much as possible.

The success of *The Last Tycoon* encouraged me. I thought my performance was good, and the picture did well, so I hoped I might get some more high-quality work. But it wasn't to be. I did earn a little money, but my next three pictures were all made by second-rate independent producers. The first one was a German production titled *Casanova & Co.,* and it was also known as *Some Like It Cool.* Once again I had to wear a dress, this time to escape from prison. The producers were trying to riff on *Some Like It Hot,* but the plot was stupid and forced. The director, Franz Antel, was way out of his league. When I got to Venice to start shooting, there was no script, but they had set aside three hundred thousand dollars to pay me, so I went ahead and did what I could. My female costars were Britt Ekland, Marisa Berenson, and Marisa Mell. They were interchangeable Hollywood starlets in a shitty film. And they were my costars, so what did that say about me? It was depressing.

My next film was *The Manitou,* a horror thriller that still shows up periodically on late-night TV. Stella Stevens was in it, as was Susan Strasberg, Paula's daughter. I never talked to Susan about her mother. The movie, which was filmed in LA, was cheaply made and needed a lot more money than it got for its special effects. It's one of those movies where you ask yourself, *What is Tony Curtis doing in* that *movie?*

I then had a very strange experience starring in a movie called *Sextette,* based on a play written by eighty-five-year-old Mae West. I agreed to do it because they paid me a hundred and fifty grand for six weeks' work. It was the last movie Mae ever made. Mae had starred in vaudeville and on the stage before beginning her film career in 1932, when she was almost forty. She gave Cary Grant his big break by insisting he play her leading man in *She Done Him Wrong* and *I'm No Angel.* Those movies were so successful that they saved Paramount Pictures from bankruptcy.

In *Sextette* I played Mae's forty-year-old Russian lover. This is the film where she utters her famous line to George Hamilton: "Is that a gun in your pocket, or are you just glad to see me?" But she had another line I liked even better. When my character sees her in her bedroom, I say to her, "Remember the songs I used to sing to you in my native tongue on the Volga, many years ago?"

She looks at me and says, "I don't remember the songs you used to sing to me, but I remember your native tongue."

Mae was tough to work with because she could be completely oblivious to a line or a cue, and she wasn't too good with names either. One day she and George Hamilton were working with the director to block a scene, and the director said to her, "You're going to come out first and go to the window, Mae, and then George is going to come in center stage."

Mae looked at the director and said, "Who's George?" She didn't have Alzheimer's or dementia; she was just so narcissistic that she had forgotten his name. The only person in the movie who mattered to her was Mae West.

Mae was pretty bad about taking direction, too. The propman would lie on the floor, out of sight of the camera, grab her ankles and turn them so she would know which way to turn, left or right. As I said, Mae didn't know her lines, so the director sat in a closed booth just outside the scene and read her lines into a microphone that transmitted his voice over a shortwave radio signal. Mae had an earpiece that would broadcast the director's voice into her ear, and she simply repeated the lines as she heard them. The director would smoke while he was in there reading her lines to her, until the booth would become so full of smoke you couldn't see him anymore. When he coughed, so did she. I would stand there, watching this, thinking, *This is crazy.*

One time I was doing a scene with Mae, and we had the setup with the booth and the microphone going. The director said, "Action," and I gave my line, and Mae replied, "Altercation on Melrose and Sunset. Approach with caution."

The director yelled, "Cut!" Everyone looked at each other; those words weren't in the script. The director asked her what she was talking about, and she said something like, "Units are en route." Then we realized that Mae's earpiece had been intercepting signals from a police shortwave radio. I couldn't help myself. I averted my face and walked off stage, hoping no one could see that I was laughing hysterically.

My biggest problem with Mae was that she was as bad as Marilyn in terms of showing up on time. I'd arrive at eight in the morning in order to be ready at nine. Mae, who had the same start time I did, wouldn't come onto the set until eleven or eleven thirty. After a week or two of this, I went to the assistant director and said, "Why are you calling me two hours before Mae shows up?"

"Because I never know when she's going to get here," he said.

I said, "How far away does she live?"

"About forty-five minutes."

"What does she do when she gets here?"

He said, "She comes in and takes some time to put on her makeup. That's a forty-five-minute ordeal. Then they fit her with hair. That's thirty minutes. Then wardrobe: forty minutes. The last thing is her enema, and then she's ready for work."

I said, "What time is the enema?"

"The enema comes after everything else is done. She doesn't wear panties, and after she has her enema, she's ready for work."

"How long does the enema take?"

"About fifteen minutes."

I said, "Call me fifteen minutes before she takes her enema."

The next day I waited most of the morning

at home, until the assistant director called.

"Enema time," he said.

I leaped into my Rolls-Royce convertible, tore down the streets of Hollywood to Goldwyn Studios, parked my car, rushed in, had my makeup put on, and hit the stage ready to work just as Mae emerged from the bathroom, her enema finished. Once I'd mastered the intricacies of this schedule, I had no complaints.

When I signed on to this film, I had certainly heard about Mae's legendary sexual appetites. I didn't want her even looking at me, but she had brought her bodybuilder boyfriend with her, so I relaxed. As I got to know her I realized she was actually a sweet, caring, very nice person — a little self-absorbed perhaps, but that hardly made her stand out in Hollywood.

Another reason I had agreed to be in *Sextette* was that Cary Grant had made movies with Mae West, and if she was good enough for Cary, she was good enough for me. But the truth is that I was feeling sorry for myself. Marlon Brando was still getting good parts, so why was Hollywood pissing on me? But I took comfort in being a consummate professional: even in these B movies, I gave each scene all I had. Never once did I go into a movie thinking, *This thing is going to be shit, so I'm not going to prepare for it.* I couldn't do that. I even busted my tail for *The Manitou.*

My professionalism was sorely tested, though, by schlock films and sequels like *The Bad News Bears Go to Japan,* which was the third in the series started by Walter Matthau and Tatum O'Neal. By the time we got to this movie, however, we were working on a pale rehash at best. Walter got about eight hundred grand for the first one; I got about a hundred and fifty for mine. But to my astonishment I ended up loving the experience of making this film. I enjoyed working with the cast, and one of my favorite scenes in the movie took place when my character stepped in the ring with this massive Japanese sumo wrestler. This guy was throwing me all over the place, and my boys didn't want to see this guy beating me up so badly, so they jumped into the ring and stopped him. It was a lot of fun, and the movie actually did very well.

In 1978 I made *It Rained All Night the Day I Left* in Israel, with Lou Gossett. I flew from LA to Washington, D.C., where I boarded an El Al plane. I was strapping into my seat in the upstairs section of the 747 when the pilot made an announcement: "We're going to hold the plane half an hour because the prime minister, Menachem Begin, will be flying with us." He, Anwar Sadat, and President Jimmy Carter had just finished their historic peace meeting at Camp David.

I was standing in the entry hall of the plane when Moshe Dayan, the Israeli general and foreign minister, walked in. I introduced myself, as did he, and I was impressed by the easy warmth of his personality. Later Menachem Begin came into our section of the plane and motioned for me to come back and visit with him and his wife. The next morning we had breakfast together, and when the plane landed, I met Shimon Peres, the former defense minister. This was all very heady stuff for a Jewish kid from New York!

When we started making *It Rained All Night the Day I Left,* I said to myself — as I did before every movie — *I'm going to make this a great movie.* We almost made it a good movie, but our director, Nicolas Gessner, was not up to the job. He didn't like me, which I could live with, but he also kept questioning what I was doing, which didn't work at all. Finally, right in front of Gessner I said to Lou Gossett, "Let's not pay any attention to him, so we can go ahead and get this picture made." Gessner laughed, but I was serious. He was a *putz.*

Things got worse. Gessner would say to the cast, "Tony seems to know it all, so why don't you tell us what to do, Tony?" So I would tell him.

One time he said, "I want a close-up on Tony. Put a twenty-meter lens on the camera."

I said, "You're not going to get a close-up with a twenty-meter lens. You'll need a fifty-meter lens. After that, put in a wide-angle, and *then* shoot the master. You'll be able to fit one of the close-ups into the master. Don't do it the other way around."

He harrumphed and said, "I know that." Maybe he did, but I couldn't figure out why he'd want to keep that knowledge to himself. I knew from past experience that I was no director, but I was a genius compared with this guy.

It Rained All Night the Day I Left was a terrible movie, but I loved Israel, and the Israelis loved me. During the shoot I lived in Tel Aviv, and on days when I didn't have to work, a tour guide would come by in the morning and take me all around the country, which, of course, is tiny. The El Al pilots let me sit with them during takeoffs and landings, and we would talk about my films. I even stayed for a few nights with an Israeli pilot whom I befriended while we were on location.

He and his family lived in an unassuming house, and he said to me, “Why don’t you move to Israel, take Israeli citizenship, and live here? The movies aren’t going to last forever.” He was very practical, and it made a lot of sense. I was on the verge of doing it, partly because it would allow me to be as far away from Penny as possible. Sadly, the leaks in our marriage that I had seen earlier had only grown larger with time. But after I really thought about it, I realized that living in Israel was a pipe dream. I still had a career of sorts, and as long as that was the case, I needed to stay in LA.

When I came home, my children Nicholas and Benjamin were waiting for me with their mother. I was tanned and relaxed, and the boys were thrilled to see me. But something told me that my marriage to Penny was over. I could tell just by her attitude. She was young and beautiful, so she inevitably attracted a lot of attention from hip, young men in Hollywood. I wasn’t around too often, and the combination was poison to our marriage.

As I had seen earlier, Penny had a tendency to go with the best thing that came along, and at some point she decided that I was no longer the best thing. I told myself that had I been making better movies, I might have had a chance, but that was just another way to put the focus back on my work. Once Penny began making the night-club scene, our relationship went downhill fast. She began seeing other guys, and marriage number three bit the dust. In retrospect, she was too young, and I was too messed up, and we both would have been better off if we hadn't gotten married. But that's hindsight talking.

My life had become exhausting and empty. I was well into my fifties, the 1980s were just around the corner, and I had no idea what to do with myself.

On the set of The Users, 1978, a TV movie starring Jaclyn Smith and John Forsythe.

19
Cocaine

Soon after I came home from Israel, Penny brought up the subject of divorce, just as I had feared. For the third time I was in a marriage going down the drain. I was a mess, but I didn't stop making movies. I felt like it was the only thing I really knew how to do.

In 1978 I acted in a film called *Title Shot,* about a mobster who tries to fix a fight. Les Rose directed it. It was a good payday, as was *Little Miss Marker,* one of two pictures I did shortly thereafter for Universal. Walter Matthau played a bookie, and I was cast as the heavy, Blackie. Julie Andrews played the girlfriend. I had fun doing it because Walter and I were together again. I loved that guy.

My next movie, *The Mirror Crack'd,* was based on an Agatha Christie novel about a group of actors who come to an English home to make a film. While they're there, somebody gets murdered. The cast included Rock Hudson, Elizabeth Taylor, Kim Novak, and Angela Lansbury, who played Miss Marple, the detective. I loved doing the movie with Elizabeth. She and I had a wonderful connection, which involved lots of good times but never crossed the line from friendship to romance. Kim Novak was sweet and very perceptive. She lived in northern California, outside San Francisco. Rumor had it that she was a lesbian, but we never talked about it, and I found her professional and easy to work with.

I hit another low point in my acting career in 1980, when Neil Simon and Herb Ross hired me to perform in a play called *I Oughta Be in Pictures.* I first met Ross at a restaurant. I was having dinner alone when he invited me over to his table and told me he was going to direct a play. Would I consider being in it? He was pleasant enough. I liked the title of the play, and when he told me what it was about — a down-on-his-luck guy who was a writer in the movies — I said I'd do it. I was already leaning in that direction because I had a good relationship with Neil Simon, who wrote the play.

I signed on for a good salary and a percentage, but when we started rehearsals, Ross turned out to be the most disagreeable man I had ever met. He was very dictatorial, with a mean streak that he loosed on everyone in the cast. I was a favorite lightning rod for Ross's nastiness because he and I disagreed about how I should play my character. He'd tell me what he wanted, and I'd listen and nod, and then I'd turn around and play the part the way I thought it ought to be played. I knew what I was doing. I wanted the character to have the energy and drive that only comes from a New York background. I knew what this guy was like. He was like me: angry, aggressive, and fighting to get out of the mess he was in.

Meanwhile, Neil Simon was rewriting lines like crazy. If the problem with the play was the way I was portraying my character, then why was Neil spending so much time rewriting the script? The material obviously wasn't working, and it wasn't my fault. But try telling Ross that. He took being abusive to a new level. In rehearsal, he'd turn to me and say, "Don't you know how to do this? After all those years in the movies, you'd think you'd know how to make an exit."

At the end of rehearsal, I'd go out to the parking lot and get into my car, but I didn't want to go home because things with Penny had hit rock bottom. I had no place else to go, so I drove to a downtown parking garage and slept in my Trans Am, which is no easy thing to do. Where were my friends? I didn't know. At the time I was so depressed that it didn't seem like I had any friends at all. I was living life in the lower depths. It was terrible. I told myself there was light at the end of the tunnel, but I honestly didn't think I was going to make it.

We opened in Los Angeles, and despite constant rewrites that forced me to keep re-learning my lines, I could tell from the audience's reaction that I had done a terrific job. The next stop for the play after our run in LA was Broadway, and I was looking forward to that. Then one evening the prop-man, who was a friend, called me over. He said, "I overheard Herb Ross talking with Neil backstage, and Herb said, 'We'll get rid of him,' and Neil said, 'Who will we get?' and Herb said, 'Maybe Walter Matthau.'" Well, there was no one else in the play whom Walter could have replaced except me.

"You know this for a fact?" I said.

"That's what I heard him say."

At that very moment I was taking a break, halfway through the evening performance. I thought for a moment. I was being double-teamed. Neil wanted me out because I had negotiated a percentage, and Ross, the fucker, wanted me out because he had no control over me. I might have handled this news with more resilience if my marriage hadn't been disintegrating and if I wasn't sleeping fitfully in my car every night. But I just didn't have much bounce at the time. Between the rewrites, the abuse, and the rejections, I had finally had had it.

When my cue came, I went out onto the stage and played a scene where my girlfriend and I are nasty to each other. My part ended with a tirade, which closed with the line "You're a mean kid, and I don't know why." I ad-libbed an additional "Fuck you," and then I walked off the stage before I was supposed to, and out of the play. I went up to my dressing room, picked up my little bag, and walked out to my car. I got in, fired it up, and drove off. Ding dong, the witch is dead.

Boy, did I feel good. Fuck 'em. There was no way I would work under those conditions, for them or anyone else. I was told later that my performance that night had been excellent. When the play opened on Broadway, Ron Leibman was playing my role, and Walter Matthau played it in the movie. I'm certainly biased, but I felt both variations lost something in translation.

One afternoon I checked my mail and found a letter to Penny from City National Bank. Curious, I opened the envelope. Inside was a check for one hundred thousand dollars, made out to her, taken out of *my* account. Our divorce negotiations were still under way at that point, but we certainly hadn't agreed to anything like this. She was being underhanded, pure and simple, and I had caught her. I called my lawyer and asked him to call the bank and stop the check. We stopped the divorce negotiations, and instead I simply dictated terms that Penny was obliged to accept. She wound up getting a lot less out of me than she otherwise might have. After the divorce was final, Penny moved to Cape Cod. The settlement gave her all the furniture in our home, so she opened an antique shop and put all our furniture in the shop as merchandise.

To get away from my mess with Penny, I spent three full months in 1980 with Hugh Hefner at his mansion. Hef was a steadying influence for me, the kind of guy I could tell anything to and he would understand. I was so vulnerable in those days that I fell for every girl I met at the mansion. There was hardly anyone around to take them out, and Hef didn't want them floating around the city unescorted, so I always had a girl on my arm.

But there were boundaries, even at the Playboy Mansion. Romances were to be conducted on the grounds, not taken to a hotel room or to someone's home. The idea was to have a place where you could have some wholesome fun, a place that wasn't sleazy. Life at the mansion felt like being on a luxurious college campus. Guests enjoyed private talks in the garden or watched movies in Hef's screening room. The girls were happy to spend time with me, and I behaved properly. I enjoyed their friendship, and where appropriate, I enjoyed romancing them. The pleasure of spending time with these beautiful girls and having them find me attractive calmed me and made me feel good. That was far more important to me than the sex.

During that time I got to know Dorothy Stratten, a really sweet, beautiful girl. I also met her husband, Paul Snider, whom I disliked immediately. There was something untrustworthy and disturbing about him. He was a tight-lipped man whose eyes darted around the room, but if someone came over to talk to him, he would instantly change into an affable, friendly fellow. Anytime Dorothy was talking to another man, though, he'd suddenly materialize, jealous as he could be. He never let her out of his sight.

Hef was ill at ease with Snider. Everyone could see that Dorothy was much too good for him. When the director Peter Bogdanovich met her, he was smitten, and they fell in love. But when Dorothy told Snider she wanted a divorce, he murdered her and killed himself. It was a terrible tragedy that no one could have predicted, although it was obvious to us all that Paul Snider was trouble waiting to happen.

When I wasn't falling in love with one of the girls at the Playboy Mansion, I lived pretty much like a hermit. I spent most of my time in my room at the mansion, and occasionally I'd go down to a party or watch a movie. As the evening went on, if I didn't feel like socializing anymore, I'd go back up to my room.

After Penny moved out and took our sons, Benjamin and Nicholas, with her, I left the mansion and went back to live alone in our condo. There I was, living in luxury, miserable, waiting for jobs that weren't coming in. Many of my contemporaries had already prepared themselves for the day when they would no longer be called on to act. They had begun writing, directing, or producing.

Lew Wasserman had tried to encourage me along those lines, but I wasn't interested. As far as I was concerned, directing a film didn't have much appeal. For one thing, I didn't think I was very good at it, and for another, it seemed a little like cheating or playing it safe. A director didn't have to come up with the emotions that allowed an actor entry into a character's inner workings. A director didn't have to find a way to interact with another actor as if their characters were real people. To me, being in front of the camera was where the creativity in filmmaking lay, and that was all I was interested in. Unfortunately, at the moment that meant I wasn't doing anything at all. When I first hit Hollywood, I had really made a splash. Now the phone was silent. It was as if I had died, only someone forgot to tell me about it.

It was during this time — the early 1980s — that I began dabbling with what had become a very fashionable drug in Hollywood and other major cities around the country: cocaine. When the cocaine craze hit, no one knew how addictive it could be. Everyone knew about the dangers of heroin, but people thought coke was something you could try when you felt like it and stop using whenever you wanted to. I'm sure that dealers encouraged that misconception.

I was introduced to cocaine during the making of *Lepke.* We were working long, grueling hours, and I was getting tired. Then one day a woman in wardrobe said to me,

"Here, try some of this." She took a small paper packet out of her pocket, opened it up, and shook some white powder out of it onto a mirror. She handed me a little straw and told me to sniff some powder up each nostril. Almost immediately, I felt comforted by a new sense of confidence, and I noticed that even though it was well past midnight, I was full of energy. I took another hit, kept the paper packet, and worked until four in the morning. The next day I paid the woman for more. It was the start of my descent into hell.

Before long, the cocaine epidemic wrecked Hollywood. Actors became so addicted that they demanded coke in their contracts. A friend of mine at Paramount told me a story about Dodi Al-Fayed, one of the producers of *Chariots of Fire.* Dodi's father owned Harrods department store in London and was one of the richest and kindest men in the world. Dodi had told his father he wanted to be a Hollywood producer, and Dodi's father had made it happen. Anyway, my friend recounted a conversation between Dodi and Bob Evans, the head of Paramount. Dodi told Bob, "I'm having trouble with one of the actors. He wants me to get him some cocaine, and I don't know what to do about it."

"What don't you know?" asked Evans.

"It's so expensive," Dodi said. "Where am I going to get the money?"

Bob said, "Well, just charge it to the transportation department." Apparently finding ways to bury the cost of cocaine was common practice in Hollywood during that time.

Around this time I moved out of the modern condominium I'd shared with Penny and the boys, and into a small apartment. And I started doing cocaine on a regular basis. Once I began using heavily, I found myself involved with unsavory people I didn't even know. When you're hooked on drugs, you have no close friends, just druggie friends. That makes you feel totally alone, which makes you want to take drugs even more. It's a vicious cycle.

My head wasn't on straight, and although I knew it, I didn't know what to do about it. The cocaine gave me a brief feeling of euphoria, which was the best feeling I could manage in those days. I told myself that if I controlled my use, and chose my friends more carefully, I'd be able to stop whenever I wanted to. As it turned out, it wasn't so easy.

One of the big reasons I started using cocaine was that I was told it was great for sex. Specifically, I heard that it made men less sensitive, allowing them to prolong the time before orgasm. This sounded good to me, so I bought some coke and started seeing lots of women, testing out what I'd heard. It didn't make me superhuman in the longevity department, but it certainly did make my sexual experiences more intense.

After a while, the girls I hung out with were all using. It was a perfect environment for disaster. There were times when I'd be at some girl's apartment and all I wanted to do was go back home, but I was too fucked up to move.

One time I went to an apartment on Fountain Avenue to buy cocaine. During the transaction, the gentleman I was buying it from reached under his desk and pulled out a .45-caliber handgun. He cocked it and laid it down on the desk. That was all he did. Maybe he was just trying to make sure I didn't try anything funny. I kept my cool, made my purchase, and got the hell out of that apartment.

After he shut the door behind me, a door down the hall opened, and a girl poked her head out and said, "Hey, come here."

I walked down to her and said, "Yes?"

"How much did you buy?" she said.

She obviously knew what the score was, so I didn't play stupid. "Five grams," I said.

She said, "I'll give you a blow job for half a gram." That happened to me more than once. Sometimes I'd go along, and sometimes not.

I remember another coke dealer who went by the street name of Madison. If a girl was around, sometimes Madison would pull out a pipe, take a hit, suck in a deep breath, and motion for the girl to come closer. He'd then blow the smoke into her mouth and give her a kiss. What a despicable thing I was involved in.

In my new environment, with my new friends, everywhere I went somebody had a gram or more. They'd put it in your hand, and each nostril would get a shot. It would give you a rush, and then twenty minutes later — if it took that long — you were craving more. Cocaine, it turned out, was not addictive: it was *very* addictive.

If you wanted sex during the 1980s in Hollywood, you needed only one of two things: cocaine or money. If a girl was addicted she was probably going to need a couple of hundred bucks to pay the rent because her rent money had already gone up in smoke. All you had to do if you wanted to have sex with her was give her money or coke. If you went to a party and flashed a gram bottle, you knew you were flaunting a commodity that every girl at that party wanted. Guys I knew really well — actors, producers, writers — were all using cocaine as a way to compete for girls.

After I began freebasing, my life got even stranger. I'd wake up in a room I didn't recognize, in a house I couldn't remember going to. I probably remembered the girl, but she was already gone; maybe she had left me a note, or maybe not. If I was making a movie, I'd get myself together and go to the studio. How I made those pictures, I'll never know, but I'm proud that I was able to manage it. When it came time to work, somehow I was able to dispel all my distractions and all my weaknesses.

To escape from myself on the weekends, I went to the only drug-free safe haven I knew: Hefner's. At Hef's I'd watch a movie, eat some dinner, and flirt with a beautiful woman.

Some friends and I even created our own little place where we could take drugs anytime we wanted to. A hairdresser to the stars owned a little place in LA called The Candy Store. It had a doorman, and to get in you had to say the password, which changed every couple of days. In front the place sold candy — Tootsie Rolls, lemon drops, stuff like that — and in back was a disco with a small dance floor. I was the president of the club, and I had the best time. And the worst.

Being an addict gives you a peculiar mixture of thoughts and feelings. On the one hand, your body is crying for relief. On the other, when you're freebasing cocaine, you feel extraordinarily good. Your life becomes much more intense. The candle burns very brightly. Yet you can see the damaging effects the addiction is having on you. You know that what you're doing isn't good for you — you know that it's killing you, really — but you don't stop. I knew that my cocaine use was hurting my looks, which was my stock-in-trade as a leading man. When the face that looks back at you from the morning mirror is puffy and haggard you start thinking to yourself, *Now I'm in serious trouble.*

I wasn't so addicted that I couldn't make the few movies offered to me. My problem was that the movie offers were still few and far between, and now I needed all the money I could get — I had three ex-wives, six children, and a cocaine habit to support — so I was even less choosy about the work I did. And that was killing me. At times like this it wasn't easy to remember that all I'd ever wanted to do was be in the movies.

In 1982 I worked in a movie called *Brain-Waves.* Keir Dullea of *2001: A Space*

Odyssey played the husband of a comatose accident victim, and somehow I, the surgeon, had given the wife the brain of a murder victim. The movie, which was awful, took twelve days to shoot. I had a hard time during filming because I was using really heavily.

Othello, the Black Commando was next. I got the part of Iago because Tony Perkins, the actor they had hired to play the role, died. Max Boulois, the producer and actor who played Othello, called me up and said, "We'll give you three hundred thousand dollars to come and do this movie."

I said, "I'll be there." I got the money up front, but after paying me and covering other expenses, it turned out that Max didn't have enough money left to make the picture. He said, "I'll give you fifty percent of the picture if you give me back some money."

I said, "I'm sorry. I can't do that." The movie was a bomb and so was my next film, *Balboa,* in which I played a scheming real estate tycoon. During the shooting of *Balboa,* I made the work bearable by chasing some of the beauties who played beach girls. My teenage son, Nicholas, stayed with me for part of the shooting of the picture. I was hitting on the girls and so was he. A chip off the old block.

Sonny Bono, a smart and funny man, appeared with me in the film. I liked Sonny very much. While I was living at the Keck estate, Sonny had come to me and asked if he and Cher could buy it. Since I didn't own it, I couldn't sell it. I could have exercised my right to buy it for three hundred thousand dollars and Sonny and Cher could have bought it from me, but Sonny thought that was too convoluted, so he passed.

I had worked with the two of them a little when I appeared on *The Sonny and Cher Comedy Hour* in the 1970s. I knew the couple had their problems. Cher was angry with Sonny, but Sonny loved her through it all.

Cher's unhappiness stemmed from her desire not to be part of an act. She thought she could do better on her own, but for years she subjugated herself to the act for the sake of their marriage and their careers. She stayed with Sonny until she couldn't stand it anymore. After they split, nobody expected Sonny to achieve anything, and at first it looked like they might be right. He did bad movies like *Balboa* until he gave acting up for politics. He became mayor of Palm Springs and later a member of the U.S. House of Representatives. I was glad for his success, knowing what a decent guy he was.

My next picture was *Where Is Parsifal?* The

producer was Alexander Salkind, who also produced *Superman.* Peter Lawford and Orson Welles were my costars. The movie was a longer version of an hour-long television show about love, hate, and chasing women. Alex Salkind was married to Berta Domínguez, who herself acted in the film. Berta was short, stocky, and older than Alex, who had to be in his sixties, and I was supposed to be her lover. Everyone was miscast in this film, including me. Of course, whatever Berta wanted, Berta got. She might stop shooting at two in the afternoon and have lunch or go see a girlfriend. When I saw her car coming back, I'd yell, "Here she comes," and then we'd all go back to our places.

Orson Welles played Klingsor. In one scene I was supposed to talk to him while he sat in the backseat of a car, but Orson was so big that he couldn't get out of the car. They had to have a special door made for him.

In one scene my character was having a conversation with Orson's character. The director said "Action," and I gave my line, and then the director yelled "Cut," and asked me to do it again.

Without bothering to whisper, Orson said, "Tony, when you say it this time, change it. Make it a little funnier."

I said, "You think so?"

He said, "You know what you want to say. Make it funnier." So I did, and the director liked it better. Orson was right. Can you imagine getting direction from a genius like Orson Welles? For the rest of the film I inserted little pieces, interwove them in the dialogue, and it turned out fine. I enjoyed getting to know Orson off the set too. When he came to LA we'd have dinner at Spago, Wolfgang Puck's restaurant. Orson would sit at the end table, where he was able to come and go as he pleased without anyone seeing him. He'd bring along a little dog that would bark at me.

"Orson," I'd say, "he's going to bite me."

"Well, bite him back," Orson said. "Fuck him."

During the time I stayed in London making *Parsifal,* I spent a lot of time driving around at night looking for cocaine, descending into the depths of the city, looking for the drug I couldn't live without.

When I returned to LA, I kept meeting girls who did cocaine, and I kept providing it to them. I lived aimlessly, using coke to numb myself to the sad state of my career. I was very lucky that Nicolas Roeg, a fine film director, asked me to play Senator Joseph McCarthy in the movie *Insignificance* in 1985. An actor by the name of Michael Emil played Albert Einstein, Theresa Russell played Marilyn Monroe, and Gary Busey played Joe DiMaggio. I liked my fellow actors a lot, and the script was wonderful. It was a good moment in a period that was otherwise memorable only for the depths of my despair. I was slowly killing myself, and I knew it. But I kept right on going.

My last film for what seemed like an eternity was *Club Life,* also known as *King of the City,* a musical thriller about a bouncer, which was released in 1986. After that, I simply could not get a fucking movie job. I wasn't offered anything for the longest time, which was a terrible blow to me. I missed the action, I missed the money, but the thing I missed the most was just making movies.

My career didn't fall on hard times because of cocaine. Everyone was on coke. Maybe it was because, at the age of sixty, I was no longer a young man. That was when I began to see the sad truth about having devoted my life to my profession. I had given the movies everything I had ever since I was a kid, saving nickels and dimes from shining shoes so I could go see Tyrone Power at the Loews theater in the Bronx. Once I got to Hollywood, I gave it my all. I learned my lines; I did my own stunts; I tried to save the studio money. I could make movies quickly and easily. I could even make the actors around me better. But when an actor reaches a certain age, that's it. The movie business is not a profession for old people, not if you're in front of the camera.

By this time I began to see the value of having a backup plan for my acting career. I just wanted to hang around a set and be part of it. If I had planned ahead better, maybe I could have kept working as a makeup man or a screenwriter or a producer. But now it was too late for me to do anything about that. I was out in the cold, utterly miserable, and feeling hopeless. If my life didn't turn around soon, I wasn't going to have much left to turn around.

My attorney, Eli Blumenfeld, was the one who arranged for me to check into the Betty Ford clinic. He was the one who drove me from LA to Palm Springs, where the clinic was located. During the trip I fantasized about what going to Betty Ford would be like. I pictured bungalows with a nice lawn and a swimming pool, a place where I could spend a lot of time resting before I got up in the afternoon and took a leisurely walk. I assumed that after I arrived, the staff was going to give me a special shot in my ass to cure me. I was beginning to look forward to the magic bullet that was going to make all the pain suddenly go away.

I was so wrong. In the real-life clinic, I lived in a room with two other guys, and we all got up at the same time, went for breakfast, did some physical exercise, and then went as a group into a room where we had to talk about ourselves, telling everyone why we felt we needed help. There was no shot in the ass, and the staff didn't cure you. You cured yourself by examining the reasons why you wanted to take drugs and alcohol and by sharing those reasons with people just like yourself. You had to dig deep in your soul every day and bring whatever you found there into the light.

I didn't say much for the first couple of meetings; I just sat back and watched. In our group, some guys were dressed like they were going to a country club, but there were also guys who were store clerks and stevedores. I couldn't understand how those guys could afford it. Betty Ford was expensive, so much so that there were times when I was more concerned with the cost than I was with my recovery.

When I was asked to speak, I told everyone about my childhood and what drugs I was doing, but I didn't say too much more than that. I wasn't very open at first because I didn't want to come off worse than the guy sitting next to me. Everybody was like that; we started off by being cautious, but as time went on, we all got down to the real story. Fuck it. I was a prick. I was mean and ornery while I was using. Don't come to me if you have a problem. I was in the depths of Dostoevsky, and in a perverse way, I enjoyed it.

We spent the first five days discovering what was really bothering us. We did this by talking it over as a group. You can sit around and think about your problems all you want, but somehow you don't really face them until you tell someone else about them. One time I told the group, "My mother used to beat the shit out of me, and I hated it. I would hide under the bed so she wouldn't find me." These were the facts that I was hiding from, the experiences that made me feel small and helpless no matter how much I accomplished in life. Once I understood that certain events in my past were the source of the anger and self-loathing that had led to my addiction, then I could begin to work on the addiction itself.

After a couple of weeks I started to come to grips with how I really felt about everything that had happened to me. Dealing with all of that old pain was really difficult, but I felt the bitterness slowly start to recede. At the end of the twenty-eight days, I felt my fears slowly dissipating. The clinic counselors helped replace those fears with new thoughts and ideas about how to live life and be happy without having to rely on drugs to do it.

As part of the clinic's twelve-step recovery program, I wrote a letter to my boys, Nicholas and Benjamin. They were in their teens. I said, "I know I haven't been a good father to you, but I promise to do better from now on. I'm not going to give up. You two guys are so important to me that I will do whatever it takes."

I also wrote a letter to Penny. I told her that I knew about her infidelities, and that I was angry at her for keeping the boys from me. I told her I felt she was stealing them from me, and I didn't like it. The letter didn't change anything between us, but at least it gave me a chance to express myself in an honest way, which was something I hadn't made a habit of doing before.

I wasn't sure if the program at Betty Ford was going to work, but it did. When I checked out of the clinic, my cocaine use came to an end. I had a new life in front of me, one without cocaine, and hopefully with more of my children in it. There wasn't too much I could do about my career, which was still in the toilet, so to help with my transition from movie star to private citizen, I devoted more and more time to painting.

20
Maybe I'll Live Forever

As the time between movies got longer and longer, I began painting more and more. I did a lot of sketching and painting in acrylics. My paintings were mostly abstract and surrealist, expressions of my fantasies, thoughts, and ideas. One of my paintings depicted a landscape, and in the middle of the landscape sat a table with a bottle of wine, some grapes, and an open book. Below the table was a wooden floor, despite the fact that the scene was outdoors. I wanted to jolt the viewer by showing how the ordinary and the surreal live side by side.

I didn't have a painting teacher, but I was influenced greatly by the artists I met, especially Marc Chagall, whom I had the honor of actually meeting when I was filming *The Great Race.* We were in Paris, working on the end of the picture, when he came onto the set to watch us filming. Chagall projected an unmistakable aura of power and confidence.

In the mid-1980s I met an art dealer, Bill Mett, who had a gallery in Honolulu. He liked my paintings, so he invited me to come and paint at his gallery. I took him up on it. With my movie career fading into the sunset, I was determined to make it as an artist. I rented a house from Bill, and I liked Hawaii so much that I bought a house there and lived in it for two years.

I don't remember a whole lot about the movies I made toward the end of my career. In 1986 I made a television movie called *Mafia Princess.* Susan Lucci, famous for her role as Erica in the soap opera *All My Children,* played Sam Giancana's daughter, and I played Sam Giancana himself, the mafia kingpin whom Frank Sinatra had introduced me to. I didn't make another movie for three years. Then I met a producer named Norman Vane. Norm wanted to make a horror film called *Midnight* that he had written and was going to direct, and he wanted to know if I'd star in it. With all that child support I had to pay, it was easy for me to say yes.

Midnight was a good film, and the work went quickly and smoothly. I followed it with a comedy called *Lobster Man from Mars,* in which I played a movie producer who owed the IRS a lot of money. As in Mel Brooks's *The Producers,* my character — the movie producer — had hit on the idea of deliberately making a bomb of a movie so he could take the production expenses as a massive tax write-off. When the movie came out, people loved it, and I got a lot of fan mail.

I didn't make another movie until 1991, some five years later, when I made *Prime Target* in Canada. In this movie I was cast as a mob informant. Not long after, I made another forgettable movie called *Center of the Web,* in which an acting coach is wrongly accused of being a hit man, so he is forced to go undercover as a federal agent.

In 1992 I made a television movie called *Christmas in Connecticut,* directed by Arnold Schwarzenegger. He and I had the best time working together. Of course we got along; we shared the first half of his last name. One time, just before I entered one of my shots, Arnold happened to be standing right next to me. As I got my cue he said, "Take no prisoners" and shoved me onto the set. It turned out to be a brilliant bit of direction. He was a charming, wonderful man, and we've remained good friends to this day.

It was around this time that I got some terrible news. You'll recall that many years earlier my parents and I agreed to put my brother Bobby in a state mental facility. Bobby was twenty-eight at the time, and my parents could no longer take care of him. They had wanted me to take him into my home, but that was impossible. He was as impulsive as a five-year-old, but he had the body of an adult man. One time when he was at my house, he became agitated and started throwing punches at me. I was mostly able to block his swings until he calmed down. But Bobby was a person who needed twenty-four-hour supervision.

After Bobby moved into the state mental facility at Camarillo, I would go visit him every so often. One time Bobby asked me to take a stroll with him. We walked by a large crib that had a young woman in it, and as I passed she beckoned to me. She scared me, so I ignored her and kept following my brother, until he stopped abruptly. There was another patient standing there, looking at us. Bobby pointed at the man and said, "This guy is going to kill me."

The man came over to us and said to me, "Where have I seen you?"

I said, "In the movies."

He said, "You're right. That's where I saw you."

Not far away stood a tiny woman wearing a floor-length housedress. Her gray hair was pulled back in a ponytail. The guy who had talked to me went over to her and said,

"That's Tony Curtis."

She looked up and stared at me. "Who's Tony Curtis?" she asked, vacantly. It was one of the few times in my life when I didn't mind not being recognized. I just shook her hand and said, "I'm Bobby's brother."

As the years went by, Bobby's condition worsened, and it was terrible to see. The visits became more and more difficult for me, until finally I just couldn't handle going at all. Bobby didn't seem to know who I was anyway. On August 22, 1992, my brother was found dead on the street in LA. He had left the hospital and refused to go back, so he had ended up living the life of a homeless panhandler. Someone had beaten him to death. My brother. I wept for him, and for the relationship we never really had.

In 1993 I went to Israel to make *The Mummy Lives.* I played the mummy, who bumps off a slew of people. That same year I made a first-rate picture called *Naked in New York.* Martin Scorsese produced it, and Whoopi Goldberg and Kathleen Turner starred, along with Timothy Dalton, Eric Stoltz, and Ralph Macchio. It was a story about a guy who wrote a play and wanted to get it produced. He and his partner come to me, an off-Broadway producer, and I help them put on their play. Unfortunately, it flops, and at the end of the picture I say to the writer, "Don't take it to heart. You got the play produced. You'll get another chance. And another. And when a play is successful, you'll be successful. Me, I'm just a figment of your imagination. I'm just something early in your career." Then I walk away and leave him standing there.

On the last day of February 1993, I married for the fourth time. I wasn't expecting it, and I wasn't looking for it, but even though I was in my late sixties I still was capable of falling head over heels for a stunningly beautiful woman. I was attending a dinner at the Friar's Club when I looked over at the next table and saw a young woman whose plunging neckline revealed quite a bit of the most beautiful, inviting breasts I had ever seen — and that was saying a lot. She was a tiny girl, not more than five foot two, but she was so sexy that I couldn't help staring at her for the rest of the evening, imagining what it would be like to make love to her. I don't know what it is about breasts that revs me up. Maybe I didn't get enough breastfeeding when I was a baby. But whenever I feel an attraction like that, I put my charm into overdrive and see if I can make something good happen.

I got up from my seat and went over to the people who organized the event to find out what I could about this stunning woman. She turned out to be a Jewish attorney named Lisa Deutsch. I was sixty-seven, and she was thirty-three, but in my mind's eye I was still a youngster. I'm fortunate enough to feel that way now, and as of this writing I'm eighty-three. When you get to a certain stage in life, women your own age seem ancient. Of course, they're no more ancient than you are, but they don't match up with the way you feel. I know it sounds crazy, but I refuse to give up that part of me that is still in tune with my youth — that part of me that still wants to steam up the windows in a car by making out. Why should I give that up if I don't have to?

My romance with Lisa was a whirlwind. I met her parents and discovered that her father had suffered from anti-Semitism, so he was happy that his daughter was going out with a Jew. As for me, I had never been in a serious relationship with a Jewish girl before, so it made me a little nervous. I found out that one difference between shiksas and Jewish girls was that Jewish girls are very attached to their families. I made an effort to open myself up to Lisa's parents, but it didn't come naturally to me.

I was probably too quick to jump into this marriage, but I had always been impulsive when it came to affairs of the heart. Very quickly, though, I sensed the potential for trouble. Lisa's father, who was a lawyer, wanted me to sign a prenuptial agreement in which I agreed to give Lisa half of everything I earned. That didn't happen, but we got married anyway.

One time early in our marriage, Lisa and I went to a party where Ronald and Nancy Reagan were in attendance. Lew Wasserman and his wife were there, as were a number of famous actors, some of whom I'd adored in the movies when I was a kid. I was very pleased to be at the same party with them, socializing with them; it meant a lot to me. But when I introduced Lisa to them, she wasn't at all impressed. At the time I didn't understand why, but in retrospect I realized that she hadn't grown up with their movies. She didn't know anything about these actors, so being in their presence didn't mean much to her. This was my first realization that the age difference was probably going to be a source of trouble. You might think I would have learned that lesson by now, but there she was, with that great inviting smile and that fantastic body, and she was my wife! How could life be better than this?

Our marriage lasted less than two years. Lisa seemed haunted by something in her past. I don't know what it was, and she never encouraged any conversation about it. Professionally, Lisa devoted herself to legal work on behalf of clients who couldn't afford legal services. I could tell that she was under a lot of stress, but I chalked that up to the demands of her job. I knew there was nothing I could do about that, and Lisa wasn't an easy person to talk to about feelings — not that I was any prize in that category, either. Sadly, it wasn't long before I could see she didn't care about being with me, much less care about being married to me. I had done it again — given my heart to a woman on the basis of how she looked as opposed to who she was on the inside — and I braced myself for the inevitable: marriage number four was about to crash and burn.

Not long before we split up, I took Lisa to Paris as part of the publicity tour for my first book, *Tony Curtis: The Autobiography,* and we had some crazy fun on the roof of our hotel. It was a very romantic evening, but it turned out to be the last one we would ever enjoy. After we returned to LA, Lisa came home late one night. She was drunk, so I said, "Get out of here until you sober up." She went downstairs to her bedroom and fell asleep. As I watched her walk away, I knew the marriage was over. After that she spent every night out. Our life together had turned to ashes.

When the marriage ended, I was surprised by the way I felt. I had expected to fall into a depression, but instead I was overcome by a sense of relief. There were no recriminations. I had had a good time while it lasted, and that was the end of that. I wasn't crushed the way I had been with Christine and Penny. I just moved on.

When I got back from the book tour, I wasn't feeling right. I was working out at Gold's Gym in LA, part of my regular routine when I was in town, when I felt so dizzy and weak that I had to lie down. I called my doctor, who told me to come into his office right away. He and another doctor examined me, and they both decided I'd had a heart attack. They rushed me to the hospital, and two days later I was wheeled into the operating room for open-heart surgery. The surgeons took a vein out of my leg and used it to replace a blocked portion of a vein leading to my heart. Fortunately, I was able to recover quickly and completely, which stunned the doctors. They said it was because I'd been an athlete all my life.

My heart attack reminded me of a Yiddish joke: A great Jewish actor puts on the finest performance of *Hamlet* you'll ever see in your life. At the end of the play, he dies. A lady from the audience gets up and shouts, "Give him an enema!"

The announcer says, "An enema? It wouldn't help."

The lady says, "An enema wouldn't *hurt!*"

I came through my open-heart surgery just fine, but that hardship was about to pale by comparison to a tragedy that is every parent's worst nightmare. In July 1994, my son Nicholas, who had been living in a garage apartment at his mother's house on Cape Cod, died of a drug overdose. He was twenty-three. I was so distraught I sank into a depression unlike anything I'd ever known. I just wanted to bring the final curtain down.

I couldn't shake the feeling that I was somehow responsible for Nicholas's death. Why did Nicholas get into drugs in the first place? Was he doing drugs because I'd done them? Was he doing drugs because he had a void where his father should have been? We got along well, so I didn't think that was it. Did he inherit from me a tendency for substance abuse? I tormented myself with these thoughts, although I knew from my own experience that ultimately addiction is an individual madness. Nicholas was addicted, but his brother, Benjamin, wasn't.

At Nicholas's funeral, a local minister got up and talked about Nicholas's poor mother and the loss she suffered. He never mentioned my name or even indicated that Nicholas had a father, and by mentioning his mother in so many ways, the minister seemed to be implying that I had abandoned Nicholas. Not surprisingly, he was Penny's minister. After the service, I wrote him a letter asking, "Why didn't you even mention my name?" He wrote back with some poppycock about religion. Fuck him. He couldn't have been much of a minister or a father if he'd so completely lost sight of the Golden Rule.

Nicholas had been a child when Penny and I got divorced, so he had spent years flying back and forth across the country, going back and forth like a yo-yo between me and his mother. I think he might have been strongly affected by that. I say this because at the age of twenty-three he showed no signs of a direction to his life. He should have had a job or hobby to keep him occupied, a steady girlfriend, a good-looking car, but he had none of that. He was broke, living over his mother's garage.

Nicholas is gone, and I miss him terribly, but his death has helped me to appreciate how lucky I am to still have five wonderful children. Kelly, my firstborn, was always remarkably practical. One of my favorite memories of Kelly's childhood took place when she was four years old. I had brought home a television, and she had never seen a television before. So she got up from the couch and walked behind the set. She was there for a long time, so I finally asked her what she was doing. She told me with great seriousness that she was looking to see where the pictures and sounds were coming from.

Kelly wanted to be an actress, and she eventually had some chances to work in films, but it never made her truly happy. She liked the theater, so she joined a couple of theater groups in San Francisco, but she didn't pursue a stage career much further than that. The life of a professional theater actor is almost impossibly difficult. She married a theatrical producer, and together they formed a company, but nothing came of it, and the marriage itself didn't work out either. Kelly is living in Los Angeles now, working for her sister, Jamie. Kelly is a remarkably generous and compassionate person, sweet and giving.

Jamie was more of a firecracker. I have always called her Jamie, not Jamie Lee, because to my mind you can spell it any way you want, it still comes out "Leigh." Jamie always sought out the excitement and joy in life, and she's intelligent, gifted, and ambitious. She's been that way all her life. As a kid, she wanted to go everywhere, do everything. I knew she would succeed in whatever she wanted to do, and sure enough, she became a fabulous success as an actress.

As a kid, Jamie didn't smile too much. She was serious, and it was hard to get her to drop that seriousness. Kelly would be playing around and laughing while Jamie sat quietly, keeping her thoughts to herself. As she got older, I realized that her attitude toward life was very different from mine, and from Kelly's. Jamie was practical, thick-skinned, and aloof — at least that's the way she was around me. But you have to remember I wasn't around much. I was always in an airplane or on a set, and my hectic schedule often had me working pictures back to back. Sometimes I'd go six months at a time without seeing Kelly and Jamie, so when I finally did see them, they were often angry with me for being away from them for so long. Jamie was usually more upset than her sister.

One time in my apartment, when Kelly

and Jamie were still kids, Kelly read me the riot act for not being around when she needed me. Jamie said nothing, but I knew that her feelings toward me were at least as strong as her sister's. I felt terrible that night, but I didn't know what to do about it. And the truth is, I don't know what to do about it now. After Janet and I divorced, Janet filled their heads with all sorts of negativity about me. I was the villain. To prove it, Janet had only to point to the articles about their monstrous dad in the movie magazines. There was nothing I could do about that. But it doesn't stop me from taking pleasure today in the people that Kelly and Jamie have become.

Jamie is married to the talented actor and director Christopher Guest. He seems to share Jamie's belief that she deserved more from a father than I gave her, and I don't blame either one of them for that feeling. Jamie's friends made me feel insecure too, and I didn't enjoy being in their company. I wish I could rewrite the past, but I know that's not possible. Frankly, I wish I could do a better job right now of enjoying my children and grandchildren, and I know I've fallen short on that score too. But I'm getting better.

In Jamie's case, I still struggle to get past

her coolness toward me. I know I can sound formidable, but inside I'm as fragile as ever. And sensitive as I am, I'm not at my best when I think someone doesn't like me. I'm working on this, but progress is slow.

I have few regrets about my life, but chief among them is my failure as a father. I hope that in whatever time I have left I can do better in one role that never came naturally to me.

Alexandra, one of my two daughters from my marriage to Christine, has become a child therapist who helps parents of newborns. She is quiet and serious, and she's very good at what she does. Allegra, the younger of these two daughters, is a firebrand. She wanted to make it on her own, so she left school and tried all sorts of things. She got into designing clothing and jewelry, and now she's designing jewelry for a home-shopping company in Germany. She has a son named Raphael. I met him when he was tiny, and I'm planning to see him again soon.

Benjamin was my second son with Penny. He's always been good with his hands, and after working as a carpenter, he's working on getting his contractor's license. Sadly, Benjamin and I don't talk, which is fallout from disagreements we've had over his son, Nicholas, who is twelve years old. I'm doing what I can to help make sure Nicholas thrives. Nicholas is a wonderful child: smart, a good student, very perceptive, and an all-around fabulous boy.

I first laid eyes on Jill VandenBerg in 1996, when I went to Nicky Blair's restaurant alone one night for dinner. I was single and enjoying it. As I walked toward my table, I saw a couple at another table. The man looked like he might be Middle Eastern, and the young woman, a blond, had a beautiful face and a magnificent body. I hadn't seen anyone that appealing since Marilyn. I tried not to be rude, but I literally couldn't take my eyes off her.

At one point my chutzpah (my inner Schwartz) kicked in and propelled me over to their table. I had never seen the man before, but I pretended I knew him. "How have you been? We haven't talked in ages. How's your family?" He was dazzled by all the attention from a famous person. Where could he possibly have met me?

Then I paused and leaned over to the beautiful woman. "Hi, I'm Tony," I said with a little smile on my face.

"Hi, I'm Jill," she replied, "and this is my friend Matt."

I felt a surge of joy from the knowledge

that those two weren't married. I said, "I'm so happy to meet you, Jill." During the conversation that followed, I found out that she lived in San Diego and drove up to LA on weekends. So this guy might be her boyfriend, but they weren't living together. I took heart from this news and ramped up the charm a notch. They say all's fair in love and war, and when Schwartz is falling in love, you'd better look out.

I told Jill I was in San Diego a lot. Then I looked at her friend, and I said, "Matt, do you mind if I get a number where I can reach Jill when I'm in San Diego?"

"No, not at all," he said. I was so relieved I wanted to jump up and click my heels. I got Jill's number, put it in my pocket, and walked away like a gunslinger who'd just outdrawn Jesse James.

Jill had told me she was returning home Sunday night. I calculated when she might leave LA, and how much time the drive home would take her. Once my estimated time had elapsed, I called her and said, "Hello. Remember me?" During that phone conversation, she let on that she had been a big fan of Marilyn Monroe and that she had been upset with me for saying that kissing Marilyn was like kissing Hitler. It wasn't the first time I'd had to explain my way out of that one, but this time there was more on the line than ever before. No way was I going to let this amazing woman's loyalty to Marilyn cause a problem for us! I took her through my explanation and apologized profusely, which satisfied her.

The next time Jill came to Los Angeles, she called me up, and we started going out. After a couple of weeks of dating, I invited her to spend the night at my apartment, and she did. It was a wonderful experience, which told me that what I felt for Jillie wasn't just an infatuation. By this time, I finally knew the difference. What I felt for this woman was truly serious. To my everlasting wonderment, Jillie felt the same way.

I'm still crazy about her now. There's something about Jill's beauty that touches me very deeply. It glows through from the inside rather than being a more typical beauty. I don't know how she avoided all the issues and hang-ups that beautiful girls so often fall victim to, but she did. She never wanted to be a model and never wanted to be an actress. She just wanted to live a happy life, and when we met, we both believed that our best chance at happiness was to spend our lives together. We've been married for ten years. I don't know what I did to deserve this, but I finally got it right.

Seven years ago, Jillie and I moved from LA to Las Vegas. I no longer wanted to live in the shadow of Hollywood. It reminded me of how much of my life in the last decade had been spent waiting for the phone to ring with a call to make a movie. Jillie found that she didn't like living in LA either. She didn't enjoy going out to lunch with the wives of so many unhappy, unemployed actors. They significantly outnumbered those who were working. And everywhere I went around town, I ran into actors like me who used to have a career but no longer did.

I think there was a shame that went along with that — I know I felt it — and a lot of people who used to be the biggest names in Hollywood became afraid to even show their faces in public. I knew that feeling too. In the years before I met Jillie, if I wanted to eat out in LA, I would go to this boxcar that had been turned into a diner and have a hamburger. It was the only place where I wouldn't run into somebody to whom I'd have to make excuses for why I wasn't working. In that diner, nobody compared me with present-day working actors. People left me alone.

I have lived beyond my golden age. When I think back to the beginning of my career and my meteoric rise, I still wonder how it happened. For a long time, when I made a movie I created a wonderful commotion. Even after *The Boston Strangler,* later in my career, I received tremendous acclaim and applause. And now, sixty years after I began, despite all that success no one will give me a chance to show what I can do. I know, I know, there aren't many parts in movies for octogenarians, but for some reason that doesn't provide me much comfort. What helps most is knowing that never for a moment did I take my success for granted. When I could set aside my insecurities, I appreciated — and was grateful for — each and every second of my good fortune.

Another reason for moving to Las Vegas was that I had a great friend there, a man named Dean Shendel. Dean had been a stuntman, and I enjoyed his company tremendously, so Jill and I had made frequent trips to Las Vegas to see him. Finally we decided we'd rather be in Vegas with him and his upbeat, fun-loving group of friends than in LA surrounded by disappointed actors.

It was on one of those trips to Vegas in 1998 that I went to see a longtime friend of mine, Kirk Kerkorian. Kirk owned the MGM Grand (and in 2004 his company purchased the Excalibur, Luxor, and Mandalay Bay hotels and casinos). When I told Kirk that Jill and I were planning to marry, he suggested we hold the wedding at the MGM Grand, and he generously offered to pick up the tab for the entire affair. One of Kirk's troubleshooters was a wonderful man named Gene Kilroy. I was told that Gene had once been Muhammad Ali's manager, and when I met him, I quickly saw that he was a real go-to guy who knew everyone in town and Las Vegas was his office. Gene took care of all the arrangements for our November 6 wedding that year, and over the years I've called on him for tickets to fights or shows or just to talk. In addition to everything else, Gene, who is a remarkably generous person, gives great advice. He has been a good friend, and I am grateful to him for that. If you have Gene for a friend you want not.

I have a wonderful life here in Vegas. Everybody treats me with dignity and respect, and I strive to do the same in return. And living here in the desert has allowed Jillie to pursue her dream. Two or three years ago, we were riding together in the car when she mentioned to me that she had learned that racehorses, including some of the best-known winners of Triple Crown races, are routinely slaughtered for human consumption overseas once their glory days are over. As a girl, Jill had always had an affinity for horses. As she grew older, she owned horses and felt very strongly that they should be well treated; when she learned how even championship horses ended their days, she decided to do something about it.

"I'm going to save these horses," she said.

"Okay, let's do it," was my reply.

We decided that Jill would build a horse farm in the California desert about forty-five minutes from where we live. Once she got the horse farm built, she bought her first retired horses and housed them on the farm. She hasn't stopped since. At last count, we had 130 horses on our farm, which we call Shiloh. I'm her silent partner in this noble venture. If any of you would like to adopt a beautiful Thoroughbred, you can reach Jillie on her Web site at Shilohhorserescue.com. I am also available.

This is one marriage in which the bride didn't change after we got married, and she didn't want me to change either. A lot of things keep our marriage alive, including Jill's sweetness, her strength, her resolve, and her all-important sense of her life's purpose. I don't know anyone more beautiful than Jillie. And if we spend a little more dough than we should to save Jillie's horses, that's okay; I have enough to keep us going. I own parts of lots of pictures, and they generate enough money to comfortably meet our needs.

I have never lost that youthful joy that I've always found in the daily aspects of life: waking up to a new day, going for a drive in a nice car, savoring the beauty of the outdoors, being able to go to restaurants and enjoy good meals, meeting lots of interesting people, and occasionally chatting up a beautiful girl. As Sinatra's song goes, I've been a puppet, a pauper, a pirate, a poet, a pawn, and a king — and I've had one helluva good time at it. I've known lots of amazing people too; I've fought with some, loved others, and although I may not have known it at the time, I enjoyed them all. I always tried my best, and in some parts of my life I came up way short and in others I touched the sky. Why should I complain? Why would I want to? I've had a great life.

They say that America's royalty is its Hollywood stars. The great thing about America is that you don't need to be born into the royal family. You could be born into an immigrant family in a New York tenement and still become an American prince through sheer hard work and desire. I should know. In my case — and perhaps this is true of everyone — my greatest failing was also my greatest strength. My tough childhood led me to feel like an outsider, but that sense of alienation hardened my resolve into a driving ambition that would not be denied. That served me well in the work that I love, and less well with the people I love. But things tend to balance out in the end.

Now I'm blessed with a woman named Jillie. I didn't know her, but I had always dreamed about her. The phone's still not ringing with that offer of a new movie, but I'm no longer waiting on it either. I'm painting and painting, visiting Jillie's horses, and savoring all-too-rare moments with my children and grandchildren. For better or for worse, I only stop to look back at times like this. Mostly I live in this moment, right now, and I'm grateful for it. I know that most of this life lies behind me, but what I live for is today, and for the tomorrows that remain. My eyes are bombarded by the sights of this beautiful world. Every breath has the rich fragrance of trees and flowers. I'm privileged to be alive to share these wondrous feelings with you. I toast our fallen comrades, all of whom live on in our hearts.

So far, so good. Do I sound like I think I'm going to live forever? You bet your fucking ass. I know better, at least in my mind. But this heart still beats a little faster for all the beauty in the world. I can honestly say that I've lived my time here fully. Perhaps the life story I have recounted in these pages will help you to avoid some of the pitfalls that tripped me up along the way. I hope so. And I hope that you'll live the rest of your time to the fullest. I don't see any other good way to go.

FILMOGRAPHY

1. **Criss Cross** (1949) A Universal-International Production (Michael Kraike). Directed by Robert Siodmak. Cast: Burt Lancaster (Steve Thompson), Yvonne De Carlo (Anna), Dan Duryea (Slim Dundee), Stephen McNally (Pete Ramirez), Richard Long (Slade Thompson), Tom Pedi (Vincent), Alan Napier (Finchley), James [Tony] Curtis (Gigolo)

2. **City Across the River** (1949) A Universal-International Production (Maxwell Shane). Directed by Maxwell Shane. Cast: Stephen McNally (Stan Albert), Luis Van Rooten (Joe Cusack), Thelma Ritter (Mrs. Cusack), Peter Fernandez (Frankie Cusack), Al Ramsen (Benjamin Wilks), Joshua Shelley (Crazy), Mickey Knox (Larry), Richard Jaeckel (Bull), Anthony Curtis (Mitch), Jeff Corey (Lt. Macon), Sharon McManus (Alice Cusack), Sue England (Betty), Bar-

bara Whiting (Annie Kane), Richard Benedict (Gaggsy Steens)

3. **The Lady Gambles** (1949) A Universal-International Production (Michael Kraike). Directed by Michael Gordon. Cast: Barbara Stanwyck (Joan Boothe), Robert Preston (David Boothe), Stephen McNally (Corrigan), Edith Barrett (Ruth Phillips), John Hoyt (Dr. Rojac), Leif Erickson (Tony), Anthony Curtis (Bellboy)

4. **Johnny Stool Pigeon** (1949) A Universal-International Production (Aaron Rosenberg). Directed by William Castle. Cast: Howard Duff (George Morton), Dan Duryea (Johnny Evans), Shelley Winters (Terry), Anthony Curtis (Joey Hyatt), John McIntire (Nick Avery), Gar Moore (Sam Harrison), Leif Erickson (Pringle)

5. **Francis** (1950) A Universal-International Production (Robert Arthur). Directed by Arthur Lubin. Cast: Donald O'Connor (Peter Stirling), Patricia Medina (Maureen Gelder), ZaSu Pitts (Valerie Humpert), Eduard Franz (Colonel Pepper), Anthony Curtis (Captain Jones)

6. **I Was a Shoplifter** (1950) A Universal-

International Production (Leonard Goldstein). Directed by Charles Lamont. Cast: Scott Brady (Jeff Andrews), Mona Freeman (Faye Burton), Anthony Curtis (Pepe), Charles Drake (Herb Klaxton), Gregg Martell (The Champ), Robert Gist (Barkie Neff), Larry Keating (Harry Dunson), Rock Hudson (Store Detective)

7. **Winchester '73** (1950) A Universal-International Production (Aaron Rosenberg). Directed by Anthony Mann. Cast: James Stewart (Lin McAdam), Stephen McNally (Dutch Henry Brown), Shelley Winters (Lola Manners), Dan Duryea (Waco Johnny Dean), Will Geer (Wyatt Earp), Jay C. Flippen (Sergeant Wilkes), Rock Hudson (Young Bull), Anthony Curtis (Doan)

8. **Sierra** (1950) A Universal-International Production (Michael Kraike). Directed by Alfred E. Green. Cast: Wanda Hendrix (Riley Martin), Audie Murphy (Ring Hassard), Dean Jagger (Jeff Hassard), Burl Ives (Lonesome), Richard Rober (Big Matt), Anthony Curtis (Brent Coulter), Houseley Stevenson (Sam Coulter)

9. **Kansas Raiders** (1950) A Universal-International Production (Ted Richmond).

Directed by Ray Enright. Cast: Audie Murphy (Jesse James), Brian Donlevy (Quantrill), Richard Arlen (Union Captain), Scott Brady (Bill Anderson), Marguerite Chapman (Kate Clarke), Tony Curtis (Kit Dalton), James Best (Cole Younger), Dewey Martin (James Younger), John Kellogg (Red Leg Leader)

10. **The Prince Who Was a Thief** (1951) A Universal-International Production (Leonard Goldstein). Directed by Rudolph Maté. Cast: Tony Curtis (Julna), Piper Laurie (Tina), Everett Sloane (Yussef), Peggy Castle (Princess Yashim), Donald Randolph (Mustapha), Jeff Corey (Mokar), Betty Garde (Mirza), Marvin Miller (Hakar), Nita Bieber (Cahuena), Hayden Rorke (Basra)

11. **Son of Ali Baba** (1952) A Universal-International Production (Leonard Goldstein). Directed by Kurt Neumann. Cast: Tony Curtis (Kashma Baba), Piper Laurie (Azura/Kiki), Victor Jory (Caliph), Morris Ankrum (Ali Baba), Susan Cabot (Tala), William Reynolds (Mustafa), Hugh O'Brien (Hussein), Philip Van Zandt (Kareeb)

12. **Flesh and Fury** (1952) A Universal-International Production (Leonard Gold-

stein). Directed by Joseph Pevney. Cast: Tony Curtis (Paul Callan), Mona Freeman (Ann Hollis), Jan Sterling (Sonya Bartow), Wallace Ford (Jack Richardson), Connie Gilchrist (Mrs. Richardson), Katherine Locke (Mrs. Hollis), Harry Shannon (Mike Callan), Harry Guardino (Lou Callan)

13. **No Room for the Groom** (1952) A Universal-International Production (Ted Richmond). Directed by Douglas Sirk. Cast: Tony Curtis (Alvah Morrell), Piper Laurie (Lee Kingshead), Spring Byington (Mama Kingshead), Don DeFore (Herman Strouple), Lillian Bronson (Aunt Elsa), Paul McVey (Dr. Trotter), Stephen Chase (Mr. Taylor)

14. **Meet Danny Wilson** (1952) A Universal-International Production (Leonard Goldstein). Directed by Joseph Pevney. Cast: Frank Sinatra (Danny Wilson), Shelley Winters (Joy Carroll), Raymond Burr (Nick Driscoll), Alex Nicol (Michael Francis Ryan), Vaughn Taylor (T.W. Hatcher), Tommy Farrell (Tommy Wells). Guest appearances by Jeff Chandler and Tony Curtis

15. **Houdini** (1953) A Universal-International

Production (George Pal). Directed by George Marshall. Cast: Tony Curtis (Harry Houdini), Janet Leigh (Bess), Torin Thatcher (Otto), Angela Clarke (Mrs. Weiss), Sig Ruman (Schultz), Connie Gilchrist (Mrs. Schultz), Michael Pate (Dooley)

16. **The All-American** (1953) A Universal-International Production (Aaron Rosenberg). Directed by Jesse Hibbs. Cast: Tony Curtis (Nick Bonelli), Mamie Van Doren (Susie Ward), Richard Long (Howard Carter), Gregg Palmer (Hunt Cameron), Paul Cavanagh (Professor Banning), Stuart Whitman (Zip Parker), Jimmy Hunt (Whizzer)

17. **Forbidden** (1953) A Universal-International Production (Ted J. Richmond). Directed by Rudolph Maté. Cast: Tony Curtis (Eddie Darrow), Joanne Dru (Christine Lawrence), Lyle Bettger (Justin Keit), Marvin Miller (Cliff Chalmer), Victor Sen Yung (Allan), Peter Mamakos (Sam)

18. **Beachhead** (1954) A Universal-International Production (Howard Koch). Directed by Stuart Heisler. Cast: Tony Curtis (Burke), Frank Lovejoy (Sgt. Fletcher), Mary Murphy (Nina), Eduard Franz (Bou-

chard), Skip Homeier (Reynolds)

19. **Johnny Dark** (1954) A Universal-International Production (William Alland). Directed by George Sherman. Cast: Tony Curtis (Johnny Dark), Piper Laurie (Liz Fielding), Paul Kelly (William Scott), Ilka Chase (Abbie Binns), Don Taylor (Duke Benson), Ruth Hampton (Miss Border-to-Border), Russell Johnson (Emory), Joseph Sawyer (Svenson), Robert Nichols (Smitty)

20. **The Black Shield of Falworth** (1954) A Universal-International Production (Robert Arthur and Melville Tucker). Directed by Rudolph Maté. Cast: Tony Curtis (Myles Falworth), Janet Leigh (Lady Ann), Herbert Marshall (Earl of Mackworth), Ian Keith (King Henry IV), Torin Thatcher (Sir James), Barbara Rush (Meg Falworth), Daniel O'Herlihy (Prince Hal), Craig Hill (Francis Gascoyne), Rhys Williams (Diccon Bowman)

21. **So This Is Paris** (1954) A Universal-International Production (Albert J. Cohen). Directed by Richard Quine. Cast: Tony Curtis (Joe Maxwell), Gloria De Haven (Colette/Janie), Gene Nelson (Al Howard), Corinne Calvet (Suzanne Sorel), Paul

Gilbert (Davey Jones), Mara Corday (Yvonne), Allison Hayes (Carmen), Myrna Hansen (Ingrid)

22. **Six Bridges to Cross** (1955) A Universal-International Production (Aaron Rosenberg). Directed by Joseph Pevney. Cast: Tony Curtis (Jerry Florea), George Nader (Edward Gallagher), Julie Adams (Ellen Gallagher), Sal Mineo (Jerry, as a Boy), Jay C. Flippen (Vincent Concannon), Jan Merlin (Jan Norris), Richard Castle (Skids Radzevich)

23. **The Purple Mask** (1955) A Universal-International Production (Howard Christie). Directed by H. Bruce Humberstone. Cast: Tony Curtis (Rene), Colleen Miller (Laurette), Gene Barry (Captain Lawrence), Dan O'Herlihy (Brisquet), Angela Lansbury (Madame Valentine), George Dolenz (Marcel Cardonal), John Hoyt (Fouche), Paul Cavanagh (Duc De Latour)

24. **The Square Jungle** (1955) A Universal-International Production (Albert Zugsmith). Directed by Jerry Hopper. Cast: Tony Curtis (Eddie Quaid/Packy Glennon), Ernest Borgnine (Bernie Brown), Jim Backus (Pat Quaid), Pat Crowley (Julie

Walsh), Leigh Snowden (Lorraine Evans), Joe Louis (Himself)

25. **The Rawhide Years** (1956) A Universal-International Production (Stanley Rubin). Directed by Rudolph Maté. Cast: Tony Curtis (Ben Matthews), Colleen Miller (Zoe), Arthur Kennedy (Rick Harper), William Demarest (Brand Comfort), William Gargan (Marshal Sommers), Peter Van Eyck (Antoine Boucher), Minor Watson (Matt Comfort), Donald Randolph (Carrico).

26. **Trapeze** (1956) A United Artists Release (produced by Hecht-Lancaster). Directed by Carol Reed. Cast: Burt Lancaster (Mike Ribble), Tony Curtis (Tino Orsini), Gina Lollobrigida (Lola), Katy Jurado (Rosa), Thomas Gomez (Bouglione), Johnny Puleo (Max the Dwarf), Minor Watson (John Ringling North)

27. **Mister Cory** (1957) A Universal-International Production (Robert Arthur). Directed by Blake Edwards. Cast: Tony Curtis (Mister Cory), Martha Hyer (Abby Vollard), Charles Bickford (Biloxi), Kathryn Grant (Jen Vollard), William Reynolds (Alex Wyncott), Russ Morgan (Ruby Matrobe), Henry Daniell (Earnshaw), Willis Bouchey

(Mr. Vollard), Louise Lorimer (Mrs. Vollard)

28. **The Midnight Story** (1957) A Universal-International Production (Robert Arthur). Directed by Joseph Pevney. Cast: Tony Curtis (Joe Martini), Gilbert Roland (Sylvio Malatesta), Marisa Pavan (Anna Malatesta), Jay C. Flippen (Seargeant Jack Gillen), Argentina Brunetti (Mama Malatesta), Ted DeCorsia (Lt. Kilrain), Kathleen Freeman (Rosa Cuneo)

29. **Sweet Smell of Success** (1957) A United Artists Release (Hecht-Hill-Lancaster for Norma-Curtleigh). Directed by Alexander Mackendrick. Cast: Burt Lancaster (J.J. Hunsecker), Tony Curtis (Sidney Falco), Susan Harrison (Susan Hunsecker), Martin Milner (Steve Dallas), Sam Levene (Frank D'Angelo), Barbara Nichols (Rita)

30. **The Vikings** (1958) A United Artists Release (Byrna Productions and Curtleigh). Directed by Richard Fleischer. Cast: Kirk Douglas (Einar), Tony Curtis (Eric), Ernest Borgnine (Ragnar), Janet Leigh (Morgana), Alexander Knox (Father Godwin), Frank Thring (Aella). Narrated by Orson Welles

31. **The Defiant Ones** (1958) A United

Artists Production. Directed by Stanley Kramer. Cast: Tony Curtis (John "Joker" Jackson), Sidney Poitier (Noah Cullen), Theodore Bikel (Sheriff Max Muller), Charles McGraw (Captain Frank Gibbons), Lon Chaney, Jr. (Big Sam), Whit Bissell (Lou Gans), Carl Switzer (Angus)

32. **Kings Go Forth** (1958) A United Artists Release (Frank Ross). Directed by Delmer Daves. Cast: Frank Sinatra (Lt. Sam Loggins), Tony Curtis (Cpl. Britt Harris), Natalie Wood (Monique Blair), Leora Dana (Mrs. Blair)

33. **The Perfect Furlough** (1958) A Universal-International Production (Robert Arthur). Directed by Blake Edwards. Cast: Tony Curtis (Paul Hodges), Janet Leigh (Vicki Loren), Linda Cristal (Sandra Roca), Keenan Wynn (Harvey Franklin), Elaine Stritch (Liz Baker), Marcel Dalio (Henri), Les Tremayne (Colonel Leland), Jay Novello (Rene), King Donovan (Major Collins), Troy Donahue (Sgt. Nickles)

34. **Some Like It Hot** (1959) A United Artists Release (Mirisch Company, an Ashton Picture). Directed by Billy Wilder. Cast: Tony Curtis (Joe/Josephine), Marilyn Mon-

roe (Sugar Kane), Jack Lemmon (Jerry/Daphne), George Raft (Spats Columbo), Joe E. Brown (Osgood Fielding)

35. **Operation Petticoat** (1959) A Universal-International Release (Robert Arthur for Granart Productions). Directed by Blake Edwards. Cast: Cary Grant (Lt. Cmdr. Matt Sherman), Tony Curtis (Lt. Nick Holden), Joan O'Brien (Lt. Dolores Crandall), Dina Merrill (Lt. Barbara Duran), Gene Evans (Molumphrey), Arthur O'Connell (Sam Tostin), Richard Sargent (Stovall)

36. **Who Was That Lady?** (1959) A Columbia Pictures Release (Ansark–George Sidney). Directed by George Sidney. Cast: Tony Curtis (David Wilson), Janet Leigh (Ann Wilson), Dean Martin (Michael Haney), James Whitmore (Harry Powell), John McIntire (Bob Doyle), Barbara Nichols (Gloria Coogle), Larry Keating (Parker), Larry Storch (Orenov), Simon Oakland (Belka), Joi Lansing (Florence Coogle)

37. **The Rat Race** (1960) A Paramount Pictures Release (William Perlberg–George Seaton Production). Directed by Robert

Mulligan. Cast: Tony Curtis (Pete Hammond, Jr.), Debbie Reynolds (Peggy Brown), Jack Oakie (Mac), Kay Medford (Soda), Don Rickles (Nellie), Joe Bushkin (Frankie), Gerry Mulligan (Gerry), Sam Butera (Carl)

38. **Spartacus** (1960) A Universal-International Release (Bryna Productions, produced by Edward Lewis). Directed by Stanley Kubrick. Cast: Kirk Douglas (Spartacus), Laurence Olivier (Crassus), Jean Simmons (Varinia), Tony Curtis (Antoninus), Charles Laughton (Gracchus), Peter Ustinov (Batiatus), John Gavin (Julius Caesar), Nina Foch (Helena Glabrus), Herbert Lom (Tigranes), John Ireland (Crixus), Woody Strode (Draba)

39. **Pepe** (1960) A Columbia Pictures Release (produced by G.S.-Posa Films International). Directed by George Sidney. Cast: Cantinflas (Pepe), Dan Dailey (Ted Holt), Shirley Jones (Suzie Murphy), Carlos Montalban (Rodriguez). Guest stars as themselves: Joey Bishop, Billie Burke, Maurice Chevalier, Charles Coburn, Richard Conte, Bing Crosby, Tony Curtis, Bobby Darin, Sammy Davis Jr., Jimmy Durante, Jack Entratter, Colonel E. E. Fogelson, Zsa Zsa

Gabor, Greer Garson, Hedda Hopper, Peter Lawford, Janet Leigh, Jack Lemmon, Dean Martin, Kim Novak, André Previn, Donna Reed, Debbie Reynolds, Carlos Rivas, Edward G. Robinson, Cesar Romero, Frank Sinatra

40. **The Great Impostor** (1961) A Universal-International Production. Directed by Robert Mulligan. Cast: Tony Curtis (Ferdinand Waldo Demara Jr.), Edmond O'Brien (Captain Glover), Karl Malden (Father Devlin), Raymond Massey (Abbott Donner), Gary Merrill (Demara Sr.), Arthur O'Connell (Chandler)

41. **The Outsider** (1961) A Universal-International Production. Directed by Delbert Mann. Cast: Tony Curtis (Ira Hamilton Hayes), James Franciscus (Jim Sorenson), Gregory Walcott (Sergeant Kiley), Bruce Bennett (Major General Bridges), Vivian Nathan (Mrs. Nancy Hayes)

42. **Taras Bulba** (1962) United Artists Release (Harold Hecht–Avala Film). Directed by J. Lee Thompson. Cast: Tony Curtis (Andrei Bulba), Yul Brynner (Taras Bulba), Christine Kaufmann (Natalia Dubrov), Sam Wanamaker (Flipenko),

George Macready (Governor)

43. **Forty Pounds of Trouble** (1962) A Universal-International/Curtis Enterprises Production (Stan Margulies). Directed by Norman Jewison. Cast: Tony Curtis (Steve McCluskey), Suzanne Pleshette (Chris Lockwood), Claire Wilcox (Penny Piper), Phil Silvers (Bernie Friedman), Stubby Kaye (Cranston), Larry Storch (Floyd), Howard Morris (Julius), Warren Stevens (Swing), Mary Murphy (Liz McCluskey), Kevin McCarthy (Blanchard)

44. **Captain Newman, M.D.** (1963) A Universal-International Production (Brentwood/Reynard). Directed by David Miller. Cast: Gregory Peck (Captain Joshua Newman), Tony Curtis (Corporal Jackson Leibowitz), Angie Dickinson (Lt. Francie Corum), Eddie Albert (Colonel Norval Algate Bliss), Jane Withers (Lt. Gracie Blodgett), Bobby Darin (Corporal Jim Tompkins), Bethel Leslie (Helene Winston), Robert Duvall (Captain Paul Cabot Winston)

45. **The List of Adrian Messenger** (1963) A Universal-International Production. Directed by John Juston. Cast: Kirk

Douglas (George Brougham), George C. Scott (Anthony Gethryn), Dana Wynter (Lady Jocelyn), Clive Brook (Marquis of Gleneyre), Gladys Cooper (Mrs. Karoudjian), Herbert Marshall (Sir Wilfrid), with guest appearances by Tony Curtis, Burt Lancaster, Robert Mitchum, Frank Sinatra

46. **Wild and Wonderful** (1964) A Universal-International Production (Harold Hecht). Directed by Michael Anderson. Cast: Tony Curtis (Terry Williams), Christine Kaufmann (Giselle Ponchon), Jules Munshin (Rousseleau), Larry Storch (Rufus Gibbs), Marty Ingels (Doc Bailey), Pierre Olaf (Jacquot)

47. **Goodbye Charlie** (1964) A 20th Century-Fox–Venice Production (David Weisbart). Directed by Vincente Minnelli. Cast: Tony Curtis (George Wellington Tracy), Debbie Reynolds (Charlie Sorel), Pat Boone (Bruce Minton), Walter Matthau (Sir Leopold Sartori), Martin Gabel (Morton Craft), Ellen McRae [Burstyn] (Frannie)

48. **Sex and the Single Girl** (1964) A Warner Bros. Release (Richard Quine–Reynard Production, produced by William

Orr). Directed by Richard Quine. Cast: Tony Curtis (Bob Weston), Natalie Wood (Helen Brown), Henry Fonda (Frank), Lauren Bacall (Sylvia), Mel Ferrer (Rudy), Fran Jeffries (Gretchen), Leslie Parrish (Susan), Edward Everett Horton (Chief)

49. **Paris When It Sizzles** (1964) A Paramount Production (Richard Quine and George Axelrod). Directed by Richard Quine. Cast: William Holden (The Writer), Audrey Hepburn (The Secretary), Noel Coward (Alexander Meyerheim), cameos by Marlene Dietrich, Tony Curtis

50. **The Great Race** (1965) A Warner Bros. Release (Patricia-Jalem-Reynard Production, produced by Martin Jurow). Directed by Blake Edwards. Cast: Jack Lemmon (Professor Fate), Tony Curtis (The Great Leslie), Natalie Wood (Maggie Dubois), Peter Falk (Max), Keenan Wynn (Hezekiah), Arthur O'Connell (Henry Goodbody), Vivian Vance (Hester Goodbody), Dorothy Provine (Lila Olay), Larry Storch (Texas Jack), Ross Martin (Rolfe Von Stuppe)

51. **Boeing Boeing** (1965) A Paramount Production (Hal Wallis). Directed by John

Rich. Cast: Tony Curtis (Bernard Lawrence), Jerry Lewis (Robert Reed), Dany Saval (Jacqueline Grieux), Suzanna Leigh (Vicky Hawkins), Christiane Schmidtmer (Lise Bruner), Thelma Ritter (Bertha)

52. **Not with My Wife, You Don't!** (1966) A Warner Bros. Release (Fernwood-Reynard Production, produced by Norman Panama). Directed by Norman Panama. Cast: Tony Curtis (Tom Ferris), Verna Lisi (Julie Ferris), George C. Scott (Tank Martin), Carroll O'Connor (General Parker), Richard Eastham (General Walters), Eddie Ryder (Sgt. Gilroy), George Tyne (Sgt. Dogerty), Ann Doran (Doris Parker)

53. **Arrivederci, Baby!** (1966; aka *Drop Dead Darling*) A Paramount Release (Seven Arts Production produced by Ken Hughes). Directed by Ken Hughes. Cast: Tony Curtis (Nick), Rosanna Schiaffino (Francesca), Lionel Jeffries (Parker), Nancy Kwan (Baby), Zsa Zsa Gabor (Gigi), Fenella Fielding (Lady Fenella Fawcett), Anna Quayle (Aunt Miriam), Mischa Auer (Rich Italian)

54. **Chamber of Horrors** (1966) A Warner Bros. Release. Directed by Hy Averback. Cast: Patrick O'Neal (Jason Cravatte),

Cesare Danova (Anthony Draco), Wilfrid Hyde-White (Harold Blount), Patrice Wymore (Vivian), Suzy Parker (Barbara Dixon), Marie Windsor (Madame Corona), with a cameo appearance by Tony Curtis (Mr. Julian)

55. **Don't Make Waves** (1967) An MGM Release (Filmways-Reynard Production, produced by Martin Ransohof and John Calley). Directed by Alexander Mackendrick. Cast: Tony Curtis (Carlo Cofield), Claudia Cardinale (Laura Califatti), Sharon Tate (Malibu), Robert Webber (Rod Prescott), Joanna Barnes (Diana Prescott), Mort Sahl (Sam Lingonberry), David Draper (Harry Hollard)

56. **La Cintura di Castità** (1967; aka *On My Way to the Crusades I Met a Girl Who . . .*) A Warner Bros. Release (Francesco Massei for Julia Film Productions). Directed by Pasquale Festa Campanile. Cast: Tony Curtis (Guerrando Da Montone), Monica Vitti (Boccadoro), Hugh Griffith (Sultan of Bari), John Richardson (Drogone), Ivo Garrani (Duke of Pandolfo), Nino Castelnuovo (Marculfo)

57. **The Boston Strangler** (1968) A

20th Century-Fox Production. Directed by Richard Fleischer. Cast: Tony Curtis (Albert De Salvo), Henry Fonda (John S. Bottomly), George Kennedy (Phil Di Natale), Mike Kellin (Julian Soshnick), Hurd Hatfield (Terence Huntley), Murray Hamilton (Frank McAfee), Jeff Corey (John Asgiersson), Sally Kellerman (Dianne Cluny), William Marshall (Edward W. Brooke)

58. **Rosemary's Baby** (1968) A Paramount Picture (produced by William Castle). Directed by Roman Polanski. Cast: Mia Farrow (Rosemary Woodhouse), John Cassavetes (Guy Woodhouse), Ruth Gordon (Minnie Castevet), Sidney Blackmer (Roman Castevet), Maurice Evans (Edward Hutchins), Ralph Bellamy (Dr. Abraham Sapirstein), Elisha Cook Jr. (Mr. Niklas), Patsy Kelly (Laura Louise McBirney), Charles Grodin (Dr. C. C. Hill). Voice cameo by Tony Curtis.

59. **Those Daring Young Men in Their Jaunty Jalopies** (1969; aka *Monte Carlo or Bust*) A Paramount Release (Marianne/Mars/De Laurentiis Production, produced by Ken Annakin). Directed by Ken Annakin. Cast: Tony Curtis (Chester Schofield), Susan Hampshire (Betty), Terry-Thomas

(Sir Cuthbert Ware-Armitage), Eric Sykes (Perkins), Gert Frobe (Willi/Horst), Peter Cook (Dawlish), Dudley Moore (Barrington), Jack Hawkins (Count Levinovitch)

60. **Suppose They Gave a War and Nobody Came?** (1969) ABC Pictures Corporation (produced by Fred Engel). Directed by Hy Averback. Cast: Tony Curtis (Lieutenant Shannon Gambroni), Suzanne Pleshette (Ramona), Brian Keith (Nace), Ernest Borgnine (Sheriff Harve), Tom Ewell (Billy Joe Davis), Bradford Dillman (Captain Myerson), Don Ameche (Colonel Flanders)

61. **You Can't Win 'Em All** (1970) A Columbia Pictures Release (SRO Company Production, produced by Gene Corman). Directed by Peter Collinson. Cast: Tony Curtis (Adam Dyer), Charles Bronson (Josh Corey), Michele Mercier (Aila), Patrick Magee (The General), Gregoire Aslan (Osman Bey)

62. **Lepke** (1975) A Warner Bros. Release (Amerieuro Picture Corp., produced by Menahem Golan). Directed by Menahem Golan. Cast: Tony Curtis (Lepke Buchalter), Anjanette Comer (Bernice), Michael Callan

(Kane), Warren Berlinger (Gurrah), Milton Berle (Meyer), Vic Tayback (Luciano), Vaughn Meader (Walter Winchell)

63. **The Last Tycoon** (1976) A Paramount Release (Academy Pictures A.G. Production, produced by Sam Spiegel). Directed by Elia Kazan. Cast: Robert De Niro (Monroe Starr), Tony Curtis (Rodriguez), Robert Mitchum (Pat Brady), Jeanne Moreau (Didi), Jack Nicholson (Brimmer), Donald Pleasance (Boxley), Peter Strauss (Wylie), Ingrid Boulting (Kathleen Moore), Ray Milland (Fleishackler), Dana Andrews (Red Ridingwood), Theresa Russell (Cecilia Brady)

64. **Casanova & Co.** (1977; aka *Some Like It Cool*) An Austrian-French-Italian-West German Coproduction. Directed by Franz Antel. Cast: Tony Curtis (Casanova/Giacomino), Marisa Berenson (Calipha of Shiraz), Sylva Koscina (Gelsomina), Hugh Griffith (Caliph of Shiraz), Britt Ekland (Countess Trivulzi), Marisa Mell (Duchess Francesca)

65. **The Manitou** (1977) Manitou Productions. Directed by William Girdler. Cast: Tony Curtis (Harry Erskine), Susan Stras-

berg (Karen Tandy), Michael Ansara (Singing Rock), Ann Sothern (Mrs. Karmann), Burgess Meredith (Dr. Ernest Snow), Stella Stevens (Amelia Crusoe)

66. **Sextette** (1978) Briggs and Sullivan Production. Directed by Ken Hughes. Cast: Mae West (Marlo Manners), Tony Curtis (Alexei Andreyev Karansky), Ringo Starr (Laslo), Dom DeLuise (Dan), Timothy Dalton (Sir Michael Barrington), George Hamilton (Vance), Alice Cooper (Waiter), Keith Moon (Dress Designer), Rona Barrett (Herself), Walter Pidgeon (Chairman), George Raft (Himself)

67. **The Bad News Bears Go to Japan** (1978) A Paramount Production. Directed by John Berry. Cast: Tony Curtis (Marvin), Jackie Earle Haley (Kelly), Tomisaburo Wakayama (Coach), George Wyner (Network Director), Lonny Chapman (Gambler)

68. **Title Shot** (1979) Regenthall Film Productions. Directed by Les Rose. Cast: Tony Curtis (Frank Renzetti), Richard Gabourie (Blake), Susan Hogan (Sylvia), Allan Royal (Dunlop), Robert Delbert (Rufus Taylor), Natsuko Ohama (Terry)

69. **It Rained All Night the Day I Left** (1980) France-Canada-Israel Coproduction. Directed by Nicolas Gessner. Cast: Tony Curtis (Robert Talbot), Louis Gossett Jr. (Leo Garcia), Sally Kellerman (Colonel), John Vernon (George Killian), Lisa Langlois (Suzanna), Guy Hoffman (Priest)

70. **Little Miss Marker** (1980) A Universal-International Production. Directed by Walter Bernstein. Cast: Walter Matthau (Sorrowful Jones), Julie Andrews (Amanda), Tony Curtis (Blackie), Bob Newhart (Regret), Sara Stimson (The Kid), Lee Grant (The Judge), Brian Dennehy (Herbie), Kenneth McMillan (Brannigan)

71. **The Mirror Crack'd** (1980) GW Films Ltd. Directed by Guy Hamilton. Cast: Angela Lansbury (Miss Marple), Elizabeth Taylor (Marina Gregg), Rock Hudson (Jason Rudd), Kim Novak (Lola Brewster), Tony Curtis (Marty N. Fenn), Edward Fox (Inspector Craddock), Geraldine Chaplin (Ella Zielinsky), Wendy Morgan (Cherry), Charles Gray (Bates), Pierce Brosnan (Actor)

72. **BrainWaves** (1982) Cineamerica Productions. Directed by Ulli Lommel. Cast: Keir Dullea (Julian Bedford), Suzanna

Love (Kaylie Bedford), Tony Curtis (Dr. Clavius), Vera Miles (Marian), Percy Rodrigues (Dr. Robinson), Paul Wilson (Dr. Schroder)

73. **Othello: The Black Commando** (1982) AMB Diffusion Eurocine Production. Directed by Max H. Boulois. Cast: Max H. Boulois (Othello), Tony Curtis (Iago), Ramiro Oliveros (Cassio), Joanna Pettet (Desdemona), Nadiuska (Gerard Barray)

74. **Where Is Parsifal?** (1983) Slenderline Ltd./Terence Young Productions. Directed by Henri Helman. Cast: Tony Curtis (Parsifal Katzenellenbogen), Cassandra Domenica (Elba), Erik Estrada (Henry Board II), Peter Lawford (Montague Chippendale), Ron Moody (Beersbohm), Donald Pleasance (Mackintosh), Orson Welles (Klingsor), Christopher Chaplin (Ivan), Nancy Roberts (Ruth)

75. **Insignificance** (1985) A Zenith Production. Directed by Nicolas Roeg. Cast: Gary Busey (the Baseball Player), Tony Curtis (the Senator), Theresa Russell (the Actress), Michael Emil (the Professor), Will Sampson (the Indian)

76. **King of the City** (1985) An MPR Production, with VTC. Produced, directed, and written by Norman Thaddeus Vane. Cast: Tom Parsekian (Cal McFarlane), Michael Parks (Tank), Jamie Barrett (Sissy), Tony Curtis (Hector), Bleu McKenzie (Tillie), Ron Kuhlman (Doctor)

77. **Balboa** (1986) Entertainment Artists/ Production Associates. Directed by James Polakof. Cast: Tony Curtis (Ernie Stoddard), Carol Lynley (Erin Blakely), Jennifer Chase (Kathy Love), Chuck Connors (Alabama Dern), Lupita Ferrer (Rita Carlo), Sonny Bono (Tony Carlo), Catherine Campbell (Cindy Dern), Cassandra Peterson (Angie Stoddard), Henry Jones (Jeffrey Duncan), Steve Kanaly (Sam Cole)

78. **Midnight** (1989) An SVS Films release. Produced, directed, and written by Norman Thaddeus Vane. Cast: Lynn Redgrave (Midnight/Vera), Tony Curtis (Mr. B), Steve Parrish (Mickey Modine), Frank Gorshin (Ron), Rita Gam (Heidi), Gustav Vintas (Siegfried), Karen Witter (Missy), Wolfman Jack (Himself)

79. **Lobster Man from Mars** (1989) An

Electric Pictures presentation of a Filmrullen Production (produced by Eyal Rimmon and Steven S. Greene). Directed by Stanley Sheff. Cast: Tony Curtis (J. P. Shelldrake), Deborah Foreman (Mary), Patrick Macnee (Professor Piccostomos), Billy Barty (Throckmorton), Anthony Hickox (John), Tommy Sledge (Himself), Dean Jacobson (Stevie Horowitz), Fred Holliday (Colonel Ankrum), Bobby Pickett (King of Mars/the Astrologer), S. D. Nemeth (the Lobster Man)

80. **Prime Target** (1991) A Hero Films release. Produced, directed, and written by David Heavener. Cast: David Heavener (John Bloodstone), Tony Curtis (Coppella), Isaac Hayes (Captain Thomkins), Robert Reed (Agent Harrington), Andrew Robinson (Commissioner), Jenilee Harrison (Kathy Bloodstone), Michael Gregory (Agent Robins), Don Stroud (Manny)

81. **Center of the Web** (1992) Pyramid Distribution Inc., a Winters Group Production (Produced by Ruta K. Aras). Directed and written by David A. Prior. Cast: Tony Curtis (Mastermind), Robert Davi (John Phillips), Charlene Tilton (Kathryn Lockwood), Bo Hopkins (the Agent)

82. **The Mummy Lives** (1993) A Klondike Films Release (Produced by Yoram Globus). Directed by Gerry O'Hara. Cast: Tony Curtis (Aziru/Dr. Mohassid), Leslie Hardy (Sandra Barnes/Kia), Greg Wrangler (Dr. Carey Williams), Jack Cohen (Lord Maxton), Mohammed Bakri (Alexatos)

83. **Naked in New York** (1993) A Fine Line Release (Produced by Fred Zollo and Martin Scorsese). Directed by Daniel Algrant. Cast: Whoopi Goldberg (masks of Comedy/Tragedy), Tony Curtis (Carl Fisher, the Producer), Kathleen Turner (the Actress), Timothy Dalton (the Actor), Eric Stoltz (the Writer), Ralph Macchio (the Friend)

84. **The Immortals** (1995) End Productions. Directed by Brian Grant. Cast: Eric Roberts (Jack), Joe Pantoliano (Pete Tunnell), Tia Carrere (Gina Walker), Tony Curtis (Dominic Bapstiste)

85. **The Continued Adventures of Reptile Man and His Faithful Sidekick Tadpole** (1997) Shoreline Entertainment. Directed by Stewart Schill. Cast: Tony Curtis (Jack Steele), Arye Gross (Lewis Rosen), Ally Walker (Elise Rosen)

86. **Hardball** (1997) Cinepix Film Properties (CFP). Directed by George Erschbamer. Cast: Michael Dudikoff (Jersey Bellini), Lisa Howard (B.B.), Tony Curtis (Wald), Steve Bacic (Peter Carlos), L. Harvey Gold (Santos)

87. **The Blacksmith and the Carpenter** (2007) Scottsdale Community College. Directed by Chris Redish. Cast: Robert Picardo (Ishmael), Tony Curtis (God, voice), Liz Sheridan (Mrs. God, voice), Hunter Gomez (Jacob), Clint James (Jesus)

88. **David & Fatima** (2008) Karim Movies. Directed by Alain Zaloum. Cast: Cameron Van Hoy (David Isaac), Danielle Pollack (Fatima Aziz), Martin Landau (Rabbi Schmulic), Allan Kolman (Benny Isaac), Anthony Batarse (Ishmael Aziz), Yareli Arizmendi (Aiida Aziz), Colette Kilroy (Sarah Isaac), Tony Curtis (Mr. Schwartz)

ACKNOWLEDGMENTS

To the Regiment and my fallen comrades.

Since this is the story of my life, I'd also like to acknowledge those people whose company I have been especially privileged to enjoy over the years: my children, Kelly, Jamie, Alexandra, Allegra, Nicholas, and Benjamin; my grandchildren Helena, Rafael, Nicholas, Annie, Thomas, Elizabeth, and Dido; my brothers, Julie and Bobby; my family and friends including Natalie Wood, Yvonne De Carlo, Heather Sills, Bobby Hoy, Arnold Schwarzenegger, Davy Sharpe, Dr. John Breiner, Frank Sinatra, Mike Meshekoff, Dodi Al-Fayed, Sophie Rosenstein, Bobby Friedman, Kirk Douglas, Janet Leigh, Jack Warner, Sir Laurence Olivier, Debby Darlene Davenport, Gene Kilroy, Kirk Kerkorian, Hugh Hefner, Marilyn Monroe, Gloria DeHaven, Suzanne Pleshette and the rest of the outfield, Larry Storch, my cousin Stanley Schiffman, Luz

Garcia, Rachael Ganatta, Sally VandenBerg, R.J. Wagner, Billy and Audrey Wilder, Warren Cowan, Danny Gillian, Arthur Cohn, Dr. Gautham Reddy, Stan Dragotta, Nickki Haskell, Arthur Rossen, Dr. David VandenBerg, Dean Shendal, Paul Haley, Dr. Charles Kivovitz, Dr. Rick Ehrlich, Mohamed Al-Fayed, Salah Al-Fayed, and the Hollywood Women's Club.

And lastly, my thanks to the book makers: Peter Golenbock, Shaye Areheart, Peter Guzzardi, Alan Nevins, and all those who helped get this book produced.

ABOUT THE AUTHORS

Tony Curtis is one of Hollywood's greatest stars. Today, he lives with his wife, Jill, outside of Las Vegas, where he continues to create paintings that have made him newly famous as a visual artist the world over. They are the founders of the Shiloh Horse Rescue and Sanctuary, a nonprofit foundation that rehabilitates abused and neglected horses for adoption.

Peter Golenbock has written some of sports' most important books, including *Dynasty: The New York Yankees 1949-64, The Bronx Zoo,* which he wrote in 1979 with New York Yankee pitcher Sparky Lyle; *BUMS: An Oral History of the Brooklyn Dodgers, Personal Fouls,* a look at corruption in college basketball; *American Zoom,* a history of NASCAR; and *Wild, High and Tight,* his biography of Yankee manager Billy Martin. Peter Golenbock lives in St. Petersburg, Florida.